Advances in Contemporary Educational Thought Series
Jonas F. Soltis, Editor

The Cultural Dimensions of Educational Computing:
Understanding the Non-Neutrality of Technology
C. A. Bowers

Power and Criticism:
Poststructural Investigations in Education
Cleo H. Cherryholmes

The Civic Imperative:
Examining the Need for Civic Education
Richard Pratte

POWER
AND
CRITICISM

*Poststructural Investigations
in Education*

CLEO H. CHERRYHOLMES

Teachers College, Columbia University
New York and London

Published by Teachers College Press, 1234 Amsterdam Avenue,
New York, NY 10027

Library of Congress Cataloging-in-Publication Data

Cherryholmes, Cleo H.
   Power and criticism: poststructural investigations in education/
Cleo H. Cherryholmes.
      p.   cm.—(Advances in contemporary educational thought)
   Bibliography: p.
   Includes index.
   ISBN 0-8077-2927-2
   1. Teaching. 2. Education—Philosophy. 3. Structuralism.
4. Deconstruction. I. Title. II. Series.
LB1027.C455 1988   88-15883
371.1′02—dc19   CIP

ISBN 0-8077-2927-2

Manufactured in the United States of America

93 92 91 90 89 88   1 2 3 4 5 6

Contents

Foreword

Intellectually, we live in an exciting age. In philosophy, psychology, the social sciences, and education, fundamental questions are being raised about the nature of these fields—what they are and what they should be about. Postpositivist, interpretivist, and neo-Marxist critiques abound. Qualitative research seeks parity with quantitative research. Poststructuralists challenge structuralists. An unsettled feeling has been aroused in the scholarly community by an array of new and sometimes foreign ways of thinking.

An older generation of scholars may remember another time, when they were initiated into an enthusiastically developing or confidently stable paradigm of research that promised definitive answers to important problems. They will recall that by mid-century, analytic philosophy had eschewed speculative philosophy and sought to provide reliable philosophical illumination by means of the clarification of concepts. Psychology had reopened the possibility of investigating mental processes and exploring cognitive, moral, and affective development. The social sciences, imitating the natural sciences, had developed empirical methods for confidently describing structural and functional features of society; and educational researchers, with massive support from the federal government, had developed and were refining an empirical-experimental-statistical-positivist approach that reached into every important aspect of education and promised solutions to some of our most persistent educational problems.

Today a younger generation of scholars and even some of their elders have had their interest piqued by many challenges to these established ways of thinking. Many find that something in Marxist critiques of power, social reproduction, and domination rings true; that something in critiques of positivism and technocracy seems to have validity; and that something in calls for making the human sciences more human is appealing. The source of these challenges is primarily from Continental thinkers even though some of what they target, such as positivism, is also of Continental origin. However, many American scholars find the primary literature of contemporary poststructuralist* thought opaque and difficult to understand. Not only are the authors cited literally foreign (e.g., Foucault, Derrida, Habermas, et al.), but also their ideas (e.g., discursive practice, deconstruction, ideal speech situation, and so forth) are alien to mainstream social scientists and educational researchers.

In *Power and Criticism*, Cleo Cherryholmes has done a masterly job of making the works and ideas of these original postructuralist thinkers accessible to the uninitiated. This in itself is a major contribution to contemporary educational thought; but Cherryholmes does more in this powerful book. He uses poststructural perspectives and ideas to give us a richer and more critical view of many things educationists take to be important. He offers poststructural analyses of, among other things, construct validity, Bloom et al.'s taxonomy, Tyler's rationale, Schwab's "The Practical 4," empirical research and critical practice, relationships between textbooks and teaching, and the perennial bogeyman, relativism. His treatment is always crisp and clear; his analyses, perceptive and revealing. This is a book all educators with a theoretical, and many with a practical, bent should read.

As an interpreter of poststructuralism, Cherryholmes stands sturdily and forthrightly in the center of one of the most significant revolutions in contemporary thought. He offers educators and researchers a platform from which they may realize "increased freedom from existing social structures and more power to create our societies and schools instead of the other way around." His essential argument is that no matter what our theoretical orientation, as educators our concerns are ultimately pragmatic; we want to have a positive effect on schools, curricula, teachers, and society. It is dangerous, however, to practice a naive, acritical pragmatism narrowly concerned with only what works. Those who do are effectively blinded to a broader range of human concerns. As human beings we always live in a specific cultural-historical context and are enmeshed in relations of power. Taking this as a given, Cherryholmes, using his understanding of poststructuralist thought, fashions his own view of a "critical pragmatism" as it is emerging in contemporary American neopragmatic

---

*Cherryholmes chooses this umbrella-like label over others currently in vogue, like postmodern, postpositivist, or postanalytic thought. In all of them their "post" prefix suggests that we have gotten beyond where we were in some very fundamental way and now need to assess where we are. To begin this assessment for educational theory and practice is Cherryholmes's project.

thought. This is a more sophisticated view that carries us beyond naive objectivism and functionalism to help us see how to live and work constructively in a social-cultural-educational world of human making.

Jonas F. Soltis, Editor
Advances in Contemporary
Educational Thought Series

Acknowledgments

Acknowledgments sometimes refer to beginnings even though beginnings are often elusive. Edward Said writes:

> Two kinds of beginning emerge, really two sides of the same coin. One, which I call temporal and transitive, foresees a continuity that flows from it. This kind of beginning is suited for work, for polemic, for discovery . . . the other kind of beginning . . . I [call] intransitive and conceptual. It is very much a creature of the mind, very much a bristling paradox. . . . Because it cannot truly be known, because it belongs more to silence than it does to language, because it is what has always been left behind, and because it challenges continuities that go cheerfully forward with *their* beginnings obediently affixed—it is therefore something of a necessary fiction. (1985, pp. 76–77)

After I began writing this book, work, discovery, and possibly, some polemics followed, even though an identifiable beginning remains something of a necessary fiction. I cannot identify a person, group, or event that pointed me in this direction. Turning points, perhaps, are less fictitious.

One important turning point occurred on a pleasant Sunday afternoon in April 1979, after I had given a paper at the meeting of the American Educational Research Association in San Francisco. That day I met Henry Giroux and shortly afterwards renewed my acquaintance with Tom Popkewitz and met Mike Apple. Since then they have become valued friends and colleagues, although my analyses of power and criticism in education diverge from as well as complement their own work, not unlike the way their work individually diverges from and complements each other. During a crucial period of writing, Tom and Mike invited me to give three colloquia at the University of Wisconsin, Madison. A fourth visit to Madison gave me a chance to discuss the penultimate version of Chapter 8 with a study group composed of graduate students, organized by Tom Popkewitz. Questions and comments from the faculty and students helped sharpen arguments and anticipate counterarguments.

Although I have no formal ties with the College of Education at Michigan State University, I taught a graduate seminar in curriculum theory there from 1983 to 1988, in which I initially presented many of these arguments. I enjoyed these classes immensely and benefited greatly from students, who, sometimes incredulous at my version(s) of things, asked many questions and offered opposing interpretations and criticisms. I appreciate the generosity of the Department of Political Science at Michigan State University, my home appointment, for making time available for these seminars.

The book was written over a four-year period. David Cohen read much of the manuscript and Lee Cronbach was generous in his support and reactions to Chapter 6. In addition, I appreciate the comments of Susan Florio-Ruane (for reading early drafts of several chapters); Fred Erickson and Folke Lindahl (for comments on Chapter 4); Geoff Whitty (for comments on Chapter 7); Eliot Singer (for comments on Chapter 2); William Riker (for comments on an early version of Chapter 5); Marilyn Johnston and Sandra Wilcox (for comments on Chapter 1); Jere Confrey (for comments on an early draft of Chapter 5); Fred Newmann (for comments on Chapters 4 and 6); Patty Stuhr, Kerry Freedman, Pat Burdell, David Labaree, Kathleen Fear, Paul Abramson, Yusuf El-Sulayman, Jim Kusch, Jonathon Shapiro, Bob Floden, Jack Knott, Gary Miller, Richard Peterson, Steven Esquith, Michael Bratton, Atul Kohli, and Ben Bohnhorst.

Finally, Jonas Soltis's warm encouragement has been important as the manuscript moved through its final stages, and the staff at Teachers College Press have made publication an enjoyable experience.

Power and Criticism

Poststructural Investigations in Education

CHAPTER 1

Rethinking Educational Discourses-Practices

The ideal of an educated person held by a given era, as Derrida points out, is always predicated on the basis of a theory of truth. (Ulmer, 1985, p. 167)

Professions are constituted by what is said and done in their name. Regularities in what is said (discourse) and done (practice) are based on shared beliefs and values ranging across tasks accomplished, problems addressed, values articulated, and research undertaken. Vast areas of agreement about how to proceed in contemporary education dwarf noteworthy and important conflicts and disagreements. Areas of agreement include (in principle if not always in practice): structured use of textbooks in classrooms, instruction based on learning objectives, educational practice guided by research findings, standardized approaches to research design and program evaluation, systematic approaches to curriculum design and development, and learning as acquisition of a positive body of knowledge and skills. The investigations that follow examine some of these agreements and others yet more fundamental. A partial listing of topics includes the following ideas and practices:

1. Tyler's rationale to design curricula in a linear, systematic way in developing materials and planning instruction
2. Textbooks and assessment tests to capture the meaning of words, statements, and arguments
3. Empirically based theory to provide guidelines for critical educational practice
4. Operational definitions to fix the meaning of theoretical terms in educational research
5. Curriculum theory to tell practitioners what to do about selecting and organizing content

At times the result is criticism of these discourses and practices, at other times, criticism of criticism.

Thomas Popkewitz (1982) applies the concepts of paradigm and ideology to educational agreements such as these. Thomas Kuhn (1974) describes scientific paradigms as shared commitments to beliefs and values (p. 184) and concrete puzzle solutions (p. 187). Operative, governing paradigms make normal science possible. Kuhn's description of normal science applies as well to professional education:

> The practice of normal science depends on the ability, acquired from exemplars, to group objects and situations into similarity sets which are primitive in the sense that the grouping is done without an answer to the question, "Similar with respect to what?" (p. 200)

Educators at all levels agree, more or less, on certain beliefs and values, on concrete puzzle solutions, and on highly regarded exemplars. These are primitives. They are taken as given and not questioned. They are not defined. Often, they are not mentioned. These agreements are the basis for what educators say and do, and normal professional discourse and practice is possible only because of them. The purpose of this book is to reexamine and rethink several of these seemingly nonproblematic assumptions and to call into question their coherence and plausibility. Educators may offer good reasons for what they do, but what they do is often done for reasons other than those they give. Because "rethinking educational discourse-practice" means looking at what practitioners and researchers say and do, a few words about discourse, practice, discourse-practice, and related matters follow.

DISCOURSE

The words *discourse* and *practice* might seem strange as well as familiar. Broadly put, discourse refers to what is said and written and passes for more or less orderly thought and exchange of ideas. Emile Benveniste (1971) puts it this way:

> Discourse must be understood in its widest sense: every utterance assuming a speaker and a hearer, and in the speaker, the intention of influencing the other in some way. It is primarily every variety of oral discourse of every nature and every level, from trivial conversation to the most elaborate oration. But it is also the mass of writing that reproduces oral discourse or that borrows its manner of expression and its purposes:

correspondence, memoirs, plays, didactic works, in short, all the genres in which someone addresses himself to someone, proclaims himself as the speaker, and organizes what he says in the category of person. (p. 209)

Educational discourse ranges from what is *said* in elementary classrooms, teacher education classes, and research findings reported at conferences and conventions to what is *written* in high school textbooks, assessment exams, and research articles in professional journals.

Discourses are not composed by randomly choosing words and statements. Instead, rules constitute and regulate language use (Wittgenstein, 1953). For example, rules guide the formulation of arguments and hypotheses, teacher directions to students, ethnographic descriptions, student responses, and so forth. Such rules help shape a discursive practice that produces a specific discourse. Michel Foucault calls a discursive practice

a body of anonymous, historical rules, always determined in the time and space that have defined a given period, and for a given social, economic, geographical, or linguistic area, the conditions of operation of the enunciative function. (1972, p. 117)

Discourses are relative to time and place. It takes little reflection, for example, to realize that what is said and written about education in the 1980s in the United States is far different from what was written in the 1880s, or in the 1880s in Western Europe, or in the 1980s in Latin America. This is not surprising because as time goes by we are likely to know more about our world and ourselves, or so we are tempted to think, leading us to speak and write differently. Furthermore, there is no reason to believe that knowledge should accumulate at the same pace everywhere, even if each society and its professions were to start with a common body of knowledge. As societies and professions develop, what is said and written and accepted as true changes. Discourses and discursive practices are relative to time and place.

PRACTICE

Educational practices are educational activities performed on a regular basis, although there is variation. An example is educational testing. Sometimes students are tested before instruction, sometimes after. Occasionally students evaluate their own progress by answering questions in a textbook or in some programmed fashion. Sometimes educational progress is assessed by criterion-referenced testing, at other times by norm-referenced testing. Teachers measure student achievement by tracking student progress from prior levels to current levels of performance. Student outcomes are sometimes compared to test results based on standardized norms.

Practices, as with discourses, are constituted by connected and overlapping sets of rules that organize and give them coherence. They vary from legal rules, such as state laws concerning educational assessment, to those that are simply written down, such as school district policies concerning grading systems and final exams, to those that are not in writing at all, such as beliefs that teachers use to guide their testing procedures within a classroom. Brian Fay puts the general point this way: "'Rules' refer to expectations of the members of a social group as to what performances are appropriate in a certain situation which is itself definable by means of those rules" (1977, p. 75). Practices do not exist without rules, nor rules without practices. Knowing rules means knowing how to proceed. In educational testing this includes knowledge ranging from legal-institutional directives and constraints to physiological and psychological considerations involved in interacting with students who vary in age, gender, ethnicity, interest, and cognitive ability.

Educational practices result from choices. Choices cannot be made without reference to a value, set of values, criteria(on), or interests. Values and interests are sedimented, to use a metaphor from archeology, in the constitutive rules of practice. To the extent that values and interests are more rather than less integrated, they can be thought of, roughly, as ideology. Ideologies have both content and function. The content of ideologies is, "beliefs and interpretations which purport to be true or valid" (Bernstein, 1976, p. 108). These beliefs and interpretations function in the

> production, consumption, and representation of ideas and behavior, . . . they can function within the spheres of both consciousness and unconsciousness; and, finally, they can exist at the level of critical discourse as well as within the sphere of taken-for-granted lived experience and practical behavior. (Giroux, 1983a, p. 143)

For example, the ideology of educational testing organizes and rationalizes beliefs and interpretations about testing—its purpose, process, and outcomes—which justify activities and rules that count as testing and evaluation. An ideological orientation about testing includes beliefs behind production of tests and their consumption by teachers, administrators, students, parents, and social institutions other than schools; such an orientation also includes (1) the importance of testing and evaluation, (2) how testing should be carried out, (3) the content of tests, and, last on this list but certainly not least in importance, (4) what test results mean. Such beliefs and actions are sometimes, but not always, well integrated and relatively consistent. Often they are consciously articulated and focus critical discussions among educational researchers and curriculum specialists; they also structure the taken-for-granted lived experience of everyday classroom life.

If people are free to choose what to do, why is it they choose activities coincident with rules and normative commitments of established practice? Why do their choices not produce something closer to anarchy? One reason is ideological: people accept, internalize, and act according to shared ideas they believe are true and valid. A second reason is that social practices are supported by power arrangements. When I use the word *power*, it will refer to relations among individuals or groups based on social, political, and material *asymmetries* by which some people are indulged and rewarded and others negatively sanctioned and deprived.[1] These asymmetries are based on differences in *possessions* or *characteristics*, and power is constituted by relationships among those differences. It is redundant to refer to a *power relation* because power *is* a relation; instead references will be made from time to time to *power arrangements* or *structures* or *systems*. For my purposes, the effects of power are as important as the exercise of power itself. In fact, making inferences about power, in any analytic sense, is largely based upon inferences about the effects of power. Power is important because of its effects, and the effects of power lead us to ask how they came about and what relations and processes produced them. Ideology intertwines with power as individuals accept, believe, and internalize explanations and justifications for the asymmetries of their social world.

Often rewards and indulgences are externally imposed upon individuals; at other times, internally. The distinction is often difficult to make. In either case, individuals *desire* and seek to act in ways that are likely to be rewarded and avoid actions likely to be penalized. Social asymmetries vary in visibility and force. State laws mandating the administration of educational assessment instruments backed by the force of state funding and legal sanctions are highly visible. Another fairly visible exercise of power occurs when school districts require grades to be assigned on a regular basis, enforced by employment sanctions. A less visible constraint on testing is expectations students have acquired in other classrooms about how they should be treated while taking a test and being graded.

To the extent that ideology and power arrangements infiltrate our thinking and actions, they shape our subjectivities, that is, how and what we think about ourselves and so act.[2] This is one way in which social practices and persons continuously create and re-create each other. Individuals think of themselves in terms of social setting, practice, institution, culture, and so forth into which they are born, inducted, socialized, trained, certified, and so forth. If they continue to be part of that society, profession, polity, religion, and so forth, they continue to think and behave in certain ways and believe certain things. If they are integrated into, accepted, rewarded, and so forth, by, say, their profession, then they must become skillful at professional activities. When individuals perform such activities they re-create the profession, because without such performances no profession would exist. Educational practice is constantly re-created by the actions of educators. The professional self-conception of individual educators is created when they learn the skills and beliefs of their profession and is re-created every time they exercise skills based on those beliefs.[3]

Most of us do not use categories like these when we think about practice because our professional subjectivities are already shaped: we have internalized appropriate rules and ideologies, have accommodated ourselves to dominant power relationships, and are more concerned with performing expected actions than with analyzing them. But in order to exert control over practice and not simply react to it, we must be explicit not only about what we do but also about what it is that structures what we do.

SPEECH ACTS

This rethinking of educational discourse-practice assumes that speech is action. Not long ago this was either rejected or overlooked. J. L. Austin puts it this way:

> We have not got to go very far back in the history of philosophy to find philosophers assuming more or less as a matter of course that the sole business, the sole interesting business, of any utterance—that is, of anything we say—is to be true or at least false. . . . Philosophers have assumed that the only things that they are interested in are utterances which report facts or which describe situations truly or falsely. (1968, p. 233)

This is a statemental or descriptive approach to language. Adopting it, one might conclude that two distinct forms of practice have been described: discursive and nondiscursive, with discursive being more in a descriptive tradition because it involves speaking and nondiscursive being more in a materialist tradition because it involves doing. It is important to point out why this distinction cannot be maintained, a point that derives from the speech act theory developed in the work of Austin and John Searle. Speech act theory developed from the insight that utterances are not just descriptions, which Austin (1968) called the descriptivist fallacy, but are actions; that is, when one says something, one is doing something. The general formulation is "X counts as Y in context C" (Searle, 1969, p. 35).

After pointing out that some utterances are actions—such as saying "I bet you five dollars," wherein (X) is the act of making a bet (Y) in appropriate circumstances (C)—Austin attempted to distinguish between speech that was action and speech that was description, which he termed *constative*. He was not able to do this, and Searle, one of Austin's foremost students, later abandoned the distinction that an utterance is either an action or a constative. In an important article Searle (1971) opened up the implications of speech act theory while closing down interest in distinguishing between speech as action and speech as description. The word *statement*, he pointed out, is structurally ambiguous. It can mean either the *act of stating* or *what is stated* (p. 274). The act of stating is doing something. What is stated comes from the propositional content of an utterance and sometimes, depending upon what is said, can be true or false. *All speech is action*, and some of what is said can be true or false. When one says something one is doing something, and its meaning is relative to setting, context, rules, and so forth. What is done with an utterance is material. If all speech is action, there is no firm distinction between discourse and practice. All discourse is material.

TEXT

Benveniste, as pointed out earlier, argues that discourses are primarily oral even though they extend to "all the genres in which someone addresses himself to someone." Discourses include written words and statements that form texts, as well as what is spoken. Texts, from Benveniste's point of view, are discursive and contribute to discourses. Moreover, they are speech acts, and we act when we project texts and discourses onto the world around us. Edward Said describes them as follows:

> Texts are worldly, to some degree they are events, and, even when they
> appear to deny it they are nevertheless a part of the social world, human
> life, and of course the historical moments in which they are located and
> interpreted. . . . The realities of power and authority—as well as the
> resistances offered by men, women, and social movements to institu-
> tions, authorities, and orthodoxies—are realities that make texts possi-
> ble, that deliver them to their readers, that solicit the attention of critics.
> (1983, pp. 4–5)

Terry Eagleton put it like this:

> Movement from "work" to "text" . . . is a shift from seeing the poem or
> novel [discourse-practice] as a closed entity, equipped with definite
> meanings which it is the critic's task to decipher, to seeing it as irredu-
> cibly plural, an endless play . . . which can never be finally nailed down
> to a single, centre, essence or meaning. . . . The text . . . is less a "struc-
> ture" than an open-ended process of "structuration," and it is criticism
> which does this structuring. (1983, pp. 138–39)

Structuration is the dual process by which individuals create social
processes and institutions through their choices and actions, and the
latter both constrain and provide opportunities for the former (Giddens, 1979, pp. 66–73).

Reading a text compares to reading a discourse-practice. To understand a text one moves from what is written to what is not written and
back again, from what is present to what is absent, from statements to
their historical setting. Texts in the discourses-practices of education
include textbooks, research papers, monographs, curriculum guidelines, and assessment tests. Research designs, observational data, experimental interventions, statistical tests, and inferences are also texts
as well as discourses-practices. Their meaning depends upon other
texts that are related to still other texts. The intertextuality of discourses and practices constitutes and structures our social and educational
worlds.

DISCOURSES-PRACTICES

When educational discourse(s) and practice(s) are treated separately in the following arguments, it will be to clarify or highlight a
particular point. My position, however, is that no firm, stable, clear,
unequivocal distinction can be drawn between discourse and practice.
Sometimes I will refer to *discourse* to focus primarily on the content of
what is said and written, at other times, to *practice* to point toward

what is done—sometimes what is done is with what is said. Often I will write *discourse-practice* or *discourses-practices* to emphasize similarities, reinforcement, interpenetration between the two. Discourse, a more or less orderly exchange of ideas, is a particular kind of practice, and practice is, at least in part, discursive.[4] Nor, for the same reason, will a firm distinction be drawn between discursive and nondiscursive practices because we continually project what we say and write onto the nondiscursive world around us. The idea that meanings flow back and forth from what is said to what is done, from ourselves to the world is integral to what follows.

POSTSTRUCTURALISM, POSTMODERNISM, AND POSTANALYTIC THOUGHT

Recurrent themes characterize educational discourses-practices. The substructures of many that are dominant emphasize order, accountability, structure, systematization, rationalization, expertise, specialization, linear development, and control. Broadly put, these substructures reflect influences from analytic philosophy, modernism, and structuralism. Even though these schools of thought developed in different areas of study and analysis, there are points of convergence. Analytic philosophy employs the power of logical, formal analysis to attack central philosophical problems. John Rajchman puts it as follows:

> Analytic philosophy . . . introduced a revision of the history of philosophy. . . . It made the central problems of classical empiricism into the central problems of philosophy and represented the idealist turn . . . [as] something that ought never to have called itself philosophy: something metaphysical, a fuzzy thinking, a false historicism, an irrationalism, something that might be repudiated with the help of the *analytic* of concepts. (1985, p. xi; emphasis added)

Analytic philosophy attempted to eliminate metaphysics, clarify fuzzy thinking, surmount history, and promote rigorous analysis. Positivism in particular and analytic philosophy in general sought to write an epistemological metanarrative of knowledge and science. *Meta-* is "used in the name of a discipline to designate a new but related discipline designed to deal critically with the original one" (*Webster's Seventh Collegiate Dictionary*). The purpose of the positivist metanarrative was to write a story or set of rules characterizing positive knowledge. In the process of working toward these goals, however, it under-

cut the possibility of achieving them. Its categorical distinctions between "the analytical and synthetic, the linguistic and the empirical,
theory and observation" (West, 1985, p. 260) were eventually discarded along with hopes of using them to solve central problems of philosophy. One result, not surprisingly, has been work in postanalytic
philosophy; philosophy without metanarratives (Rajchman & West,
1985).

The term *modernism* is sometimes used to characterize works of
literature, art, and architecture as well as science and social philosophy. Jean-François Lyotard uses

> the term *modern* to designate any science that legitimates itself with
> reference to a metadiscourse . . . making an explicit appeal to some
> grand narrative, such as the dialectics of Spirit, the hermeneutics of
> meaning, the emancipation of the rational or working subject, or the
> creation of wealth. . . . This is the Enlightenment narrative. (1984, p.
> xxiii)

Shortly thereafter he writes:

> Simplifying to the extreme, I define *postmodern* as incredulity toward
> metanarratives. This incredulity is undoubtedly a product of progress in
> the sciences. . . . The narrative function is losing . . . its great hero, its
> great dangers, its great voyages, its great goal. . . . Thus the society of
> the future falls less within the province of a Newtonian anthropology
> (such as structuralism or systems theory) than a pragmatics of language
> particles. (1984, p. xxiv)

The modern attitude is part of the Enlightenment tradition. It is concerned with rational control of our lives, beliefs, values, and aesthetic
sensibilities. But the required metanarrative(s) that spell out such rationality have not been forthcoming.

A third way of thinking about some of this is in terms of structuralism. Structuralism, originated in the linguistic structuralism of
Ferdinand de Saussure, has since been extended to a wide variety of
fields and is complementary in many ways with analytic philosophy
and modernism. I have couched the following investigations in struc-
tural/poststructural terms for several reasons. First, analytic/postana-
lytic philosophy applies mainly to academic philosophy, even though
implications of philosophical analysis extend beyond academe. Second, even though the categories modernism/postmodernism are widely used, they do not provide a tight formulation. Third, structuralism/
poststructuralism can be, more or less, systematically outlined, and
each approach has been applied to a number of fields. Modern, ana-

lytic, and structural thought seek rationality, linearity, progress, and control by discovering, developing, and inventing metanarratives, metadiscourses, and metacritiques that define rationality, linearity, progress, and control. Postmodern, postanalytic, and poststructural thought are skeptical and incredulous about the possibility of such metanarratives. This "rethinking" is an exploration of poststructural implications for educational discourse-practice.

A further word about metanarratives, metadiscourses, and metacritiques is called for. They arise, Jürgen Habermas argues, when philosophers

> attempt to maintain . . . the unity of reason, even if only in a procedural sense . . . [and] distill the common characteristics of rational activity that *must* be implicitly presupposed . . . in the argumentative collisions between universes of discourse. In this way, there arise what Rorty calls "metanarratives," that is, the theories of rationality that are supposed to account for why and in what sense we can still connect our convictions and our descriptive, normative, and evaluative statements, with a transcending validity claim that goes beyond merely local contexts. (1985, p. 193)

Educational metanarratives include Ralph Tyler's rationale (1949) for developing curriculum; Benjamin Bloom et al.'s *Taxonomy of Educational Objectives* (1956) for organizing cognitive knowledge; and Joseph Schwab's (1983) "The Practical 4," for "watching and correcting" school curricula. They function to outline what is or is not acceptable, desirable, efficient, and so forth regarding educational discourses-practices; these exemplars are discussed in Chapters 2 and 3. Metanarratives are similar to paradigms that guide thought and practice in a discipline or profession. Metanarratives guide by rules; paradigms, by example in the form of concrete examples and puzzle solutions.

Narratives about narratives, however, can express different kinds of claims and evaluations about discourse and practice. A metanarrative, for example, can state necessary and sufficient, sufficient, or necessary conditions for the narrative of a discourse-practice, even though only the first meets Habermas's sense of "a transcending validity claim that goes beyond merely local contexts."[5] A metanarrative that proposes necessary and sufficient conditions for an educational discourse-practice claims that it, the discourse-practice, will be true, good, beautiful, efficient, reasonable, or desirable "if and only if" the prescriptions of the metanarrative are executed completely and correctly. It would tell educators exactly what to do to get a desired outcome. This level of specification and completeness, however, exceeds the ambitions of most metanarratives advanced in education. The investigations that follow adopt the troublesome position that *we do not have a foundational metanarrative for educational discourses-practices* and one is unlikely to be developed.[6] Even though Tyler, Bloom, and Schwab, for example, make no claim to be foundational, many people so interpret them. Many contemporary educators approach what they do as though it is based on a firm foundation with fixed standards, but if no such foundation or standards exist with little or no prospects for establishing them, then it is time to rethink what we say and do. Contrary to such a foundational point of view, I will argue that our attempts to develop metanarratives are incomplete, time-bound, interest-relative, ideologically informed, and shaped by power.

Narratives about narratives, however, need not always aspire to a transcendent status, even though transcendental first principles are the goal of many analytic thinkers and those who remain legatees of positivist thought. A metanarrative, loosely construed, may only propose sufficient conditions for a narrative. Such a claim is that the practice will be good, beautiful, true, reasonable, desirable, or efficient, "if" its metanarrative prescriptions are executed completely and correctly. This more relaxed view resembles educational arguments that do not claim there is only one way of doing things but only that what is proposed (the metanarrative and the narrative discourse-practice it maps) is one of those ways. Less demanding still, a metanarrative may only propose necessary conditions where the claim is that discourse and practice "will not be" beautiful, true, good, efficient, desirable, or reasonable "without" implementing certain practices and prescriptions. This metanarrative effort identifies limiting conditions, as it were, where the conditions, if they are not met, will prevent the realization of desired educational practices and outcomes.

We occasionally talk about what we are talking about and what we are doing. Sometimes such talk is an attempt to construct metanarratives. But because the talking about talking is always time-bound (to the current state of knowledge) and interest-relative (to the interests that produced that knowledge as well as the interests of those doing the talking) and culturally, historically, politically, and economically situated, our efforts to produce metanarratives appear to be less than transcendent and not foundational. For the most part I will not suggest sufficient conditions for what we say and do but will from time to time suggest necessary conditions, the least demanding form of metanarrative, for educational discourses-practices. Even in these cases there is little way of knowing whether the necessary conditions I offer, taken together, produce sufficient conditions for true, beautiful, and good education; furthermore, they will likely be subject to continual revision, rejection, or supplementation.

A last point on metanarratives: a narrative in one setting can operate as a metanarrative in another and vice versa. For example, "principles of scientific management" is a metanarrative for the narrative of Tyler's principles of curriculum development that in turn is a metanarrative for narratives of specific curriculum development projects. What some people find troublesome, however, is not that there are layers of narrative and metanarrative but that all we might have are layers of narrative and that possibly there is nothing foundational to anchor theory and practice. I intend to show that one attempt after another to provide foundational accounts for educational thought and practice cannot sustain a close reading. The results point to a critical pragmatism.

THE ARGUMENT

Structuralist and positivist modes of thought dominate texts and discourses-practices of contemporary education. Positivism refers to an epistemological viewpoint and philosophical school of thought that was quite influential outside as well as inside professional philosophy during the first half of the twentieth century. Positivism will not be discussed, in part because structuralism is broader, more comprehensive, and, some might say, more invasive of social life and institutions. Sometimes structural arguments make knowledge claims that could be taken as positivist, sometimes not. Structuralism is a systematic way of thinking about whole processes and institutions whereby each part of a system defines and is defined by other parts. In many cases educational texts and discourses-practices seem to be premised on structural assumptions. Three well-known examples are discussed in Chapter 2.

Poststructuralist thought attacks structuralist assumptions and the arguments built upon them. Deconstruction, which is one form of poststructural criticism, questions whether proposed first principles that purportedly ground structuralist programs and meanings ever transcend our texts and discourses-practices. If no transcendent first principles exist, then our structures are not as fixed and "structured" as they might appear, because every term or element is always defining every other term or element and vice versa and back and forth with no clear-cut beginning or ending. Another form of poststructural criticism investigates the effects of history and power on what we claim to know and how we organize our discourses-practices. This criticism argues that we are captives of our discourses-practices and, furthermore, that they are not rationally designed. They control us, not the other way around. Together these bodies of thought question the liberal faith in rationality, control, and progress that is repeatedly expressed in educational texts and discourses-practices. The "rethinking" in this chapter's title derives from the challenge of poststructural insights and arguments. They will be used in closely examining a few standards, conventions, beliefs, and accepted truths (small *t*) found in contemporary educational texts and discourses-practices. Chapter 3 provides poststructural readings of the three examples that are given structural readings in Chapter 2.

Rethinking extends beyond criticism. When criticism turns to action, when poststructural analysis is projected onto the world in what we say (discourse) and do (practice), critical pragmatism as a generalized approach to discourses and practices is a possible response. Sometimes pragmatism is thought of as testing an idea by its practical effects; but if practical effects are determined by uncritically comparing what happens with conventional standards, pragmatism becomes vulgar and naive, as vulgar and naive as unreflective acceptance of conventional standards and structures. Critical pragmatism draws from many sources. It does not present a neat approach to education, and certainly not a structured one, even though there remain places for structure. Critical pragmatists bring a sense of crisis to considerations of standards and conventions. Critical pragmatism considers not only what we choose to say and do, along with their effects, but also what structures those choices. Critical pragmatism pursues the fundamental questions asked by poststructural analysis into the design as well as operation of our social practices and institutions. Critical pragmatism is concerned with evaluating and constructing the communities, educational and otherwise, in which we live and work.

A variety of topics are analyzed in moving from structural and poststructural commentary to critical pragmatism. The nature of meaning and how meanings of words, statements, and discourses are dealt with in textbooks and teaching are explored in Chapter 4. Relationships between empirically based theory and critical practice, as well as between educational researcher-theorists and practitioners, are examined in Chapter 5. A prevailing idea, so it seems, is that theory and knowledge based upon empirical research can guide practice and increase the possibility for steadily improving what we do.

The relationship between theory and practice is shown to be more complex and involved than it is ordinarily portrayed in this familiar instrumental and utilitarian view.

Chapter 6 deals with construct validity and its role in the discourses of research. How are words attached to objects and events? How are theoretical constructs attached to research measurements and observations? Even though a literature on construct validity has developed over the last 30 years, the complexity of attaching words to things has not been given a poststructural reading. Chapter 7 deals with curriculum. Curriculum as a field within professional education has been subjected to a fair amount of criticism and quite a bit of internal conflict. Some educators believe this indicates the study and practice of curriculum to be regressive or underdeveloped or dead. Given the complexity of the theory and practice of curriculum, however, such turmoil should be interpreted as normal instead of deviant. At the end of Chapters 4 through 7, specific critical pragmatic suggestions are made. Chapter 8 outlines a more general orientation toward critical pragmatism and addresses objections that can be directed against it. Beyond that, an initial attempt is made to outline poststructural and critical pragmatic strategies for incorporation into educational discourses-practices.

CHAPTER 2

Thinking About
Education Structurally

> At its simplest, [structuralism] claims that the nature of every
> element in any given situation has no significance by itself, and in
> fact is determined by its relationship to all the other elements
> involved in that situation. In short, the full significance of any
> entity or experience cannot be perceived unless and until it is
> integrated into the structure of which it forms a part. (Hawkes,
> 1977, p. 18)

> Structuralism is based, in the first instance, on the realization
> that if human actions or productions have a meaning there must
> be an underlying system of conventions which makes this mean-
> ing possible . . . actions are meaningful only with respect to a set
> of institutional conventions. Wherever there are two posts one can
> kick a ball between them, but one can score a goal only within a
> particular institutionalized framework. (Culler, 1973, p. 21–22)

Structuralism is a method of study that has been used to describe and
analyze phenomena as widely disparate as literature, politics, economics, myths, and cultures. A key assumption about structurally
examined phenomena is that they are characterized by an underlying
structure, not too surprising, that is defined, in part, by relationships
among their constitutive elements. Structuralism broadly considered,
then, includes assumptions about *structures* and *methods of analysis*. It
has been rigorously developed by many twentieth-century scholars,
several of them French. Contemporary educators also display structuralist assumptions in their investigations and *prescriptions* for policy
and practice. Structuralism operates prescriptively in education when
preferred structural procedures, interpretations, and organizations
are promoted with promise of order and rationality. Structuralism as a
method of analysis, at least at the outset, requires distinction from

structuralism as prescription for policy and practice. Structural investigations claim to split analysis (description, explanation, theory) from prescription (commitments, values, practice) even though this distinction sometimes evaporates into indistinction (this is directly discussed in the context of relationships between theory and practice in Chapter 5 and indirectly elsewhere).

Such analyses and prescriptions are related in contemporary education because (1) structurally oriented investigations often inform educational texts, discourses, and practices, (2) that contribute to structural prescriptions, (3) that lead to structurally organized practices, (4) that are investigated structurally, and on and on. Educational discourses and practices, so this argument goes, are often premised on implicit and unstated structural assumptions and arguments about underlying structures *and* methods of investigation even though this is rarely made explicit. Structuralist assumptions seemingly pervade contemporary educational texts, discourses, and practices in addition to other aspects of modern life. To the extent that structural analyses and prescriptions fail to deliver on their claims they deceive us or, at the very least, we are complicit in deceiving ourselves about their power and insight. This does not mean that structural assumptions and arguments are without value, it is just that what they offer may be more modest and other than advertised.

Assumptions of structuralism as a method of study *and* about phenomena to be studied are outlined in the following section. Three widely known educational arguments that promote related yet different educational structures are then given structuralist readings:

1. Tyler's influential 1949 rationale for curriculum development and instruction;
2. Schwab's 1983 extension and application of Tyler's rationale;
3. Bloom et al.'s 1956 rigorous attempt to classify educational objectives in the *Taxonomy of Educational Objectives*.

To my knowledge none of these scholars deliberately set out to import structural ideas into educational discourses-practices nor do they cite a structuralist literature. Bloom et al. come the closest to having explicit intentions along these lines. Finding many explicitly structural principles in their arguments, therefore, takes on added significance because apparently there was no conscious intention to proceed in this manner.[1]

STRUCTURALISM

Structuralist thought is exhibited in work in a wide variety of disciplines: anthropology (Levi-Strauss, 1969a, 1969b), cognitive development (Piaget, 1971, 1976), literary criticism (Barthes, 1972), Marxist criticism (Althusser, 1969), sociology (Parsons, 1960), mathematics (Barbut, 1970; Gandy, 1973), and education (Gibson, 1984). Michael Lane characterizes structuralism in this way:

> What, then, are the distinctive properties of structuralism? In the first place it is presented as a method whose scope includes all human social phenomena, no matter what their form, thus embracing not only the social sciences proper . . . but also the humanities . . . and the fine arts. This is made possible by the belief that all manifestations of social activity, whether it be the clothes that are worn, the books that are written or the systems of kinship and marriage that are practised in any society, constitute languages, in a formal sense. Hence their regularities may be reduced to the same set of abstract rules that define and govern what we normally think of as language. (1970, pp. 13–14)

The term *code* is sometimes used to refer to the abstract set of rules underlying a structure. The vocabulary of a social code names elements in the structure. In education these include such elements as student, teacher, textbook, assessment test, curriculum guide, graduation requirement, school attendance, educational achievement, educational attainment, and literacy. The syntax of a social code determines how elements of the system may be legitimately connected: for example, which courses fulfill graduation requirements, how literacy is defined by which assessment test, and which courses and what level of performance prepare teachers for certification (Lane, 1970).

Structural analysis, whether it is used to study classrooms, schools, curricula, organization of knowledge, kinship systems, or language, emphasizes wholeness and totality, not units and parts. The focus on wholeness comes from concentrating on systemic relationships among individual elements, not on their unique characteristics. Structural analysis also deals with transformations. If a structure is determined by relationships among its units, then those relationships, if the structure is to survive, must regenerate and reproduce the structure. Furthermore, structures are self-regulating, their relationships governing which activities are and are not permitted. A structure, then, is constituted by relationships among elements that are self-regulating and generate transformations. The relationships of a structure define it; they are its reality. As a consequence, structuralism decenters the subject by emphasizing relationships and not individuals. In educational practice, meaning is not determined by what teachers or students think, say, or do but by relationships among what teachers and students think, say, and do. Meaning is located in structures, not in individuals.[2]

Structuralism has been influenced heavily by the linguistics of Ferdinand de Saussure and a book of his that he neither wrote nor published (Lane, 1970). Saussure gave a series of lectures at the University of Geneva from 1906 to 1911, from which his *Course in General Linguistics* was compiled from student and lecture notes. It was published posthumously in 1916. Although Saussure's work will not be discussed in detail, ideas central to his view of language will be outlined.

First, according to Saussure, "the linguistic sign unites . . . a concept and a sound-image. . . . I propose to retain the word *sign* to designate the whole and to replace *concept* and *sound-image* respectively by *signified* and *signifier*" (Saussure, 1916/1966, pp. 66–67). Other thinkers have used different words for *signifier* and *signified*, as summarized in the following list modified from Robert Scholes's *Textual Power* (1985, p. 92). He adds a third aspect of the sign.

SAUSSURE	Signifier	Signified	
PEIRCE	Sign	Interpretant	Object
OGDEN/RICHARDS	Symbol	Thought	Referent
CARNAP	Expression	Intension	Extension
FREGE	Expression	Sense	Reference

Saussure's structural analysis concerns only linguistic systems, not nonlinguistic phenomena. His term *linguistic sign* combines only words and concepts; that is why, for Saussure, the column furthest to the right is empty. I will not follow his lead on this; instead I will follow the others and include rather than exclude objects, referents, and extensions. Here is my reasoning. A text or discourse is constituted by words, utterances, and statements with which ideas, thoughts, and concepts are associated. Textual, discursive ideas are also projected on our object-referent world as words, and utterances assign ideas and concepts to our perceptions. Meanings assigned to objects are socially constructed. Items in the first column to the right of the Author column indicate words, usages, and utterances, and those in the next, ideas and concepts. The last column indicates phenomena to which words and concepts refer. In order to avoid potential confusion and technical differences among these categories, I will use *word* in reference to Saussure's signifier column, *definition* or *concept* for the signified column, and *object* or *referent* for the last column.

Second, signs, for Saussure, are arbitrary because words are linked to definitions by conventions and usages; for example, different languages assign different words to concepts. This does not mean that we can presently assign any word to any idea or concept; but any word *could* have been assigned to any idea or concept before we arrived on the scene. Which words are assigned to which concepts changes from language to language. N. W. Visser illustrates the point this way: "The French say *la main*; we speak of a *hand*; Zulu-speakers say *isandla*. Obviously none of these is a more accurate or appropriate word for a hand than any of the others" (1982, p. 54). Furthermore, different languages divide up the world differently. This is certainly the case for specialized professional discourses. In terms of educational theory and research, quantitative, ethnographic, and critical researchers divide educational discourses-practices quite differently. No previously agreed-upon categories exist by which the world could or should be described and explained—who would have been involved in such an agreement and when would it have taken place? Instead, languages develop, for whatever reasons, differently. If it were otherwise, the matter of translation would be far simpler than it is.

Third, signs (*signifier-signified* for Saussure, *word-concept* in my terminology) do not exist outside a system. Saussure's structural analysis attends to signs and not objects; it is concerned with signifying practices, the way language is organized and used. It is not concerned with truth. However, other approaches to a theory of signs—for example, Charles Peirce's (1931–1958)—includes objects and referents. The structure of the sign system points to an underlying structure of objects and referents. In this formulation structuralism has some investment in truth, although the nature of this investment is not unambiguous.

Fourth, words mean what they do because of relationships to and differences from other words. Saussure sums this up:

> Language is a system of interdependent terms in which the value of each term results solely from the simultaneous presence of the others. (1916/1966, p. 114)

> Everything . . . boils down to this: in language there are only differences. . . . Proof of this is that the value of a term may be modified

without either its meaning or its sound being affected, solely because a neighboring term has been modified. (1916/1966, p. 120)

Educational achievement conveys what it does because it is different from *attainment, attentiveness, good behavior,* or *responsiveness.* Meaning based on differences among words is quite distinct from meaning based on representation (where meaning is taken to be correspondence or identity between words and things). Furthermore, *educational achievement* means what it does not only because it is different from *educational attainment* but also because of its relationships to, for example, objectives, content, and norms or standards. By itself *educational achievement* does not have linguistic value. Nor would, say, an *educational objective* be intelligible outside a context of students, content, or instruction. (Chapter 4 is an extended discussion of the nature of meaning and meanings, and Chapter 6, of construct validity. Each discusses these questions at some length.)

Fifth, there is a distinction between language (*langue*) and speech (*parole*). Structuralism focuses on language and not particular utterances. T. K. Seung explains how this extends beyond language:

> The Saussurian distinction between *langue* and *parole* can also be applied to the furniture, the garment. . . . The actual array of furniture in any given room is a *parole;* the possibilities of selecting and combining different pieces into that array or any other arrangement constitute a *langue.* The various pieces of clothes one wears for any given occasion is a *parole;* the possibilities of selecting and combining those and any other pieces into an acceptable form of attire belong to the *langue* of vestimentary language. (1982, p. 121)

In educational discourse-practice a particular lesson is *parole* and possible lessons are part of a pedagogical *langue.*

Sixth, structural analysis focuses on one moment in time; it is a snapshot (Saussure's term is *synchronic*). At any one moment a linguistic structure is fixed, but languages change as words and meanings are added and dropped. It is obvious that educational discourses-practices also develop and change. But at any moment relationships among, say, educational practices constitute education, just as relationships among English words constitute the English language. Structural analysis for Saussure is ahistoric. Beginnings and origins are excluded. Again, let us take education as an example. A structural analysis of a classroom lesson does not consider the origins of content or organization or the rationale for learning objectives and assessment instruments. Instead it focuses on interactions, relationships, and processes that constitute the lesson as observed and recorded. This aspect of structural analysis is not new to educational research.

Seventh, because language is determined by relationships or differences among words, binary distinctions or oppositions determine the content of the structure. Seung writes:

> Binary distinction is the simplest logical device for discrimination, namely between having a quality or attribute and not having it, or between belonging to a class and not belonging to it. It underlies every assertion or denial. There can be no more pervasive logical principle than this one. (1982, p. 10)

This is the process by which words are distinguished from each other. In some cases they are direct opposites, such as light/dark, strong/weak, or fast/slow, but in many instances differences are binary distinctions, such as achievement/attainment, equal access/equal outcomes, or education/instruction.[3] Binary distinctions abound in contemporary education: achievement/failure, theory/practice, concept/fact, accountability/lack of accountability, terminal objective/ intermediate objective, literate/illiterate, cognitive/affective, sociocentric/egocentric, subject-centered/learner-centered, reproductive/nonreproductive, emancipation/oppression, autonomous/nonautonomous, and empowered/disempowered, for example. In structural analysis and criticism, the word valued by the structure is stated first, the disvalued word second, and which orientation one adopts toward educational discourses-practices determines one's values and disvalues. The normative commitments of a structure, then, are highlighted by identifying its valued and disvalued categories.

Eighth, structuralism claims to be ideologically neutral because it promotes description and mapping. It does not take sides. In this sense it is consistent with certain twentieth-century philosophical approaches to science, such as logical positivism and logical empiricism. The goal is to tell it like it is and not as one wishes it to be. Telling things as they are, however, is a subtle endorsement of things as they are, and this works to structuralism's disadvantage during times of social unrest and controversy. For example, structuralism's lack of political relevance and commitment was attacked during the general political turmoil in France in May 1968, where structuralism had previously been an important intellectual force. Visser tells the following story:

> The demand for a more socially involved, more politically committed methodology was crystallised in a famous statement written on a black-

board at one of the campuses of the University of Paris, which may be freely translated as "Structures don't go down into the streets and fight!" (1982, p. 63)

Ideological neutrality also resonates with contemporary educational discourses-practices when research findings are reported in the tradition of positivism and empiricism and political and ideological criticism is studiously avoided.

Structural analysis of sign systems attends to relationships, categories, classifications, and valuations of a particular argument, myth, novel, poem, governmental system, tribal organization, or teacher training program. Structural characteristics are found in many areas and activities of contemporary education, such as curriculum theory and planning, textbook content, curriculum guidelines, assessment tests, time-on-task research, and approaches to research design. Structural analysis, in turn, identifies which signs are included and excluded, which are valued and disvalued. Here are three examples.

STRUCTURALISM IN EDUCATION

Proposals for educational improvement and reform in the United States, at least since World War II, have consistently employed structural assumptions, usually unstated.

Tyler's Rationale

In 1949 Ralph Tyler made a strong and persuasive argument for organization in curriculum planning. He writes:

> The rationale developed here begins with identifying four fundamental questions which must be answered in developing any curriculum and plan of instruction. These are:
> 1. What educational purposes should the school seek to attain?
> 2. What educational experiences can be provided that are likely to attain these purposes?
> 3. How can these educational experiences be effectively organized?
> 4. How can we determine whether these purposes are being attained? (p. 1)

Tyler shows educators how to think systematically about curriculum and instruction. His four questions impose structural assumptions on educational thought. For example, by themselves learning objectives have little meaning, but in a structure of organized learning experiences and evaluation, they become part of systematic instruction. Likewise, an evaluation instrument in the context of objectives and learning experiences takes on significance that it lacks by itself. Each stage of the Tyler rationale in isolation from the others means little. They acquire meaning from relations to and differences from other steps in the process.

Tyler proposes an eclectic approach when selecting objectives. He points out that learners themselves, life outside the school, subject specialists, philosophical orientations, and educational psychology are all important sources for learning objectives (Tyler, 1949, Chapter 1). He writes:

> It is certainly true that in the final analysis objectives are matters of choice, and they must therefore be the considered value judgments of those responsible for the school. A comprehensive philosophy of education is necessary to guide in making these judgments. (p. 4)

His brief review of conflicting philosophies over purposes of education repeatedly returns to the plurality of demands made on curriculum and instruction; for example, objectives should focus on student needs, academic content, or reflect community standards. They should be melded together for purposes of planning curriculum and instruction.

Once objectives have been determined he turns to educational objectives and learning experiences: "for a given objective to be attained, a student must have experiences that give him an opportunity to practice the kind of behavior implied by the objective" (p. 65). The experiences should produce learner satisfactions and be within their range of abilities. He appreciates the complexity of selecting learning experiences by noting that different experiences can produce the same outcome and, conversely, one experience can produce several outcomes. Learning experiences are meaningful, in Tyler's rationale, because they follow from previously selected objectives. He also anticipates the Bloom et al. *Taxonomy of Educational Objectives*, then in its early stages of formulation.

The third step in the process is the organization of the learning experiences in order to enhance efficiency in instruction. "It is . . . necessary to consider the main structural elements in which the learning experiences are to be organized. Structural elements exist at several levels" (p. 98). Learning experiences should be organized according to three criteria: continuity, sequence, and integration. Together these criteria ensure that learning experiences will be reinforced over time, built upon by moving to greater levels of complexity and sophistication, and systematically related to learning experiences in other parts of the curriculum.

The fourth and final step is evaluation. How extensive the evaluation should be is determined by the information needed, and he reviews, quickly, some principles of research design such as sampling, validity, and reliability:

> What is implied in all of this is that curriculum planning is a continuous process and that as materials and procedures are developed, they are tried out, their results appraised, their inadequacies identified, suggested improvements indicated . . . it is possible for the curriculum and instructional program to be continuously improved over the years. (p. 123)

The process is to be recycled and errors corrected. It is orderly, persuasive, and structural to the core.

Its structural characteristics are as follows:

1. Curricular meaning is determined by relationships among steps in the process.
2. Individual steps do not have educational significance apart from the system in which they are located.
3. The design process is ahistorical in that origins of objectives, learning experiences, and evaluation are discussed and analyzed in terms of the immediate situation and not historically.
4. Teachers and students are decentered and not at the center of meaning and curriculum because meaning is determined by relationships among objectives, learning experiences, their organization, and evaluation.
5. The design process gives the appearance of ideological neutrality.
6. The four steps of curriculum design define and regulate the curriculum—they constitute its reality.
7. The four steps of curriculum design determine how curriculum is transformed.
8. Tyler's rationale posits a series of binary distinctions: purposeful/purposeless, organization/disorganization, evaluation/nonevaluation, legitimate educational purposes/illegitimate educational purposes, accountability/nonaccountability, continuity/discontinuity, sequence/nonsequence, and integration/nonintegration.

Tyler's proposal was attractive because it promised order, organization, rationality, error correction, political neutrality, expertise, and progress.

Schwab's "The Practical 4"

Schwab's 1983 essay on the practical follows in the tradition Tyler inaugurated. He set out to write a "practical paper on the practical" (p. 239) that would outline something for curriculum professors to do. The structural elements of the essay are not logical, "not premises, argument, and conclusion but circumstances and alternative ways of changing them" (p. 239). He begins with a definition of curriculum:

> Curriculum is what is successfully conveyed to differing degrees to different students, by committed teachers using appropriate materials and actions, of legitimated bodies of knowledge, skill, taste, and propensity to act and react, which are chosen for instruction after serious reflection and communal decision by representatives of those involved in the teaching of a specified group of students who are known to the decision makers (1983, p. 240)

This definition identifies elements of curricular structure: what is successfully conveyed; committed teachers; appropriate actions; legitimated knowledge, skill, taste, propensity to act and react; serious reflection; communal decision; and a specified group of students. The parts are important only in the context of the whole, and the whole is what constitutes the curriculum; they are not important by themselves.

He objects that much written about learning objectives trivializes and anatomizes content. Objectives, he argues, can only be selected in "the light of consideration of available or obtainable means, materials, and teaching skills; nor can ends chosen lead to means and materials which yield only the ends for which they were chosen" (p. 240). Objectives are contextualized. And of equal importance, theoretically at least, are the four commonplaces of education: teacher, student, what is taught, and milieux of teaching. Sometimes one commonplace will dominate; at another place or time a different one may dominate.

The problem is how to "institute a continuing watch and correction of . . . curriculum" (p. 243):

> In this paper, I deal with . . . a path for professorial involvement in the practical. I shall do so by first describing the character and usefulness of a new role or office to be installed in individual schools or small school

systems. I shall then indicate the initial higher education which would prepare men and women to fill this office, and the professorial scholarly activity which would continuously refresh those who fill this office. (p. 243)

Schwab proposes a curriculum committee to evaluate and correct the curriculum. Its membership should be eclectic, consisting of two or three teachers, the principal, a member of the school board or business community, an academic specialist, and, possibly, a student. The person who chairs the group holds this curriculum position and should guard against alienating individual members and anticipate biases for or against particularly academic or pedagogical approaches to curriculum.

Curricular problems will be discovered at home and abroad. Classrooms will be visited. A comparative study of standardized achievement and aptitude tests, textbooks, and obligations imposed by law or bureaucratic decree will be undertaken. The chairman will talk to students and visit playgrounds. Abroad, the chairman will visit other schools and talk with their teachers. And the chairman will read leading journals. Practical problems are not given, they are taken:

> That is, in the words of John Dewey, one encounters problematic situations, conditions which are discomforting or disconcerting, but the concrete formulation of the problem requires delicate consideration of alternative formulations. (p. 257)

Little more is said about taking problems, but after their formulation solutions must be devised or discovered (p. 257). Much of the remaining argument describes the education and refreshment of the chairman.

Schwab's "The Practical 4" follows clearly in the Tyler tradition and is so acknowledged by Tyler himself (Tyler, 1984). Schwab intends to quell unneeded theorizing and make curriculum an active instead of passive enterprise.

Structural elements in "The Practical 4" are easily identified:

1. It emphasizes relationships among students, teachers, content, and setting in watching and correcting the curriculum.
2. Students and teachers are decentered because curriculum is centered on relationships, such as those among legitimated knowledge, appropriate actions, and communal decisions that are external to individual students and teachers.

3. Curricula do not exist beyond what is explicitly part of the curricular system that is systematically conveyed to students.
4. Curriculum analysis and correction deal with what is in place at a given point in time and not with historical analyses of how things got that way.
5. The curriculum is conceptualized in terms of binary distinctions: what is successfully conveyed/what is not successfully conveyed, committed teachers/uncommitted teachers, legitimate knowledge/illegitimate knowledge, serious reflection/casual reflection, communal decisions/individual decisions, representatives/nonrepresentatives, and specified group of students/ unspecified group of students.
6. The curriculum and the processes by which it is evaluated and corrected is ideologically neutral; it is a professional exercise based on professional expertise.

Schwab's essay clearly illustrates continuing structural influences on curricular discourse in the 1980s.

Bloom et al.'s Taxonomy

Bloom, Engelhart, Furst, Hill, and Krathwohl begin their book, *Taxonomy of Educational Objectives: Cognitive Domain*, with an epigraph; it is Webster's (*Webster's New Collegiate Dictionary*, 1953) definition of taxonomy, "Classification, esp. of animals and plants according to their natural relationships" (1956, p. 1). It is dedicated to Ralph Tyler. This project to classify educational objectives originated at the American Psychological Association Convention in Boston in 1948. "The major purpose in constructing a taxonomy of educational objectives is to facilitate communication" (p. 10) among those "who deal with curricular and evaluation problems" (p. 1). This is to be achieved by the following steps: "The major task in setting up any kind of taxonomy is that of selecting appropriate symbols, giving them precise and usable definitions, and securing the consensus of the group which is to use them" (p. 11). The object is to classify "student behaviors which represent the intended outcomes of the educational process" (p. 12) that are distinct from teacher behaviors and actual student behaviors. And "probably the most common educational objective in American education is the acquisition of knowledge or information" (p. 28). The authors assume a minimum commonality among classes of intended behaviors across students, schools, subject matters, grade levels, locales, and so forth.

Minimally a taxonomy is a scheme that designates classes of objects that have something in common (p. 10). But a taxonomy is more than simple classification:

> A taxonomy must be so constructed that the order of the terms must correspond to some "real" order among the phenomena represented by the terms . . . [and be] validated by demonstrating its consistency with the theoretical views in research findings of the field it attempts to order. (p. 17)

Even though they were not able to base the taxonomy on current theories of personality and learning, it was hoped that the taxonomy would point the way toward general theories to follow. The taxonomy has six major classes:

1.00 Knowledge
2.00 Comprehension
3.00 Application
4.00 Analysis
5.00 Synthesis
6.00 Evaluation

And "the objectives in one class are likely to make use of and be built on the behaviors found in the preceding classes in this list" (p. 18). Behaviors were arranged from simple to complex, concrete to abstract.

The authors demonstrate a remarkable sophistication in pointing out that taxonomies, whatever else may be said of them, are social constructions, and since "the determination of classes and their titles is in some ways arbitrary, there could be an almost infinite number of ways of dividing and naming the domains of educational outcomes" (p. 13). The arbitrary nature of a taxonomy notwithstanding, a useful taxonomy should be comprehensive and communicable, stimulate thought, and be accepted and used by workers in the field.

A few of their guiding principles are insightful about subsequent uses to which the taxonomy would be put. First, the taxonomy is designed to capture the way teachers distinguish among student behaviors (p. 13). Second, the taxonomy, as with any categorical system, is to be logical and internally consistent (p. 14). Third, the taxonomy should represent contemporary understandings of psychological phenomena (p. 14). Fourth, the taxonomy should be "purely descriptive" in which it is possible to represent every educational goal in a "neutral" way that avoids value judgments (p. 14). The presumed value neutrality of the taxonomy is strongly emphasized.

> A comprehensive taxonomy of educational objectives must, in our opinion, include all the educational objectives represented in American education without making judgments about their value, meaningfulness, or appropriateness. (p. 30)

The taxonomy embodies several characteristics of structuralism:

1. The particular form of the taxonomy is arbitrary.
2. The value of each educational objective is determined by its relationships to and differences from other objectives.
3. It asserts a number of binary distinctions, for example, comprehension/knowledge, application/comprehension, analysis/application, synthesis/analysis, evaluation/synthesis, and implicitly subject-centered learning/student-centered learning.
4. Teachers and students are decentered because educational value and meaning is authoritatively located in structures external to individuals.
5. It is ideologically neutral, designed to "be a purely descriptive scheme in which every type of educational goal can be represented in a relatively neutral fashion" (p. 14).

The authors of the taxonomy are clear about their structuralist commitments even though a structuralist literature is not cited.

CONCLUSION

Structuralism as a pervasive and often unacknowledged way of thinking has influenced twentieth-century thinking in important ways. It promises order, organization, and certainty. Structuralism in education promises accountability, efficiency, and control as well as order, organization, and certainty. Structuralism is consistent with teaching for objectives, standardized educational assessment, quantitative empirical research, systematic instruction, rationalized bureaucracies, and scientific management. As long as structural assumptions remain unacknowledged, they are immunized against criticism. The discussion now shifts to poststructural analysis and questions whether structuralism delivers on its promises.

CHAPTER 3

Thinking About Education Poststructurally

> Foucault's aim is to isolate, identify, and analyze the web of un-equal relationships set up by political technologies which under-lies and undercuts the theoretical equality posited by the law and political philosophers. . . . To understand power in its material-ity, its day to day operation we must go to the level of the micro-practices, the political technologies in which our practices are formed. *(Dreyfus & Rabinow, 1983, p. 185)*

> To deconstruct a discourse is to show how it undermines the philosophy it asserts, or the hierarchical oppositions on which it relies, by identifying in the text the rhetorical operations that produce the supposed ground of argument, the key concept or premise. *(Culler, 1984, p. 86)*

Structuralism is promoted as orderly, organized, and rational analy-sis. In the 1980s educational discourses-practices remain heavily influ-enced by structuralist assumptions, even though that commitment may be due more to professional inertia and contemporary political interests than to justifications that are continually rehearsed and paraded as defenses for what educators do. Structural assumptions can be criticized on several grounds. One objection centers on its displacement of the individual from the center of meaning. It is quite possible, for example, that periodic revivals of interest in humanistic education are rejections of the antihumanistic side of structuralism in education, which puts relationships among elements and structures at the center and people at the margins. A second, politically conser-vative, objection to structuralism might argue that its focus on struc-ture at a point in time diminishes historic cultural traditions and values. A more serious objection, however, is that structuralist assumptions contain arguments that subvert themselves. The latter lead to poststructural analysis and criticism.[1]

Even though structuralism has influenced work in a variety of disciplines and professions, it may nowhere have been developed with greater rigor or self-consciousness than in literary criticism and theory (see Eagleton, 1983). This led to close scrutiny of structuralist assumptions unlike, say, in educational discourse, where structural assumptions are everywhere to be found yet unacknowledged. Criticism of structuralism has produced a diverse body of thought called *poststructuralism*. Jonathan Culler contrasts structuralism with poststructuralism in the following passage:

> In simplest terms, structuralists take linguistics as a model and attempt to develop "grammars"—systematic inventories of elements and their possibilities of combination—that would account for the form and meaning of literary works; post-structuralists investigate the way in which this project is subverted by the workings of the texts themselves. Structuralists are convinced that systematic knowledge is possible; post-structuralists claim to know only the impossibility of this knowledge. (1984, p. 22)

If systematic knowledge is possible for structuralists, it is based on meanings that are fixed. One way to stabilize meaning in a text or discourse is to appeal to a transcendent idea that rises above the text or discourse. Such an idea or concept is a transcendental signified or a transcendental semantic meaning. The meaning of other words can be determined by comparing them against such a foundational idea. Eagleton writes:

> It is just that, out of this play of words, certain meanings are elevated by social ideologies to a privileged position, or made the centres around which other meanings are forced to turn. Consider, in our own society, Freedom, the Family, Democracy, Independence, Authority, Order and so on. (1983, p. 131)

Vincent Leitch suggests other candidates for this origin of truth: "the spoken word, . . . the voice of reason, or . . . the Word of God" (1983, p. 25). What has passed for, or, put somewhat differently, has been passed off as, transcendental signifieds in education? Candidates include examples in the previous chapter: the Tyler rationale, Schwab's "The Practical 4," and Bloom et al.'s *Taxonomy of Educational Objectives*. Effective schooling, "excellence" in education, education for critical thinking, and back to the "basics" also come to mind. Poststructural analysis asks of transcendental signifieds: Where do they come from? How were they produced? Why did they originate?

How are they reproduced? Why are they authoritative? What do they assert?

Origins of poststructural thought are difficult to pinpoint. Howard Felperin traces one aspect of poststructural analysis, deconstruction, to the pre-Socratics (1985, p. 104). Nietzsche and Heidegger are more recent, yet important forerunners of present-day poststructural thought (Megill, 1985). And Richard Rorty adds Dewey and Wittgenstein to the list of twentieth-century contributors while signing on himself (1980). Contemporary developments in poststructural thought, however, took off during the 1960s and can be identified with, but certainly not limited to, the careers and writings of Michel Foucault and Jacques Derrida. They offer accounts of the meaning of discourses, practices, and systems of signs that pose fundamental challenges to structuralism. A brief exposition follows of a few of their more important ideas; this is, at best, an elementary introduction to two complex bodies of thought. Then the three examples of educational discourse-practice of Chapter 2 will be given a poststructural reading.

INTERPRETIVE ANALYTICS AND MICHEL FOUCAULT

Michel Foucault was a French intellectual who called himself a historian of systems of ideas.[2] He studied historical practices that made the production of specialized discursive practices possible. These include those that constitute modern prisons (1979), mental institutions (1973a), hospitals (1975), sexuality (1980c), and political economy and general grammar (1973b). He argues that social and political institutions and discursive practices are mutually productive and reproductive:

> Discursive practices are not purely and simply ways of producing discourse. They are embodied in technical processes, in institutions, in patterns for general behavior, in forms for transmission and diffusion, and in pedagogical forms which, at once, impose and maintain them. (1980b, p. 200)

Foucault is interested in the political production of truth. How are discourses constituted? How do discourses constitute institutions? How do institutions constitute and regulate discourses? He tries to account for how texts came to be what they are, not explain or interpret them or say what they really meant.

Foucault describes long, slow, almost imperceptible changes in discursive practices, occasionally interspersed with jarring disjunctures, that constitute meaning in sign systems. It is inescapable, he argues, that discourses are materially produced by specific social, political, and economic arrangements. What is said in the name of truth is not simply an idealist construction. Discursive practices have a material basis because they cannot be extricated from their historical setting. Repeating from Chapter 1, a discursive practice is

> a body of anonymous, historical rules, always determined in the time and space that have defined a given period, and for a given social, economic, geographical, or linguistic area, the conditions of operation of the enunciative function. (1972, p. 117)

The rules of a discourse govern what is said and what remains unsaid. They identify who can speak with authority and who must listen. They are anonymous because there is no identifiable author (Foucault, 1980b), nor do they have a clear-cut beginning (Said, 1985).

Educators speak as educators, for example, after becoming proficient in their professional discourses. Certifiably so. Following certification one is permitted or asked or compensated to speak with authority on education. Such speakers, however, have no direct access to the origins of the discourses. In Foucault's terms they are anonymous speakers, or as Michael Shapiro puts it, "It would be appropriate, within his [Foucault's] view of the subject, to reverse the familiar notion that persons make statements, and say that statements make persons" (1981, p. 141).

Implications of this argument for contemporary education are striking and dramatic. Professional educators would like to believe they are in control of what they say and do and that their discourses-practices are based on true statements. But if truth is discursive and discourses are historically situated, then truth cannot be spoken in the absence of power and each historical arrangement of power has its own truths. Foucault summarizes the relationship between truth and power in the following passage:

> Truth is a thing of this world: it is produced only by virtue of multiple forms of constraint. And it induces regular effects of power. Each society has its regime of truth, its "general politics" of truth: that is, the types of discourse which it accepts and makes function as true; the mechanisms and instances which enable one to distinguish true and false statements, the means by which each is sanctioned; the techniques and procedures

accorded value in the acquisition of truth; the status of those who are charged with saying what counts as true. (1980a, p. 131)

Discourses dominant in a historical period and geographical location determine what counts as true, important, or relevant, what gets spoken, what remains unsaid. Discourses are generated and governed by rules and power. It is not possible to separate the meaning of signs and sign systems from their production and reproduction. It may be that the relationship of a word to a definition or concept is arbitrary, as structuralists posit, but these "arbitrary" configurations are products of history, culture, politics, economics, and language. Individuals are linked to macrosocial processes and institutions when they become socialized, and by this mechanism power helps shape how we think of ourselves and act. For example, preservice teacher-training students want to become good teachers. Becoming a "good teacher" means for them to acquire skills to control a classroom, plan lessons, give appropriate feedback, evaluate learning, and hold parent conferences. They desire to become "good teachers" in their time and place. Good teachers desire to master "appropriate" discourses-practices of teaching.

Power operates visibly and invisibly through expectations and desires. It operates visibly through formal, public criteria that must be satisfied. It operates invisibly through the way individuals (teachers, administrators, and university-based educators, for example) think of themselves and act. Educators adapt as a matter of everyday professional life to contractual organizational demands, to demands of professional discourse, to expectations of professional peers, and to informal as well as formal job expectations. Power helps shape subjective feelings and beliefs, our subjectivities. Often power is most effective and efficient when it operates as desire, because desire often makes the effects of power invisible.

The definition of power in Chapter 1 focused on asymmetries by which some people are rewarded and indulged or deprived and sanctioned by others. In Foucault's analysis, discursive and nondiscursive practices of schools, teacher education programs, school board elections, state certification requirements, and textbook adoption procedures create and recreate asymmetries as individuals desire to become the best they can be as teacher, administrator, counselor, or supervisor. Power shapes and informs our psyche. The result is that we are *objects* of social institutions and processes while we *intentionally* engage in meaningful behavior. Foucault studies the political production of truth and argues that it is produced by individuals caught up and proficient in discursive and nondiscursive practices of their time who participate in discourses without origins or authors and over which they have little control.

The poststructuralism of Foucault rejects the ahistoricism and political neutrality of structuralism. The arbitrariness of structuralism is historically and culturally relative. The relationships of structuralism that determine its transformation are denied because the possibility of objective laws apart from history are denied. Relationships among signs or elements of a structure result from power arrangements that precede speech and truth. Foucault's analysis, however, shares the antihumanism of structuralism because persons are products of and not at the center of social structures. Given his analysis, a progressive politics for Foucault is: How can people gain control of their discourses and practices instead of being controlled by them? (Foucault, 1973a)

DECONSTRUCTION AND JACQUES DERRIDA

A second form of poststructural criticism, associated with the work of Jacques Derrida, focuses on the written text. It challenges the structural claim that meaning in a text can be determined by appeal to a transcendental signified or that meaning is outlined in binary distinctions and oppositions. Derrida argues that meaning is not centered or fixed because it is caught in a *play* of references between words and definitions where texts only give the appearance of stability but have no center, no transcendental signified, no transcendental semantic meaning.

Two provocative arguments of Derrida's are that meanings are dispersed throughout language and texts and are deferred in time. If meanings are dispersed and deferred, then structures of meaning are no more than illusions. Dispersed meanings turn structural assumptions against themselves in the following manner. In structural terms, the linguistic value of a word is determined by differences from and relationships to other words. In everyday life a dictionary is used to find differences and relationships among words. To the word *achieve*, for example, is assigned the definition "to bring to a successful conclusion: accomplish." Of course, one may wonder what definitions are attached to *conclusion* and *accomplish*. To *conclusion* is assigned "a reasoned judgment, the necessary consequence of two or more propositions taken as premises" or "result, outcome." To *accomplish* is assigned "to execute fully: perform" or "to attain to (a measure of time or distance.)" A definition turns into a series of words, each with its own definition, and the chain of relationships extends indefinitely.

Deferral of meaning is closely related to dispersal of meaning. An example of dispersed meanings is given by tracing meanings of a word to its definition, which is itself composed of words that have definitions, which are themselves composed of words, and on and on. If this search is considered in terms of the time it takes to complete the search, the meaning of *achievement* will not be decided until the meanings of *successful, conclusion,* and *accomplish* are determined. Determining the meaning of *achievement* is put off until yet a later time. But when will the meaning of *achievement* be decided? It is continually deferred into the future. Tracking meanings is not a closed-ended process. One consequence is that we are always waiting for definitive meanings. If we are always waiting for definitive meanings, the structuralist idea of definitive and fixed meanings is not reasonable or plausible.

How this works in ongoing discourses-practices is easily demonstrated. *Educational excellence* is often promoted as a goal worthy of the next educational reform movement. It operates as a transcendental signified, yet there is often doubt about what it means. Put a bit differently, if *educational excellence* were brought about, how could it be recognized (another consequence of not having a metanarrative)? Consensus on the meaning of *educational excellence* is transitory, and when there is agreement it is often observed only among members of a homogeneous subgroup of professional educators or laypersons. Imagine a group of reformers promoting *educational excellence*. Someone asks, "What is educational excellence?" A reformer responds, "Educational excellence is something that deserves the concern of all of us and we should all help bring it about. What do you think it is?" This might, or might not, be an effective political strategy for co-opting potential antagonists, but the clarification (?) begets clarification (?), and the meaning of *educational excellence* is deferred until later while resources for educational reform are mobilized. At some point, for whatever reason(s), we are persuaded to stop searching and settle on a stipulated meaning, which serves, of course, as the point of origin for some later search. Deciding when to construct agreements or deconstruct meanings is a pragmatic choice.

How can the meaning of a word be fixed if it points to a definition composed of words that point to multiple definitions composed of yet more words that point to . . . and so on without end. Where do we begin? Where do we end? What limits this chasing after origins and centers of language and discourse? If we use a dictionary we tend to stop after finding a definition or two because there are practical and situational limits on our need for rigor and closure determined, in part, by dominant discourses-practices that constrain our search for meanings. The structure, rigor, and orderliness promised by structuralism is illusory. Settling upon a foundation is situational and pragmatic. Authors of record choose to press certain ideas rhetorically or logically, and readers choose to stop deconstructing the text at certain moments.

Meanings are dispersed from word, to definition, to definitions of words in definitions, and on and on. This dispersion of meanings destroys Saussure's structural concept of the sign. Reading, in part, is a pursuit of traces of meaning in a text. A consequence of the dispersal of meanings in a text is that proposed categories of inclusion and exclusion deconstruct and break down. Derrida writes: "I have attempted to systematize a deconstructive critique precisely against the authority of meaning, as the *transcendental signified*" (1981, p. 49). Transcendental signifieds represent commitments of a sign system. Deconstructive criticism exposes these commitments and, in the process, shows how the logic of a text embarrasses and contradicts itself. Eagleton writes:

> Sometimes such meanings [transcendental signifieds] are seen as the *origin* of all the others, the source from which they flow; but this . . . is a curious way of thinking, because for this meaning ever to have been possible other signs must already have existed. (1983, p. 131)

Even though a transcendental signified is illusory, it is arguable that disciplines and professions, including educational discourses-practices, are not possible without the transitory "certainties" they offer.

It is fair to ask whether deconstruction promises a foundation immune to its own criticism. The answer, simply put, is no. Derrida writes, "I do not believe, that someday it will be possible *simply* to escape metaphysics" (1981, p. 17). A transcendental signified is a metaphysical commitment. By this is meant a commitment that does not require rational, scientific, logical justification. We are always caught in a play of references, traces of meaning, meanings dispersed in language and deferred in time. The denial of a fixed center undermines a structural sense of meaning, giving rise to the term *poststructural*.

Whereas Foucault argues that discourses are never independent of history, power, and interests, Derrida shows that texts are often not what they claim to be. Their rhetoric is often not supported by their logic. Here is a highly abbreviated version of this argument. Texts and discourses make substantive claims. They might claim to provide a means of planning a curriculum (Tyler), help in selecting and organizing educational objectives (Bloom et al.), or provide a way to study and correct a curriculum (Schwab). These are rhetorical claims. They assert: "I will tell you how to do X." Texts and discourses also have a logical structure, valid or invalid, if they are more than simple or polemical assertion(s). The logic of an argument, among other things, links premises to conclusions on the basis of evidence and warrants or backing for the evidence. Derrida claims that many texts make rhetorical claims unsupported by the logic of their arguments; this is a characteristic of language and writing, not simply a problem with specific texts or discourses. The ways in which rhetoric and logic diverge, contradict each other, reinforce each other, or remain ambiguous about the claims of the other provide insight into the effects and thrust of power and ideology in what we say and do. The problem of rhetorically overreaching one's logic is shared in varying degrees by Tyler, Bloom et al., and Schwab and will shortly be demonstrated.

Eagleton describes deconstruction this way:

> Deconstruction . . . has grasped the point that the binary oppositions with which classical structuralism tends to work represent a way of seeing typical of ideologies. Ideologies like to draw rigid boundaries between what is acceptable and what is not, between self and non-self, truth and falsity, sense and nonsense, reason and madness, central and marginal, surface and depth. (1983, p. 133)

The political neutrality of structural analyses or proposals is illusory, because whatever transcendental signified is promoted brings with it interests and commitments. It is not possible to ground a text on something stable and fixed beyond itself.

Because meanings are dispersed and deferred, the binary distinctions and oppositions by which structures are ordered give way and can often be shown to depend upon each other as a result of meanings related to meanings related to meanings . . . Because meanings depend upon each other in this linguistic and textual dispersal, structural distinctions are covertly tenuous, waiting, as it were, to be overtly deconstructed. If discourses-practices are premised on structural grounds in ignorance of their eventual deconstruction, periodic disillusionment is to be expected, because, at least if poststructuralists are correct, what texts and discourses-practices promise is often something other than what they deliver.

On first encounter, the poststructural agreements of Foucault and

Derrida may seem a bit abstruse and exotic. One is certainly entitled to ask what they have to do with educational discourses-practices. This will now be illustrated by giving a poststructuralist reading to Tyler's rationale, Schwab's "The Practical 4," and Bloom et al.'s *Taxonomy of Educational Objectives*. Poststructural analysis, depending upon the version one selects, makes specific claims about knowledge, discourse, practice, and text. Poststructural analysis, again depending upon one's inclinations, presents methodologies for criticism. Some of the arguments in the following section reflect criticisms that have appeared before (see Kliebard, 1970; Pinar, 1981; Giroux, 1979), *but* the methodological force of poststructural criticism goes beyond questioning the substantive direction of the argument or its normative commitments.

POSTSTRUCTURAL CRITICISM AND EDUCATION

Tyler's Rationale

Tyler's rationale for curriculum design is composed of four steps: selecting and defining learning objectives, selecting and creating learning experiences, organizing learning experiences, and evaluating curriculum. Implementing the rationale requires decisions at each stage, and a structural and systematic approach to decision making involves at least (1) a description of the factual, "objective" situation, (2) a statement of values to be pursued, (3) possible alternative choices, (4) predictions about probable outcomes for each alternative, and (5) selection of a course of action based on a decision criterion. Tyler ignores questions of value, prediction of outcomes, and decision criteria. One immediately confronts the question: Under what conditions can the rationale be made operative? Because the rationale is incomplete when it comes to making decisions about curriculum and instruction, it deconstructs in the Derridean sense because it rhetorically claims what it does not logically deliver.

The transcendental signified of the rationale is "an instructional program as a functioning instrument of education" (Tyler, 1949, p. 1) or curriculum development and instruction as a practical enterprise. Because its transcendental signified is a "functioning instrument of education" located in whatever educational discourses-practices are in place, it is socially determined by its political, historical, cultural, economic, and linguistic setting in the Foucauldian sense. Put differently, because the rationale does not achieve what it claims, curricula and instructional plans constructed on its pattern necessarily reflect the dominant ideology and power arrangements of the time. And what is spoken on its behalf operates as truth (small *t*). Such claims change with the times. For example, curricula designed in the 1950s were silent on issues such as feminism, racism, poverty, and social injustice and inequality, issues about which some curricula designed in the 1970s and early 1980s were vocal. The structural basis for the Tyler rationale produces programs that are unwitting captives of their times. *They are objects of history intentionally produced by educational experts.*

Tyler acknowledges the historical and social relativism of the rationale in the following passage:

> Another question with which the school's philosophy will need to deal can be stated, "Should there be a different education for different classes of society?" If the answer is "yes," then the practice of setting up different objectives for children of lower social classes who leave school early to go to work may be justified. On the other hand, if the answer to this question is "no," if the school believes in a common democratic education for all, then in place of having differentiated objectives for different classes of youngsters in the school an effort is made to select common objectives that are personally and socially significant and the school tries to develop ways of attaining these common objectives with a wide variety of types of young people. (1949, p. 36)

It should be pointed out straight away that schools do not have beliefs one way or the other; people have beliefs. In the context of the rationale it makes little difference whether the answer is "yes" or "no" to the question of different education for different classes. The rationale is not helpful in making choices of this kind because there is no discussion of decision making, politics, ethics, social criticism, social responsibility, or critical reflection. Because the procedure is ahistorical, there is no way to make judgments in the context of what has gone before. Tyler promises "basic principles" of curriculum and instruction, yet there is silence on principles needed for the proposal to become operative.

Tyler's rationale gives the appearance of order, organization, rationality, and enlightened educational control and engineering. But it does not deliver in terms of criticism and choice. Its rhetorical claims exceed its logical argument. The effect, therefore, is to reinforce current educational discourses-practices, along with their supporting ideologies and power arrangements. The rationale endorses things the way they are while calling for rational planning, change, and innovation.

Schwab's "The Practical 4"

Because Schwab followed in the Tyler tradition, his argument either corrects shortcomings in Tyler's rationale or is subject to the same criticisms. It turns out that, 34 years later, he is subject to similar criticisms. Schwab set out to write "a practical paper on the practical" (1983, p. 239) about

> the nature of curriculum change, that is, identification of the places where change is wanting, the borrowing or invention of alternative ways of fulfilling identified wants, deliberation on the costs and benefits of these alternatives, and, at last, their initiation with convinced and ready teachers. (1983, p. 244)

His concern is to institute "a continuing watch and correction of . . . curriculum" (1983, p. 243). Presumably a "practical paper on the practical" would have something to say about identifying a curriculum that is wanting; how to go about borrowing ideas, materials, and skills to meet deficiencies; alternative ways of deliberating or working out cost-benefit analyses of different curricula; and so forth. Or one might expect a practical paper to answer what about the curriculum is to be watched, to what ends, and how deficiencies might be corrected. To implement his proposal decisions must be made concerning: What counts as a curricular problem? How do we decide to take a situation as a problem? What values are to be furthered in watching and correcting the curriculum? How are alternatives to the current curriculum to be identified and developed? On what basis can predictions about outcomes be made? What are appropriate decision criteria for curriculum watching and correcting? None of these are addressed in Schwab's "practical paper on the practical." Decisions about watching or correcting cannot be made without reference to values; however, the values of one person might be the biases of someone else. Schwab warns against bias yet does not discuss values.

After urging curriculum professors to watch and correct the curriculum, he describes a special committee on curriculum chaired by a particular kind of professional to do the job. This is the logic of his proposal:

1. A committee should be formed to watch and correct the curriculum.
2. The members should be representative of several interested groups, such as teachers, administrators, the business community, and students.
3. The chairperson should have special training (a Renaissance education?), ensure that each member of the committee treats other members with respect, and guard against bias.
4. The members are to watch and correct the curriculum.

He ends where he began. The last step involves discovering and formulating curricular problems, suggesting alternative solutions, and deliberating on and modifying these alternatives (1983, pp. 257ff). The reader is given a list of things to be done, but they are not explained. The search for problems leads to conversations with teachers, visits to other schools, and to prominent educational journals. He is silent on what is defensible.

Something is missing in this plan for action, because the final step is the same as the initial goal. He begins by telling curriculum professors to watch and correct the curriculum, outlines the formation of a committee, and concludes by telling the committee to watch and correct the curriculum. The effect of the argument—the parallel with Tyler is striking—is to reinforce and reproduce existing discourses-practices. Existing rules, commitments, and power arrangements will shape what is said in the absence of alternative discourses and values, substantive criticism or reflection, or discussion of criticism. The proposal for an active role for curriculum professors turns out to be passive and politically conservative. Politically neutral expertise takes a stand in favor of things as they are because nothing is said about what should be changed or to what end(s).

Bloom et al.'s Taxonomy

Constructing a taxonomy presumes an underlying structure that can be ordered into a hierarchy of classes and categories. The meaning of each level is determined by differences from and relationships to other levels. Furthermore, the categories must be exhaustive (there must be a category for every learning objective) and mutually exclusive (a learning objective can be put in one and only one category). These are *necessary conditions* for any taxonomy.

There are problems with stability and structure in the Bloom et al.

taxonomy. First, Bloom et al. concede that knowledge and information are relative:

> It should also be noted that the validity, accuracy, and meaningfulness of
> information are relative in many ways and always are related to a particu-
> lar period of time. . . . There is also a geographical and cultural aspect to
> knowledge in the sense that what is known to one group is not necessari-
> ly known to another group, class, or culture. . . . Truth and knowledge
> are only relative and . . . there are no hard and fast truths which exist for
> all time and all places. (p. 32)

> All knowledge is partial. (p. 40)

This is a curiously poststructural position for authors of a taxonomy.
The effect of these comments, and they demonstrate a sophisticated
and subtle grasp of important epistemological issues, undermines
structural assumptions on which the taxonomy is constructed. Briefly,
it goes like this:

1. All knowledge and information are relative to time and place
   and are partial.
2. The taxonomy provides knowledge and information to
   educators.
3. Therefore knowledge and information provided by the taxonomy is relative and partial.

Now, the question is: In what way is the taxonomy relative and
partial?

The relationship between the taxonomy and its place in history
and geography are mentioned at several places and produce an important contradiction:

> Since the taxonomy is to be used in regard to existing educational units
> and programs, we are of the opinion that the major distinctions between
> classes should reflect, in large part, the distinctions teachers make
> among student behaviors. (p. 13)

> A final criterion is that the taxonomy must be accepted and used by
> the workers in the field if it is to be regarded as a useful and effective
> tool. (p. 24)

These statements support existing educational structures and processes, while elsewhere there are claims for value neutrality:

> A comprehensive taxonomy of educational objectives must, in our opin-
> ion, include all the educational objectives represented in American edu-
> cation without making judgments about their value, meaningfulness, or
> appropriateness. (p. 30)

The taxonomy was designed to be useful in contemporary educational
practice. No criticism of that practice was offered or suggested. The
activities, rules, values, ideologies, and power arrangements of contemporary educational practice were not questioned. The taxonomy,
then, was relative to what would facilitate school operation in the
1950s. The taxonomy explicitly asserts value neutrality while admit-
ting its relativity to historical practices, ideologies, and power arrangements. Perhaps not too surprisingly, it is designed to serve interests of
the status quo while claiming neutrality in the name of educational
expertise.

There is a second way in which the taxonomy deconstructed in its
claims about values. When they come to level 6.00, evaluation, they
write, "It is quite possible that the evaluative process will in some
cases be the prelude to the acquisition of new knowledge, a new
attempt at comprehension or application, or a new analysis or synthesis" (p. 185). With this caveat the authors concede that evaluation
precedes knowledge and comprehension and other levels lower in the
taxonomy. If evaluation precedes the knowledge level of the taxonomy, then the application of the taxonomy cannot be value free, again
undercutting its claim of ideological neutrality.

They claim that higher levels of the taxonomy subsume lower
levels. In this way learning objectives and experiences can be arranged
from simple to complex and concrete to abstract. "As we have defined
them, the objectives in one class are likely to make use of and be built
on the behaviors found in the preceding classes in this list" (p. 18).
The taxonomy is built on binary distinctions like the following: com-
prehension/knowledge, application/comprehension, analysis/appli-
cation, synthesis/analysis, and evaluation/synthesis, with the first
term in each pair being valued over the second because the second is
subsumed and thereby superseded by the first. But sometimes the
order is reversed; we have just seen that knowledge objectives do not
always precede evaluation objectives. Comprehension can also precede knowledge, because if one cannot comprehend, translate,
and interpret certain messages, some kinds of knowledge cannot be
learned. Likewise, application sometimes precedes comprehension,
because only after successful application is comprehension demonstrated.

Level 4.00, analysis, "emphasizes the breakdown of the material into its constituent parts and detection of the relationships of the parts and of the way they are organized" (p. 144). This definition, it turns out, is a description of a diagram of problem solving (p. 121), offered as an example of application. This simply asserts that sometimes one can only *apply* knowledge and information after *analysis* by breaking knowledge and information into constituent parts. Synthesis "is here defined as the putting together of elements and parts so as to form a whole" (p. 162). This is the other side of analysis. Are we interested in defining the whole in terms of its parts or in looking at the parts that constitute the whole? Choosing whether analysis precedes or follows synthesis depends upon context, purpose, situation, background experiences, and so forth. There is no transcendent reason or justification for *always* putting analysis before synthesis, application before analysis, comprehension before application, or knowledge before comprehension. Bloom et al. concede that evaluation sometimes precedes knowledge. This can now be generalized to the rest of the taxonomy; movement from complex to simple, and abstract to concrete, occurs as well as the other way around. Furthermore, evaluation *always* precedes knowledge because one only decides what to learn or know as a result of a decision, and decisions cannot be made without reference to value(s). Choices are always value relative.

Finally, the structure of the taxonomy itself reflects a valued way of thinking about education and knowledge, even though it was claimed to represent value free description. Recall the admission that the taxonomy is arbitrary. If the taxonomy is arbitrary and other versions can be substituted for it, if the taxonomy is relative to history and geography, if the taxonomy is designed to support existing educational practices, then it is not surprising that it promotes such *values* as control (of content, students, and organization), quantification (of learning outcomes), individual accountability, order, authority of disciplinary knowledge, subject-centered learning, teacher authority, the status quo of social organizations, fragmentation of knowledge and information, appearance of certainty and stability of knowledge (disclaimers in the handbook notwithstanding), authoritative knowledge viewed as a positive body of knowledge, and applied psychometrics in the service of education.

In generating the taxonomy of educational objectives, Bloom et al. voice structural *and* poststructural arguments. The structural case is developed seriously, while poststructural qualifications are only found in marginal commentary. Because the structural taxonomy was designed to make the existing educational system more efficient, structural rhetorical claims of the taxonomy were accepted by practitioners and logical contradictions and political commitments of the taxonomy were ignored. Its critical and evaluative potential was silenced.

CONCLUSION

Foucault and Derrida move beyond structuralism differently. There are, however, points of convergence. Foucault emphasizes the political production of truth and that what passes for truth is historically relative. Discourses intertwine with power to create speaking-acting subjects. Derrida's work is more analytic in its focus on text. He shows that meanings are dispersed and deferred and that rhetorical claims often diverge from logical argument. Meanings are in constant play. The arguments of Foucault and Derrida come together. If, as Derrida contends, there is a play of meanings as they are dispersed and deferred but particular meanings are privileged, how does a meaning, a transcendental signified, acquire its privileged position? If, as Foucault maintains, truth is a product of the politics of time and place, then the truth of a discourse-practice operates as a transcendental signified. In everyday life everything is not always shifting, because discourses-practices often have long-term stability, more or less. The stability can be so enduring that the historical dependency of the transcendental signified can be overlooked; witness Tyler, Schwab, and Bloom et al. This is where Foucault and Derrida, together, explain current texts and discourses-practices and reinforce each other. The transcendental signified required by structuralism is relative to (1) time and place (Foucault) and (2) rhetorical claims of a specific text (Derrida). The structure, however, is illusory, because it is a product of history and power (Foucault) and is analytically unstable (Derrida).

The structural arguments of Tyler, Schwab, and Bloom et al. are based upon unstable categorical distinctions, take ideological positions while denying ideology, offer advice about correcting practice that reinforces practice in place, promote nonlinear structures as linear, advocate educational decision making separate from considerations of ethical or decision criteria, and ignore the effects of power in discourse-practice. Why, one is led to ask, are such arguments widely cited if they do not do what they claim? Why are they privileged? If these arguments fail to do what they claim, what ends do they serve? They serve to reproduce educational practices in place in the name of change and progress. When the origins of discourses-practices are ignored, the material basis of discourse is ignored, the way in which power precedes and invades speech is ignored, criticism is ignored, and ethical and ideological dimensions of speech are ignored; the result is that discourses-practices are determined, often invisibly, by rules, interests, commitments, and power structures of time and place.

The introduction is complete. We now turn to an issue so basic to contemporary education, the nature of meaning and meanings, that it is almost completely ignored in the literature. We will explore it in the context of textbooks and teaching.

CHAPTER 4

Meaning, Meanings, Textbooks, and Teaching

Mean·ing: n **1a:** *the thing one intends to convey esp. by language:* PURPORT **b:** *the thing that is conveyed esp. by language:* IMPORT **2:** INTENT, PURPOSE **3:** SIGNIFICANCE **4a:** CONNOTATION **b:** DENOTATION (Webster's Seventh New Collegiate Dictionary).

Is the object's meaning guaranteed by reference to its creator's intention in making it, or is its meaning a function of its position in a system of objects? . . . I wish to argue that we can interpret it best only by taking our eyes off it, denying it status as a thing in itself, and reading it as intertextually as we can within the limits of the present discourse. (Scholes, 1985, p. 136)

Educational discourses-practices convey things, or, at least, are designed to convey things, even though what is conveyed may bear little resemblance to what teachers have in mind. An account of meaning is a general schema, description, characterization, stipulation, outline, or explanation of what is involved when things are conveyed or intended to be conveyed. Meanings are the specific items and substance of what is involved. For example, one might ask what does "the Union won the Civil War," "the Union won the War Between the States," or "the North won the War Between the States" mean? A general account of meaning would provide guidance in determining what these questions mean.

The educational literature, however, does not reveal much in the way of accounts, discussions, or theories and explanations of meaning. The logical status of meaning is that of a primitive and undefined term. Its rhetorical function is reduced to that of blindness, silence, an empty space in educational discourse. Two presuppositions seem to be operative: (1) meaning as such is not in need of analysis, and, its corollary, (2) only specific meanings of words, utterances, discourses, and texts require stipulation, definition, explication, and elaboration. This produces a curious paradox. The paradox is that meaning is not analyzed, discussed, explicated, or elaborated, because intuitively we know and share the meaning of "meaning." Without discussing meaning, however, how can it be known that the meaning of "meaning" is shared? If a shared sense of meaning characterizes contemporary education, what is it? There is a shared view of meaning, I submit, and it is predominantly structural.

This exploration of meaning ranges across the meaning of words, utterances, discourses, and how meaning is constituted by reading. A poststructural view of meaning will be argued. It will be shown that meaning is located in ongoing discourses, not in isolated words or utterances. Language and meanings are sometimes presumed to be value neutral, as transparent windows on the world, or as mirrors of nature (see Rorty, 1980, for an elaboration of this last metaphor). This value-neutrality hypothesis will be rejected. Some people speak with authority, while others listen as consumers, because power infiltrates language we inherit, the meanings of our words, utterances, and discourses, and the institutions and practices that shape their use. To presume that meanings are independent of power is to misconstrue the nature of language. To teach meanings without reference to their constitution is to distort what is conveyed. It is to be caught up in an anonymous discourse. To objectify the nature of meaning and meanings is to succumb to a social determinism made powerful by its invisibility. Textbooks advance valued meanings. Valued meanings are also found in scope and sequence guidelines, achievement tests, learning objectives, and lesson plans. Teaching processes and mediates these meanings. How meaning and meanings are put forward and taught is at the core of education. After analyzing meaning and meanings, I will turn to the classroom dialogue between textbooks and teaching and begin to sketch out a view of critical pragmatism in education.

WORDS AND STATEMENTS

A Traditional Approach to Word Meaning

Ludwig Wittgenstein begins the *Philosophical Investigations* with a quotation from Augustine's *Confessions* that may well capture the intuitive belief about meaning that most of us bring to teaching (much of what followed in the *Investigations* was devoted to attacking it).

> The individual words in language name objects—sentences are combinations of such names. . . . In this picture of language we find the roots of the following idea: Every word has a meaning. The meaning is correlated with the word. It is the object for which the word stands. (1953, p. 2e)

A word has a definition and it refers. This is often drawn upon in school textbooks, where a word is introduced and given a definition followed by a positive example of the word. Here is an example about opportunity costs from a fourth-grade social studies text:

> Choices have *costs*. The cost of a choice includes all the things you give up. It includes all the things you choose not to do. For Juan [a young man living in a Bolivian village who is choosing between going to college or getting a job] the cost of one choice is that he will have to wait to help his family. The cost of the other choice is that he will have to wait to go to college. He might never get to college at all. (Ochoa, Cherryholmes, & Manson, 1979, p. 230)[1]

Sometimes textbooks play positive and negative instances against each other in order to clarify, explicate, exemplify, or otherwise elaborate the meaning of a word.

This approach to word meaning has been around at least since the Middle Ages. It imposes order and system because it requires ordered pairs of words/definitions and definitions/instances. It assumes the meaning of a word is its *identity*, with a definition pointing to positive instances and excluding negative instances. But there are problems with this approach. For example, two terms can refer to the same object, such as the *morning star* and the *evening star* both referring to the planet Venus. Also there are terms, such as *political power, literary merit, poverty,* and *educational excellence,* that have more than one definition, and some definitions may not specify which instances are extensions and which are not.

Textbooks can be thought of as collections of statements that make authoritative knowledge claims. They make statements about subject matter, social values and arrangements, what counts as knowledge, and what information is more or less important. They assert by inclusion and exclusion what is important and unimportant to study and present the meaning of words as fixed. Students, among others, are told little to the contrary by the overwhelming majority of textbooks in any subject at any level, with the exception of some areas in literature and philosophy.

Hilary Putnam proposes a sociolinguistic hypothesis that reduces, even if not eliminating, ambiguity in word meaning: a sociolinguistic division of labor based on an underlying material division of labor fixes the meaning of a word. In his words:

> Every linguistic community possesses at least some terms whose asso-
> ciated "criteria" are known only to a subset of the speakers who acquire
> the terms, and whose use by the other speakers depends upon a struc-
> tured cooperation between them and the speakers in the relevant sub-
> sets. (1975, p. 228)

He uses the example of gold. Some people have the job of selling gold wedding rings, others of wearing gold wedding rings, and still others of telling whether or not something is gold.

Some people have the job of writing textbooks about political power, electrons, literary merit, and molecules. Teachers have the job of designing classroom experiences that teach these ideas. Students have the job of learning them so they can respond appropriately when examined. As with sellers and buyers of gold wedding rings, some have the job of positing knowledge claims, others of transmitting them, and still others of acquiring them. Scholars, however, often have a variety of definitions from which to choose in writing text-books; teachers have fewer from which to choose but often select from more than one; and students usually, more so at lower levels, are given the opportunity to learn only one. The sociolinguistic division of labor for a particular configuration of scholars, teachers, and cir-cumstances fixes meaning for students at a given point in time and space. Umberto Eco puts it this way: *"the conditions of necessity of a sign are socially determined"* (1984, p. 38). Word meaning is relative to back-ground social practices.

Truth-Conditional Semantics

The problem of meaning does not begin and end with words. We also ask what an utterance (statement) means. Truth-conditional se-mantics is an approach to statement meaning as intuitively appealing as matching words with definitions and instances. It comes from Al-fred Tarski's correspondence theory of truth: "a sentence is true if it is satisfied by all objects, and false otherwise" (1952, p. 25). The follow-ing is an often-used example.

The sentence "snow is white" is true if and only if snow is white. But Tarski developed this account of truth for formal languages and logical systems and never claimed it could be applied to truth claims made in a natural language. He writes, "For other languages—thus for all natural, "spoken" languages—the meaning of the problem is more or less vague, and its solution can have only an approximate character" (1952, p. 19).

As long as statements are compared with statements, such as whether the conclusion of an argument is a valid deduction from its premises, Tarski's formulation, under certain conditions, works, because rules of logic provide criteria that tell whether a conclusion is valid and analytically true. When the matter is one of comparing statements with things, however, only judgments and inferences can be made, and truth as a matter of judgment is not what Tarski had in mind. For example, determining whether the sentence "snow is white" is true depends on a number of judgments and inferences.

Truth-conditional semantics and the correspondence theory of truth at first have face validity and plausibility when thinking about education. When teachers instruct students, it may not be far off the mark to suggest that many believe the meaning of what they say is contained in some sort of correspondence with the way things are.[2] But there are problems if this is generalized to all teacher and textbook statements. For example, a social studies teacher says, "On May 29, 1985, Ronald Reagan was president." The truth value of this statement is highly certain and is determined by the condition that on May 29, 1985, Ronald Reagan was president. When a social studies teacher says, "The Reagan administration made a complete commitment to supply-side economics," we are less certain about its truth value, because it is not clear what conditions would make the statement true. Textbooks are filled with cases like this. This is from a fifth-grade social studies text: "Thomas Jefferson was elected the third President of the United States in 1800. He served two terms. Probably his greatest contribution as President was the Louisiana Purchase" (Vuicich, Stollman, Cherryholmes, & Manson, 1979, p. 199). We know what conditions are required for the first two sentences to be true. The third sentence is a bit different. We do not know what conditions would make it true, because it is evaluative and speculative about the "greatest contribution" of Jefferson as president. If a truth-conditional view of meaning is applied indiscriminately to these three sentences, the objective conditions required for the first two would not be distinguished from judgmental factors related to the third. Truth-conditional semantics may work in some areas of mathematics, logic, and computer-language curricula and instruction, but it distorts meaning for the overwhelming majority of statements in teaching.

Speech Act Theory

Speech act theory, mentioned in Chapter 1, asserts that saying something is also doing something. When Austin first worked on these ideas he believed that certain conditions had to be present for an utterance to count as an action: certain conventional procedures must exist, the conventional procedures must be correctly in place and be completely executed, the speaker must be sincere, and must so act (Austin, 1968). Later, Searle showed that all speech is action. What is accomplished with an utterance depends on the beliefs that the speaker and hearer bring with them. Ruth Kempson describes it like this:

> Sentence meaning and word meaning will be thought of in terms of conditions for appropriate use, and thus *implications of sentences will be characterized not as a property of the sentence itself but as a presupposition on the part of a speaker using that sentence, a requisite set of beliefs if the speaker is to use the sentences appropriately.* (1977, p. 54; emphasis added)

Speech act theory points to those aspects of the social setting that make an utterance a specific kind of action. Several actions were performed with the statements about Jefferson. "Thomas Jefferson was elected the third President of the United States in 1800" asserts a proposition and is an act of instruction. "Probably his greatest contribution as President was the Louisiana Purchase" is instruction, evaluation, and an assertion bestowing approval. The desired effect was that the reader be instructed, informed, and accept the evaluation. Searle (see Chapter 1) shows that statements mean either (1) act of stating, (2) what is stated, or (3) both 1 and 2. The statements about Jefferson can be analyzed in terms of truth-conditional semantics for what is stated and in terms of speech act theory for what is done.

Wittgenstein supplements this general point in the *Philosophical Investigations*: "For a *large* class of cases—though not for all—in which we employ the word "meaning" it can be defined thus: the meaning of a word is its use in the language" (1953, p. 20e). Words can be used in at least two ways: (1) Wittgenstein's established uses of words, Searle's what is stated, and (2) Wittgenstein's possible uses of words, Searle's act of stating. It is possible to grasp established word usages at once (this is also supported by linguistic structuralists), but established usages do not capture all possible uses. Because new situations and conditions arise and it is seemingly safe to surmise that the future will not be like the past, it cannot be known that established meanings will hold for the future. The distinction is between language as (existing) phenomena subject to description and speech as action (as it is being constituted) subject to explanation.

If Searle and Wittgenstein are correct, teachers should not succumb to the illusion that meanings are fixed, centered, and unchanging. Textbooks, however, seem predicated on two rules with respect to meaning. First, they tend to approach meaning structurally, with meanings presented by definitions, referents, and linkages. Second, they advance meanings, if up-to-date, that represent the current state of "authoritative knowledge." One can think of knowledge about algebra, chemistry, American history, English literature, and art education as fixed, at least for a moment in time. This is language subject to description and presentation to students. Textbooks fail overwhelmingly to point out that different authorities might identify different knowledge as "authoritative" and that each such identification is an action.

Speech act theory points to rules and conventions to determine what one does (intends) with an utterance. One looks not just at the utterance but at convention, institution, and circumstance to determine a statement's meaning (Webster's first definition of meaning). One is always doing something with an utterance, and some utterances have truth value. The meaning of an utterance depends on its context *and* is somewhat unstable, in part because existing meanings cannot extend to all applications. But textbooks implicitly present meanings as fixed in structures, and sentences on pages, pictures, charts, and graphs do nothing to dispel this appearance of stability.

Neither teachers nor students are likely to ask how meanings came to be what they are if textbooks do not self-consciously draw attention to the social construction and context dependence of meanings. Here is a definition of learning from a fourth-grade textbook:

> One way people learn is by copying the behavior of others. First, people watch or listen. Then they copy the behavior. . . . Another way people learn is by trial and error. They try different ways of doing something until they get it right. Then, they do it that way again and again. . . . Another way of learning is through *rewards* and *punishments*. A reward is something you get for behaving a certain way. A reward makes you feel good. . . . A punishment is also something you get for behaving a certain way. But a punishment makes you feel bad. (Ochoa, Cherryholmes, & Manson, 1979, pp. 73–77)

These approaches to learning are rooted in twentieth-century psychology, are instrumental and utilitarian and not aesthetic, and emphasize control and manipulation and not play in learning. Although good reasons can be found for defining learning like this, they can also be found for defining learning in terms of aesthetics and play. Textbooks say little about how meanings can be traced through the language and can be modified, shifted, fractured, and possibly discarded.

Critical Theory and Habermas

Habermas's critical theory approaches meaning from speech act theory and is concerned with, as Thomas McCarthy notes, "the rational reconstruction of universal, 'species-wide' (language) competences" (1979, p. xx). Meaning resides in what the speaker is engaging in and what the hearer is counting on. A speech act is successful if both speaker and hearer accept its truth, rightness, truthfulness, and comprehensibility and it brings about the interpersonal relations intended by the speaker. The meaning of an utterance is determined by shared beliefs, norms, linguistic conventions, and intentions that give substance to the four validity claims. In this way a speech act is institutionally bound.

Critical discourse, proposed by Habermas, is required when truth claims asserted in normal interactions are challenged. It moves from an accepted to a rational consensus, that is, from institutionally to noninstitutionally bound speech acts. If what the speaker and hearer share makes it impossible to determine the meaning of an utterance, then it is necessary to create conditions whereby the problematic validity claims can be redeemed. This requires, Habermas argues, "with a truth claim, obligations to provide grounds, with a rightness claim, obligations to provide justification, and with a truthfulness claim, obligations to prove trustworthy" (1979, p. 65). The movement to rational consensus, however, must be constrained in order to minimize distorting influences of commitments, interests, ideologies, and power arrangements of existing institutions. Habermas makes a valiant effort to construct new meanings free from the dominance of past practice. To this end, critical discourse must be symmetrical and nondominated. All parties may initiate comments, challenge assertions, and question not only theoretical formulations but also metatheoretical and metaethical frameworks. Strategic behavior, turning the search for truth into conflict or competition, is not permitted. Winning or losing is not the outcome of discourse. No votes are taken. These conditions are necessary for emancipation from past commitments, past practice, and social determinism. The proposal is intriguing but flawed.

Habermas argues that power structures are entangled with meanings. Then he proposes critical discourse to break the linkage between power and meaning. This prescription fails, however, because the conditions necessary for critical discourse are denied by his own analysis. Our search for knowledge cannot proceed without normative commitments (the search for truth), human interests (someone must be interested for whatever reason in an object and its study), and power arrangements (if any asymmetries or inequalities exist, some modes and objects of study will be favored over others). Meanings, in terms of his own argument, cannot be separated from human interests.

The tension between stability and instability in meanings has reappeared. In the traditional approach to word meaning the problem lay in differences between words with clear-cut definitions and instances and those that were not so clear-cut; in truth-conditional semantics the tension was found in the difference between the logical validity of formal, artificial-language arguments and the rhetorical character of natural-language arguments; in speech act theory certainty was located in well-known and institutionalized settings and uncertainty in settings that were not clearly known or agreed upon. For Habermas meaning stability/instability is found in differences between normal interaction (institutionally bound speech acts) and critical discourse (noninstitutionally bound speech acts).

Grice's Cooperative Principle

H. P. Grice, a British analytic philosopher, construes talk exchanges as cooperative efforts with a common purpose. Along with truth-conditional semantics, this is probably how educators would like to think of curriculum and instruction. Shared purposes, in the classroom for example, allow us to make decisions about which utterances are acceptable and unacceptable and what they mean. Grice's cooperative principle (1975) has four parts: (1) quantity (provide as much information as required and no more); (2) quality (avoid saying something you believe is false or for which you have no evidence); (3) relation (make it relevant); and (4) manner (be orderly, brief, clear, and avoid ambiguity and obscurity). The cooperative principle complements Habermas's pragmatics. One should be prepared to give evidence for an utterance, strive for clarity and order, and speak to the point. But speakers and hearers cannot make judgments about quantity, quality, manner, and relevance without a common social and linguistic context. If something like Habermas's norms of communicative interaction or Searle's "rules [that] specify both the conditions of utterance of the sentence and also what the utterance counts as" (1969, p. 48) are not shared, speakers are out on a limb when it comes to judging quantity, quality, relation, and manner. Grice's point is simple and straightforward. If a speaker is ignorant of social and linguistic context, he or she cannot know how to cooperate, because it will not be known how much or what to say; if a hearer is likewise contextually ignorant, what is said may literally be perceived as nonsensical. Grice's cooperative principle depends upon shared social and linguistic conventions, and institutions.

It is intuitively appealing to think that one must pay sole attention to a word or an utterance if one is to determine what that word or utterance means. The search for meaning, however, has been turned upside down: one makes sense of what one intends to convey and things conveyed by attending to social convention and circumstance as well as to words and utterances.

DISCOURSES AND TEXTS

Now we turn to poststructural accounts of discourse and text. Developments in modern logic (Quine, 1953), structuralism (Culler, 1984), philosophy of language (Wittgenstein, 1953), and analytic philosophy (Putnam, 1975) foreshadowed poststructural treatments of meaning. This is not to say they anticipated the particular arguments of Foucault and Derrida; but given these earlier arguments, it is not surprising that poststructural thought developed along the lines it has.

Foucault and Discourse

Austin and Searle demonstrated that an utterance was an act in the context of social rules, institutions, and conventions, but they paid almost no attention to those contextual factors. Although Foucault did not work in the tradition of speech act theory or pragmatics, he made far-reaching additions to this previous work, effectively reversing its focus by looking at the enabling and facilitating discursive practice instead of the discrete speech act. Power precedes speech because utterances are located within existing social institutions whose rules, power configuration, norms, commitments, and interests determine what can and cannot be said and what utterances count as.

Foucault's analysis sheds considerable light on textbooks and meaning. Foucault argues that the effects of power shape a discursive practice. Its rules are rarely explicit and subject to criticism, even though those who participate must speak in accordance with them. In *McGraw-Hill Social Studies* (Cherryholmes & Manson, 1979), as in other elementary social studies series, considerable attention is given to geographic and historic information. The well-known and widely followed expanding-communities sequence is followed: families to neighborhoods to communities to regions of the United States to the United States to regions of the world. Authors and editors in the broader discourse of elementary social studies publishing are limited by the same constraints and thereby become, in many ways, interchangeable. With interchangeability comes anonymity.

Textbooks are products of several forms of constraint. Publishing companies are capitalist, not charitable, institutions and try to maximize profits. Textbooks are rationally tailored (at least that is the idea) to satisfy state textbook selection committees and reflect widely accepted scope and sequence guidelines. They usually avoid controversial content and pedagogical style. Some textbooks, to be sure, are better written than others, are more interesting to students, and gain advantage by being more attractively designed and produced. But these differences are marginal to the substantive discourses-practices to which they contribute. Teachers, social studies supervisors, and administrators have expectations and desires when selecting textbooks. Their expectations come from professional training, work experience, beliefs, attitudes, and orientations to teaching. They wish to provide students with learning experiences to help them score well on standardized achievement tests, be prepared for material in the next grade (along with textbooks likely to be used), and so forth.

Textbooks contribute to ongoing educational discourses-practices, and to be commercially successful, they must conform. The meaning of the discourse-practice of textbook publishing is, in large part, a function of its historical antecedents and its relationships to contemporary institutions and practices. The search for meanings has shifted from word to statement to discourse to historical and social context, and the notion of meaning as identity has been left far behind.

Derrida and Text

Derrida focuses on written text, and his work is a sustained criticism of a structural view of meaning. He overturns the notion of transcendental signified as a ground for meanings and substitutes the idea that meanings leave traces throughout a text. This can be illustrated by the definition of learning cited earlier in this chapter and repeated here:

> Another way of learning is through *rewards* and *punishments*. A reward is something you get for behaving a certain way. A reward makes you feel good. . . . A punishment is also something you get for behaving a certain way. But a punishment makes you feel bad. (Ochoa, Cherryholmes, & Manson, 1979, p. 77)

Learning is defined by rewards and punishments. A reward is something one gets for behaving a certain way. One might ask what behavior means and be confronted with another definition and when it is provided possibly ask for yet another. But the "something you get" and the "certain way" of behaving drives home the point that meanings are dispersed in language.

Transcendental signifieds function to fix meanings by assigning some ideas a privileged status. Because meanings are ultimately grounded by one idea privileged over others, the text is sometimes thought of as speaking with one voice in a linear and developmental way. A logical analogy is apt. The transcendental signified is the first premise to which other premises are added, and the subsequent argument must be consistent with the premises. A transcendental signified acquires its status because it is ideologically favored. But a transcendental signified does not escape the system, because it always presupposes the presence of other words or signs. Derrida puts it this way: "There is not a single signified that escapes . . . the *play* of signifying references that constitute language. . . . This, strictly speaking, amounts to destroying the concept of 'sign' and its entire logic" (1982, p. 7; emphasis added).

One way to approach deconstruction is to adopt an attitude of playfulness that, at first, might seem strange and out of place in thinking about meaning. Play allows one to see beyond the rhetorical claims of a text. One can seek connections between a word, utterance, or discourse and what is not there. One can utilize as well as look for metaphors, allegories, similes, and other literary devices in addition to more conventional, structural, logical analysis and reconstruction of a text. Deconstructive analysis suggests that texts are never what they seem.

This is a radical argument. Texts appear to speak with one voice. Deconstructive criticism demonstrates that texts have many voices. A text cannot be grounded on something stable and fixed beyond the sign system in which it occurs. Texts include what is not written as well as what is written, producing shifting and decentered meanings. Texts include traces of words and concepts not present, and that which is not present makes possible that which is present.

The meaning of what is present depends upon what is absent; for example, one can use the word *meaning* because of what is not stated, such as "the thing one intends to convey esp. by language" (*Webster's Seventh New Collegiate Dictionary*). In order to understand the text, one must go back and forth between what is present and what is absent, what is written and what is not written. What is put forward presupposes other signs and symbols that already exist; they, in turn, presuppose still others. If we attempt to trace central ideas back to their origins, we find either that they continually lead to prior ideas or contradict themselves. Whatever passes itself off as a transcendental signified not only deconstructs but, if it was persuasive initially, tends to represent dominant ideological orientations.

Foucault approaches discourse in terms of its political production, whereas Derrida approaches it as successive appeals to foundational ideas that eventually deconstruct and turn on themselves. Foucault shows textbooks to be political, material products that represent a privileged way of seeing things, privileged by means of power, position, tradition, and so forth. Derrida shows the structure, coherence, stability of meaning, and centeredness of textbooks to be a fiction. The apparent coherence of textbook definitions of learning, reward, and punishment cited earlier, for example, hides deeper commitments to efficiency, control, manipulation, instrumentalism, and utilitarianism. Structuralism shows meanings to be decentered and external to the individual. Poststructuralism shows meanings to be shifting, receding, fractured, incomplete, dispersed, and deferred.

Paradigms and Meaning

Some convincing contemporary accounts of the structure of scientific knowledge make arguments that parallel Derrida's about the transient nature of meanings. Kuhn describes in fascinating detail scientific paradigms that are either the beliefs, values, and techniques of a given community, or "puzzle-solution" models, which are examples of scientific research (1974). Paradigms sanction the inclusion of some problems and questions in acceptable scientific activity and the exclusion of others. But the history of science is the history of paradigm breakdown. Anomalies appear that previous scientific achievements can neither explain nor suggest how the anomalies can be fruitfully attacked. A scientific revolution follows that eventually produces a new paradigm (structure of scientific knowledge, "puzzle-solutions," or constellation of scientific beliefs and values). The revolutions may be few and far between but are to be expected. Structured knowledge, according to Kuhn, is valuable and valued but less foundational than it appears.

Quine offers a pragmatic account of scientific knowledge. He puts it like this:

> Total science is like a field of force whose boundary conditions are experience. A conflict with experience at the periphery occasions readjustments in the interior of the field. Truth values have to be redistributed over some of the statements. Reevaluation of some statements entails reevaluation of others. . . . But the total field is so underdetermined by its boundary conditions, experience, that there is much latitude of choice as to what statements to reevaluate in the light of any single contrary experience. (1953, p. 42)

Structured knowledge orients us to the world. But experience always threatens what we know. When expectations about the world have to be revised, many revisions can be made.

One can think of the issue of meanings as divided into three interactive elements: what the speaker or author intends, what the text asserts, and what the reader infers. The discussion has thus far surveyed, very broadly, arguments about speaker-author intentions and the text. Now we turn to the reader, reception theory as it is known, and the role of metaphor in the text.

READING AND METAPHOR

The second part of Webster's first definition of meaning—what is conveyed—shifts attention to the student, reader, receiver, and so forth and the sense that is made of a word, utterance, discourse, and text.

Reception Theory

What is conveyed when students read? Eco, reinforcing Derrida among others, provides a place to start: "Texts generate, or are capable of generating, multiple (and ultimately infinite) readings and interpretations" (1984, p. 24). This occurs for two reasons: (1) the indeterminacy of textual meaning, as pointed out by Derrida, signals that texts speak with many voices; (2) readers always infer a writer's intention because no formulae exist to be applied (Hirsch, 1967). The first problem generates the second. If words can be used differently from one setting to another or have meanings that leave traces through the text, the reader must figure out what they mean. According to Robert Crosman, "Since neither words nor the utterances built up out of them can be made unambiguous, except by an act of reading, 'meaning' is not inherent in words or utterances but is an inference drawn by a construing mind" (1980, p. 155).

The only way to exclude readers from making meaning is to assume that a text has one "correct" interpretation, that it is univocal—speaks with one voice (an assumption, by the way, of standardized achievement tests). Arguments from later speech act theory, Habermas, Grice, Foucault, and Derrida all run counter to the idea of a univocal text. Crosman (1980) offers yet one more: Suppose we find an author who claims that there is one "correct" interpretation for what she or he has written in a textbook, scope and sequence chart, or test. Furthermore, suppose that the author tells us what the text is intended to convey. We still have to make sense of what the author says is her or his intention—interpretation is still required.

Reception theory is closely related to a phenomenological approach to reading (Eagleton, 1983, Chapter 2; Iser, 1974, Chapter 11). Wolfgang Iser describes the general position:

> The work is more than the text, for the text only takes on life when it is realized, and furthermore the realization is by no means independent of the individual disposition of the reader—though this in turn is acted upon by the different patterns of the text. The convergence of the text and reader brings the literary work into existence, and this convergence can never be precisely pinpointed. (1974, p. 275)

It is tempting to think of the reader as a subject (subjectivity) reading and making sense of an object (text). Reception theory, however, collapses the subject-object distinction. Prior understandings, experiences, codes, beliefs, and knowledge brought to a text necessarily condition and mediate what one makes of it. Teaching can assist students in questioning textbooks and themselves. Links to larger social settings and experiences can be pointed out. Of course, such teaching subverts the textbook.

Some people may argue that we should not emphasize ambiguities or contradictions in texts, but, as Eagleton writes, "adopting a reading convention which eradicates ambiguity, itself depends upon a whole network of social knowledge" (1983, p. 78). For example, reading Tyler, Schwab, and Bloom et al. as if there were no ambiguities or contradictions assumes a very specific and complex set of beliefs and a particular ideological orientation.

The social knowledge the reader brings to a text decenters its meanings. One does not look only to the text but also to the background information and knowledge that makes the textbook intelligible—or the lack of which makes it unintelligible, which Pierre Bourdieu (1977) calls "cultural capital." The reader's store of social codes, information, and knowledge still does not eliminate ambiguity. Reading is a ferreting out movement falling somewhere between induction and deduction, "an active interweaving of anticipation and retrospection" (Iser, 1974, p. 282), an "act of recreation [that] is not a smooth or continuous process" (Iser, 1974, p. 288), or an "unfolding of the text as a living event" (Iser, 1974, p. 290). Eco is worth quoting at length on this point:

> The notion of sign as expression of equality and identity could be legitimately claimed to support a sclerotic (and ideological) notion of the subject [student]. The sign as the locus (constantly interrogated) for the semiosic [interpretation of signs] process constitutes, on the other hand, the instrument through which the subject is continuously made and unmade. The subject enters a beneficial crisis because it shares in the historical (and constitutive) crisis of the sign. The subject is constantly reshaped by the endless resegmentation of the content. (1984, p. 45)

Textual meanings cannot be exhausted by a single reading. Reading is not just the cognitive processing of words on pages. Reading is going back and forth from the text to oneself. Scholes puts it like this: "Interpretation *does* enter the reading process at a very early point. And interpretation is never totally free but always limited by such prior acquisitions as language, generic norms, social patterns, and beliefs" (1985, p. 150).

One is always reading oneself when reading a text. To the extent that texts present themselves as "naturally occurring," they are distortive and deceptive. To the extent that teaching rewards attention to textbooks as fixed structures of language and knowledge, the errors and mistakes of structuralism are reinforced. But textbooks and teaching can move away from meanings as structurally centered. For example, the following illustrative questions (Ochoa, Cherryholmes, & Manson, 1979) and activities are part of the fourth-grade textbook material in the lessons on learning cited earlier in this chapter:

> What are two ways in which people learn new things?
> Name some behaviors you learned by copying other people.
> Name something you learned by trial and error. (p. 75)

> What are rewards? What are punishments?
> What are some rewards for you?
> What are some punishments?
> Why do people tend to do things that bring them rewards? (p. 77)

> Who gives rewards and punishments to children?
> Who gives rewards and punishments to adults?
> Name some rewards and punishments you give your friends.
> Name some rewards and punishments you give your parents. (p. 79)[3]

Some of these questions ask for accepted meanings advanced by the text: "What are two ways in which people learn new things?" "What are rewards?" "What are punishments?" A next move attends to reading oneself as one reads a text: "Name something you learned by trial and error." "What are some rewards for you?" "Name some rewards and punishments you give your friends, parents." Then these accepted meanings and their interpretations are projected onto the world: "Why do people tend to do things that bring them rewards?" "Who gives rewards and punishments to children?" "Who gives rewards and punishments to adults?" The move is from questions with definitive answers to rhetorical questions whose answers are conjectural and speculative. Textbooks can pose questions that emphasize either structural or poststructural responses. Teaching sets limits and provides opportunities for responding to them.

Metaphor

Metaphors are figures of speech by which one idea or object is used to refer to a different idea or object. Metaphors point to that which is not present. In an important sense all language is metaphorical, because words (symbols) refer to things (ideas, objects, and so forth) or other words. Metaphors draw attention to the richness and complexity of the world. It is often believed that in order to "read" and understand a metaphor one must know the linguistic code and context. If we understand how an individual uses a metaphor, then we have some idea what she or he intends to convey; if we know how an individual makes sense of a metaphor, we know what has been conveyed. But can metaphors be used to resolve meanings in a world of word, utterance, and discursive ambiguity? Eco writes:

> For too long it has been thought that in order to understand metaphors it is necessary to know the [linguistic] code (or the encyclopedia): the truth is that the metaphor is the tool that permits us to understand the encyclopedia better. (1984, p. 129)

Textual slippage, disruptions, discontinuities, ambiguities, contradictions, and incompleteness are found everywhere. Reading metaphors as sources of insight and not as structurally fixed and centered provides access to those disruptions and discontinuities and to meanings such as we find them. Teaching this capitalizes on textual metaphors (and language as metaphorical); including illustrations, types of questioning, subjects for case studies, and geographic and cultural descriptions (all of which are not there but are pointed to by language that is there) that illuminate the complexity of the text, the dispersal of its meanings, and its traces in the past.

SUMMARY: MEANING AND MEANINGS

Meanings are located in ongoing discourses. Discourses consist of spoken and written exchanges. Exchanges are, more or less, orderly; certain topics are discussed and others are not. Some people speak with authority, and others listen or speak as outsiders. To determine what a word means one looks to the discourse and not just to the word. To determine what an utterance means one looks to the discourse and not just to the utterance. To determine what a discourse means one appeals to its history, culture, politics, economics, conventions, and institutions to account for how it operates to produce truth and what is said. A discourse has no single, identifiable author. Its categories, modes of argumentation, metaphors, and rules of evidence precede speaker and hearer and determine what counts and what is dismissed. Rules of inclusion and exclusion, sometimes explicit and sometimes implicit, determine what is in and what is out. These rules are based on ideas, concepts, beliefs, values, and power arrangements that transcend as well as ground what is said and done.

Eventually the importance of these ideas and beliefs, taken as transcendent for a time, will deconstruct or be deposed by shifting effects of events and power. Reading uncovers multiple messages and voices in the text as the reader moves back and forth from herself or himself to what is written. Meaning must not be thought of as structurally grounded but as poststructurally shifting leading to different usages, uncovering discursive fractures, and constituting new applications of words and utterances.[4]

This account of meaning may seem a bit perplexing. Meanings are found in discourses that reflect existing social relations (Putnam), linguistic usages (Saussure), human interests (Habermas), and power structures (Foucault). Meanings are not stable but deconstruct. They deconstruct because there is nothing outside the sign system on which to ground and center them; there is no transcendental signified (Derrida, Eco). Seemingly stable meanings give way because words, utterances, and discourses can be applied differently in different contexts (Searle, Wittgenstein, Derrida, and Eco).

THE DIALOGUE BETWEEN
TEXTBOOKS AND TEACHING

An imaginary dialogue between textbooks and teaching is the product of a somewhat odd imagination, because textbooks are mute and teaching is a process. They encounter each other through students and teachers. It is these latter who engage in dialogue and discourse. But the literary structures of textbooks and models, approaches and strategies of teaching, shape what is said, how it is said, what is not said, who is held accountable for what, and what is done with what is said. Now it is possible to outline, broadly, how student/teacher interactions can be opened up as well as constrained by textbooks and teaching.

It is arguable that operative but unstated approaches to meaning in textbooks and teaching are stepchildren, if not direct descendants, of linguistic structuralism, the traditional approach to word meaning, and descriptivist tendencies in truth-conditional semantics. One major contribution to post–World War II American education after another reflects structural approaches to meaning. They include, in addition to the examples in Chapter 2, the utilization of disciplinary structure to organize curriculum by Jerome Bruner (1960), the positing of instructional objectives by Robert Mager (1975), and Madeline Hunter's (1985) time-on-task approach to instruction.

Assumptions about meaning and meanings embedded in text-books and their production are similar in many ways to structuralist assumptions identified in Tyler, Bloom et al., and Schwab (see Chapter 2). Textbook assumptions about meaning seem to include:

1. Word meaning is identity with a definition.
2. Utterance meaning is correspondence with the way things are (truth-conditional semantics).
3. Discourse meaning is the "objective" production of truth.
4. Meaning is fixed in sign systems external to the learner.
5. Meanings are given and static (at least when presented to students).
6. "Objective" knowledge is the transcendental signified of curriculum and instruction.
7. "Objective" knowledge fixes and stabilizes meanings (what is authoritatively known determines what is to be included and excluded).

Taken together these assumptions set up binary distinctions that define meaning in textbooks and teaching, such as concepts/facts, terminal objectives/intermediate objectives, cognitive/affective, generalized knowledge/knowledge of particulars, and subject-centered learning/student-centered learning. Students are to be taught, controlled, examined, and certified in terms of meanings located in *external* structures of knowledge and educational processes.

These textual assumptions and strategies have several consequences:

1. Word meaning is treated as identity with a definition that reflects current usage, while ambiguous definitions and different applications of a word tend to be excluded.
2. Word and utterance meaning is determined by stable and fixed structures of knowledge and procedures.
3. Meanings are treated as ahistorical; they are neither set in social, political, cultural, economic, or linguistic context nor treated as products of those settings.
4. Utterances are treated as passive and descriptive, not as actions.
5. There is silence on the political production of textbooks and approaches to teaching.
6. The contribution of students (readers) to meanings is slighted,

because past experiences, social codes, information, and cultural capital are often downplayed in pursuit of learning objectives.
7. A false sense of stability and certainty of meaning and meanings is given.

It may not be possible to set things right quickly or completely, but it is possible to move beyond blatantly deficient structural and traditional approaches to meaning.

The reader should be forewarned that the following moves do not build upon each other in a linear, structural fashion, because it is not possible to design a pedagogical strategy in a structuralist mold to correct for the errors of structuralism. But structural and traditional approaches to meaning offer a place to start. I begin with what might at first appear to be a step backwards. *Structuralism should have the first but certainly not last word in approaching the meaning of words, utterances, discourses, and texts.* This is theoretically defensible and seemingly unavoidable. First, the theoretical defense. It is reasonable to suppose, along with Saussure, Wittgenstein, Putnam, Foucault, and Eco, that at a given time meanings are relatively fixed, unless we are at the highwater mark of one of those rare Kuhnian revolutions when key words and concepts are openly in question. But even at such moments words and discourses not being overturned will be relatively fixed and stable. Meanings are fixed, in part, by sociolinguistic usages that reflect an underlying material division of labor (Putnam), by relations to and differences from other words and utterances (Saussure), by usages generally employed (Wittgenstein), by discursive practices (Foucault), and by the social determination of linguistic codes (Eco).

Origins and starting places, however, require comment. All of us, when we learn, bring different past experiences, beliefs, attitudes, models, and ideologies with us. We are different. We start from different places. Someone advanced in mathematics might be relatively uninformed about literature, and someone advanced in social studies might be a beginner in art. Novices and the ignorant deserve a good-faith introduction to socially accepted, systematic, authoritative knowledge, because this knowledge and the structures it promotes are the world, for the time being, of teachers, students, and everyone else. Knowledge of this world also brings self-knowledge because as we read its texts we read ourselves. A place to begin, then, is with coherent stories or sets of ideas that provide students with information and knowledge that subsequently can be expanded, explicated, criticized, and deconstructed. It seems reasonable to begin with coherence before moving to complexity, contradiction, and ambiguity.

Superficially, this resembles the use of advanced organizers. But this argument is about meaning, not just teaching strategy, because advanced organizers need not lead to a suspicion or rejection of structurally presented meanings. Culturally sanctioned, positive, and authoritative knowledge is incomplete, interest-bound, tied up with existing power arrangements, and cloaked in certainty. As the illusion of certainty is dispelled, it becomes possible to uncover the origins and commitments of our structures and the effects of power that led to their production.

Textbooks, lesson plans, scope and sequence guidelines, and the Bloom et al. taxonomy provide a place to *begin*. Structurally presented meanings can be benign and constructive as long as the dialogue between textbooks and teaching does not begin and end with them. If structural meanings function as the ending instead of the beginning of the dialogue, if they state maximum and not minimum learning objectives, then they become dangerous as they stifle, distort, and police student/teacher reading and interaction.

Unqualified endorsement of structuralist interpretations of disciplinary knowledge and educational processes *embraces a deterministic view of society wherein a subjectivity, the way an individual (student, teacher, administrator, parent) views herself or himself and so acts, is constituted by previously existing social categories and institutions.* The words we use are rooted in language we inherit, and we have no control over what we inherit. Eco refers to it like this: "As subjects, we are what the shape of the world produced by its signs makes us become" (1984, p. 45). Our linguistic inheritance, however, is ultimately unstable; each use of a word is a bit different, and at every moment meanings of words and utterances are dispersed through the language.

If it is appropriate to start with structural meanings that are currently accepted, then we are blessed with the good fortune of being supplied with textbook after textbook built upon (some quite consciously) structuralist assumptions. The economics and power arrangements that shape the textbook market virtually guarantee continued production of textbooks in a structuralist mold. Because structural, traditional, and truth-conditional semantic approaches to meaning are not ultimately justifiable, it behooves us to be flexible and question the categories, inclusions and exclusions, metaphors, argumentative styles, and rules of evidence for textbooks and discourses. Structural approaches to meaning are weak when it comes to variability; creativity; complexity and contradiction; incompleteness; ambiguity; interpretation; origins and dynamics of words, utterances, and discourses; and the political production of truth.

Structurally based meanings advanced by textbooks can be historically, politically, economically, culturally, and linguistically located, analyzed, and criticized in the classroom. Meanings are products of social and political practices specific to time and place, to history and geography, to events and their spatial distribution. Social and political purposes, power arrangements, institutions, and practices constitute the possibility of and confer meanings on what is said. And "where there is rule and institution, there is society and a deconstructible mechanism" (Eco, 1984, p. 167). Teaching can illuminate, explore, analyze, and criticize, to some degree at least, the categories of discourse, modes of expression, metaphors, argumentative styles, rules of evidence, and literary allusions that textbooks value and celebrate. To put it differently: Why does the discourse of a textbook have the structure and make the claims it does? Students and teachers can become historians of ideas, archivists, social critics and commentators by examining the discourses within which they are caught up. Students and teachers thereby become students of curriculum, and the categorical distinctions curriculum theory/curriculum and curriculum/instruction collapse.

Origins of discourses are related to demographics, economic growth, intellectual history, technological developments, political events, armed conflicts, and social stratification, for example. At least occasionally, meaning and meanings should be presented in such light. Otherwise, meaning is locked into a static, politically conservative, and demonstrably outmoded structuralism. Eco's description of the universe of human culture is a commentary on such a rigid view of meaning. Human culture, he writes,

> (a) . . . is structured according to *a network of interpretants*, (b) It is virtually *infinite* because it takes into account multiple interpretations realized by different cultures: a given expression can be interpreted as many times, and in as many ways, as it has been actually interpreted in a given cultural framework. . . . (c) It does not register only "truths" but, rather, what has been said about the truth or what has been believed to be true as well as what has been believed to be false or imaginary or legendary. . . . (d) . . . a semantic encyclopedia is never accomplished and exists only as a *regulative idea*. . . . (e) . . . *a notion of encyclopedia does not deny the existence of structured knowledge; it only suggests that such a knowledge cannot be recognized and organized as a global system . . . every attempt to recognize . . . local organizations as unique and ''global''—ignoring their partiality—produces an ideological bias*. (1984, pp. 83–84; emphasis added)

Textbooks are products of human culture that present partial, local organizations of meanings. It seems their fate never to escape partiality and ideological bias.

The way teachers respond to textbooks is a decisive moment in teaching, a pivotal point in dealing with meaning and meanings. Such moments continually present themselves. They cannot be dealt with once and for all. Teachers continually choose whether to reinforce knowledge claims presented as authoritative and structured or to expose their partiality. The choices are pragmatic. If they reinforce dominant structures, they enact an uncritical and vulgar pragmatism. If they are informed by a sense of crisis (small *c*) that questions structural and positivist meanings and standards, they enact a critical pragmatism. We build our communities, educational or otherwise, and social life with choices such as these, whether they are vulgar or critical. The structural thrust of textbooks proposes local organizations of knowledge to be global, thereby smuggling ideological biases into the constitution of subjectivities, the way we view ourselves and our place in the world. If teaching reinforces these biases, the social construction of meanings remains hidden, they are treated as "natural," and they are reified. If teaching simply repeats structured assertions of textbooks (tests, scope and sequence guidelines, workbooks, computer programs, and so forth), then the dialogue becomes repetitive and noninstructive even though students and teachers might become facile in the discourse. Teaching that moves behind and beyond the text through the language, culture, arts and sciences, and politics and economics of society makes the meanings of our words, utterances, and discourses more accessible to us.

This can be risky business. When everyone is acknowledged as a reader and maker of meanings, the dialogue between textbooks and teaching extends beyond the classroom. Educational authority is decentered. Poststructural teaching, among other things, points to the origins and production of textbooks; it implicates discourses with each other that, in a more structured world, appear to be discrete. One discourse and practice so implicated is the world of educational administrators as they administer the school. Schools are hierarchical, tightly or loosely coupled organizations as the case may be. They tend toward strong classification and tight framing, to use Basil Bernstein's (1977) categories. School organizations provide a text, as it were, in which words are defined, utterances made, values expressed, and plots unfold. Educational administrators have to ensure that school structure is persuasive and compelling and that all who enter read their lines. School structure constrains what can and cannot be said. It tends to reinforce the authority behind the textbook. School organization and educational practice are concrete and material. The exercise of power negatively sanctions some discourses and inquiry and provides opportunity for others. Meanings are produced and policed by the existing division of labor, extant usages, current institutions, and accepted social practices. All of these are normative and coercive. But meanings embedded in school structure are not less provisional than meanings in textbooks. It is appropriate, if a bit provocative, for teachers and students to trace meanings and authority in the organization that makes it possible for them to be who they are as teachers and students. Taking meaning seriously can, if one is not appropriately circumspect, place one's job in jeopardy. But if there are risks there are also substantial payoffs, because they will have greater knowledge of the social structures that makes it possible for them to be who they are.

The work of Derrida suggests another approach that teaching may take in its dialogue with textbooks. Because deconstruction can only follow prior constructions, we begin, as above, with proposed structural, systematic meanings. A move along this line playfully explores uses of words, utterances, arguments, and metaphors. Such play twists and stretches, pulls and pushes, stresses and strains what is said into new statements, combinations of statements, references, arguments, and other utterances. This reflects Wittgenstein's sense of word utilization and Derrida's text construction, called "grammatology" (Ulmer, 1985). In important ways we are always trapped in our language, but its ambiguities and its possible applications present opportunities, spaces for new meanings and thought. Unless we seize these chances we lock our own cell, thereby collaborating in our linguistic imprisonment.

Teaching is a reading of the textbook, school, and society. The reading is here. Eco writes:

> The text does not speak any longer of its own "outside"; it does not even speak of itself; it speaks of our own experience in reading (deconstructively) it. There is no more a dialectics of *here* and *there*. . . . Everything happens *here*. (1984, p. 154)

Teachers set the stage wherein a sociolinguistic division of labor is acknowledged and valued. Linguistic usages within this setting should at first, I suggest, reflect structurally assigned meanings. But new meanings are constituted and conveyed when teachers teach. Teachers, if they are self-conscious about what they say and do, become curriculum theorists and subjects instead of objective instruments of instruction. We inscribe the flaws of traditional approaches to word meaning, limitations of truth-conditional semantics, errors of early speech act theory, and the misplaced rigor of structuralism into our teaching if we focus solely on accepted word and utterance usage in textbooks, achievement and aptitude tests, classroom interactions, and curriculum scopes and sequences.

CONCLUSION

One view of curriculum is that it is what students have an opportunity to learn (McCutcheon, 1982), and instruction provides those opportunities. Roger Simon (1985) argues that curriculum is a contest over the sign. Combining these, curriculum, at least some of the time, is a contest over what signs students have an opportunity to learn, and instruction is the literal and figurative mediation of those signs. "In truth, the sign always *opens up* something new. No interpretant, in adjusting the sign interpreted, fails to change its borders to some degree" (Eco, 1984, p. 44). Meaning has turned out to be something other than what it at first appeared. Word meaning is not given by looking at the word but by looking beyond it. When we look at something other than the word, we do not find an author of its meaning or a transcendent foundation for its meaning; sometimes we find contradictions, we find power inextricably caught up in it, and new applications of the word create possibilities for radical playfulness that verge on aesthetics. The same general conclusions hold for utterances. In order to clarify word and utterance meaning, we look to the discourses within which they are located. In order to illuminate discourse and text meaning, we look for, with little expectation of finding, origins of texts in culture, politics, economics, and so forth. Discourses change, and sometimes changes are induced by what people choose to say and do within whatever degrees of freedom they have. Passivity, on the other hand, promotes determinism and the conformity that goes with it.

CHAPTER 5

Theory and Practice

> To most thinkers of the eighteenth century, it seemed clear that
> the access to Nature which physical science had provided should
> now be followed by the establishment of social, political, and
> economic institutions which were in accordance with Nature.
> Ever since, liberal social thought has centered around social re-
> form as made possible by objective knowledge of what human
> beings are like—not knowledge of what Greeks or Frenchmen or
> Chinese are like, but of humanity as such. . . . Much of the
> rhetoric of contemporary intellectual life takes for granted that the
> goal of scientific inquiry into man is to understand "underlying
> structures," or "culturally invariant factors," or "biologically
> determined patterns." (Rorty, 1985, pp. 4–5)

> In that Empire, the craft of Cartography attained such Perfection
> that the Map of a Single province covered the space of an entire
> City, and the Map of the Empire itself an entire Province. In the
> course of Time, these Extensive maps were found somehow want-
> ing, and so the College of Cartographers evolved a Map of the
> Empire that was of the same Scale as the Empire and that coin-
> cided with it point for point. Less attentive to the study of Cartog-
> raphy, succeeding Generations came to judge a map of such
> Magnitude cumbersome, and, not without Irreverence, they
> abandoned it to the Rigors of sun and Rain. In the western
> Deserts, tattered Fragments of the Map are still to be found,
> sheltering an occasional Beast or beggar; in the whole Nation, no
> other relic is left of the Discipline of Geography. (Borges, 1972, p.
> 141)

One goal of many educational researchers is to have the fruits of their
labor accurately *represent* educational practice. There is hope of exactitude. There is hope that empirically based research will provide
knowledge and information to design more effective materials, teaching procedures, administrative arrangements, and tests, for example.

Exactitude, as Borges suggests above, presents problems. If theory exactly represents practice, how can it guide practice? Conversely, if theory erroneously represents practice, how can it guide practice? In either case, following Rorty's observation, what is the relationship between theory and an enlightened practice, or, put somewhat differently, a critical practice? Is the aphorism "knowledge shall make us free" an outright delusion? Can the circle from observation of practice to theory about practice to practice be anything other than vicious?

One structural interpretation of contemporary education would place the binary distinction theory/practice in the forefront. It might be argued as follows. Theory about what happens in schools provides knowledge for planning school practices. This distinction supports the status and authoritative hierarchy of professional education, because, so the argument goes, university-based researchers produce knowledge that practitioners draw upon for solutions to their problems. There is also a reverse push from practice to theory, whereby immediate demands made upon practitioners (for example, raising achievement test scores, preventing student dropouts, lowering the rate of teenage pregnancies, or reducing drug usage among students) set the research agenda. In either case, theory asserts knowledge claims about practice, thereby providing a basis for planning and control. Is this implausible or unreasonable? Yes, if one is interested in anything other than naive, acritical social reproduction.

This relationship between theory and practice is presumed in different ways in three following discussions of the contribution of applied research to policy. First, David Cohen and Michael Garet (1975) test the following:

> One assumption is that policies consist of discrete decisions: Social research is expected to affect policy by influencing discrete choices among competing programs and methods. A second assumption is that applied research is more authoritative than ordinary common-sense ideas about social policy. . . . On the basis of these assumptions, it often is argued that applied social research is justified because it provides the state with authoritative and objective evidence concerning the costs and consequences of social policies. . . . The main justification for applied research, however, rests on a belief that research will rationalize social policy. (1975, pp. 19–20)

The argument is straightforward: the more we know about something, the better we will be able to plan and control our activities to increase our satisfaction. These intuitively appealing assumptions were falsified. Cohen and Garet show that discrete public policy decisions made during the late 1960s and early 1970s were not influenced by discrete research findings.

Alice Rivlin writes about similar assumptions in terms of PPBS (planning-programming-budgeting system) analysis. This is her account:

> Anyone faced with the problem of running a government program, or indeed, any large organization, would want to take these steps to assure a good job: (1) define the objectives of the organization as clearly as possible; (2) find out what the money was being spent for and what was being accomplished; (3) define alternative policies for the future and collect as much information as possible about what each would cost and what it would do; (4) set up a systematic procedure for bringing the relevant information together at the time the decisions were to be made. PPBS was simply an attempt to institutionalize this commonsense approach in the government budgeting process. (Rivlin, 1971, p. 3)

The generic notions of theory and practice are present but not labeled as such. Practice (2) is what the money was being spent for and what was being accomplished; theory, in this instance, is a combination of objectives (1), alternative policies (3), and a systematic procedure for bringing relevant information together (4). Rivlin then proceeds to analyze some of the complexities and difficulties involved. Yet she contradicts herself. Rivlin argues that PPBS is "simply an attempt to institutionalize this commonsense approach in the government budgeting process." But this approach demands expertise that is not at all commonplace or commonsensical. She clearly distinguishes expert knowledge produced by systematic and controlled investigation from taken-for-granted commonsense knowledge of everyday life, but she then denies that distinction by labeling their combination a "commonsense approach in the government budgeting process."

Carol Weiss writes the following about program evaluation:

> Evaluation research is a rational enterprise. It examines the effects of policies and programs on their targets (individuals, groups, institutions, communities) in terms of the goals they are meant to achieve. By objective and systematic methods, evaluation research assesses the extent to which goals are realized and looks at the factors associated with successful or unsuccessful outcomes. The assumption is that by providing "the facts," evaluation assists decision-makers to make wise choices among future courses of action. Careful and unbiased data on the consequences should improve decision-making. (Weiss, 1975, p. 13)

Weiss notes that the political context within which program evaluation takes place severely constrains what evaluators can learn. Here there is a contradiction. "Evaluation research is a rational enterprise" because of its "objective and systematic methods." Yet, Weiss later argues, research cannot produce knowledge independent of values and political interests; therefore, upon what kind of "facts" are policies based?

Two important characteristics are shared by these accounts of theory and practice. First, there is a binary distinction, even opposition, between theory and practice, because theory is privileged knowledge and practice is action. Second, each account is flawed. In the case of Cohen and Garet, they falsify the supposed linkage between applied research and public policy decisions; Rivlin's commonsense approach cannot work without technological expertise; and Weiss's account of evaluation as a rational enterprise does not produce objective, interest-free knowledge because it is political to the core. The following account, to the contrary, rejects a binary distinction or categorical opposition between theory and practice and, based on this rejection, explores the possibility and character of critical practice. The arguments of Cohen and Garet, Rivlin, and Weiss will be reinterpreted later.

EMPIRICALLY BASED THEORY

Educational practice, one side of the theory/practice distinction, was discussed in Chapter 1. Practice is constituted by activities, rules, interests, commitments, ideology, and arrangements of power. Now, what is theory? Theories come in different forms for different purposes. The problem addressed here deals with the use of empirically based social scientific theories for critical practice. At least that is where the argument begins. The role of normative or prescriptive theories for critical practice is a bit different. This section briefly characterizes scientific theories. The following section attacks the distinction between empirically based social scientific theories and normatively based social practice.

What is it to which educational researchers, qualitative as well as quantitative, aspire? First and foremost they are trying to find out what is going on. Generalizations summarize what they learn. But few researchers would argue that their goal is to stop with summary statements; instead, if one is to believe texts on research methodology (such as Kerlinger, 1973), the goal is to generate social scientific theories and explanations about educational phenomena. Frederick Suppe gives the following account of scientific theory:

> Theories have as their subject matter a class of phenomena known as the intended scope of the theory. The task of a theory is to present a generalized description of the phenomena within that intended scope which will enable one to answer a variety of questions about the phenomena and their underlying mechanisms; these questions typically include requests for predictions, explanations, and descriptions of the phenomena. The theory does not attempt to describe all aspects of the phenomena in its intended scope. (Suppe, 1977, p. 223)

Such generalized descriptions should be, in Bas van Fraassen's view, empirically adequate, that is, "all the actual observable phenomena fit" one specification or characterization of a theory (1980, p. 84).

Theories and explanations are necessarily *incomplete* and *interest-relative*. An explanation includes at least one generalization that applies to more than one situation. If it were otherwise it would simply be a description. Two situations or events must be different, or they are identical. Therefore an explanation is incomplete; it cannot cover all aspects of different situations or events (Lambert & Brittan, 1970, p. 92).

Because theories and explanations are incomplete, researchers and theorists must choose what they wish to explain. For example, a theory of testing would not attempt to describe all aspects of testing. One theory or set of theories might focus on item-response theory; another might deal with construct validity applied to testing; a third might try to account for effects of testing on subsequent performance; a fourth might look at relationships among social class, ethnicity, gender, and test performance.

If choices have to be made, then it follows that theories and explanations are interest-relative because choices cannot be made without reference to decision criteria, values, or interests. Putnam (1978) and van Fraassen (1980) each offer detailed arguments about the interest relativity of explanations. As van Fraassen puts it, explanations are answers to *why* questions. Why do female elementary students tend to do less well on mathematics tests than male students? Or why do students from working-class homes and neighborhoods do less well on standardized achievement tests than students who come from upper-middle-class homes and neighborhoods? *Why* questions, Putnam adds, always "presuppose ranges of interests" (1978, p. 43).

Empirically based theories can be located in different philosophical and research traditions, but they are all interest-relative. Qualita-

tive researchers cannot escape this problem any more than quantitative researchers can. Both choose what to observe, and those choices
reflect values and interests. The fundamental and far-reaching disagreement about the problematic meaning of social phenomena between naturalistically and phenomenologically oriented researchers is
marginal compared to the incompleteness and interest-relativity of
theories and explanations.

EXAMINING THE DISTINCTION
BETWEEN THEORY AND PRACTICE

The assumptions tested by Cohen and Garet, asserted by Rivlin,
and analyzed by Weiss relating theory to practice were found wanting.
Cohen and Garet find no support for the notion that applied educational research findings influence educational policy in discrete and
systematic ways. Rivlin's account of PPBS requires technological expertise for a "commonsense" approach to policy analysis. Weiss's
analysis shows that program evaluation is politically dependent on
human interests. Each begins with an assumption that theoretical
knowledge is superior to practical knowledge because it is generalized, articulated, systematic, scientific, objective, and disinterested
when compared to practical knowledge, which is idiographic, tacit,
less systematic, nonscientific, subjective, and interested in terms of
values, ideologies, and political commitments. Because of its superiority, so this reasoning goes, theory can be used to control and guide
practice. This empowers those who have theoretical knowledge relative to those who have practical knowledge. Theoretical control over
practice is, thereby, rationalized and legitimated.

Recall what theoretical knowledge is. "The task of a theory is to
present a generalized description of the phenomena" (Suppe, 1977,
p. 223). Theoretical knowledge, even if incomplete and interest-relative, is abstract and generalizable; it is what it is because it is not
practical knowledge. Regularities, trends, and invariant relationships
that constitute theoretical knowledge are abstracted from the detail
and idiosyncracy of everyday life. Differences between knowing and
acting theoretically and practically identify what each is; depending
upon one's interests, one may choose to privilege either theory or
practice. Educational researchers and theorists are interested in arguing the superiority of theoretical knowledge; principals and teachers
concerned with the complexity of life in schools appreciate and value
the richness of practical knowledge.

But theory and practice are interdependent in ways that lie beyond interests and choices. In Chapter 1 it was argued that educational practice is constituted by activities, rules, commitments, interests, ideologies, and power structures. If theories and explanations are empirically adequate and account for observable phenomena, then they explicitly or implicitly represent activities constituted by rules, commitments, and so forth. To understand this better, consider the difference between brute and institutional phenomena. Brute phenomena are naturally occurring events or objects, such as wood, atoms, stones, and tornadoes. Institutional phenomena are events or objects constituted by the actions of individuals and groups, such as touchdowns, elections, committees, and test scores. Scientists are interested in facts about both brute and institutional phenomena. Educational researchers and theorists are primarily interested in institutional phenomena, because educational phenomena are constituted by choices and actions of individuals and groups. Now, following P. F. Strawson, "facts are what statements (when true) state; they are not what statements are about" (1964, p. 38). Facts are linguistic entities; all linguistic entities are social constructions; therefore, all facts are institutional. Educational theories and explanations, then, consist of socially constructed statements about educational discourses-practices and institutional phenomena of the form "X counts as Y in context C" (Searle, 1969, p. 52).

Two kinds of institutional facts are involved in our problem of theory and practice. First, statements of the form "X counts as Y in context C" are themselves institutional. For example, "650 on the SAT's verbal test is a high score" is an institutional fact in the research context of testing and measuring achievement. Second, "95 marks on the paper that match symbols recorded in a computer count as 650 on the SAT verbal test" is a situation in which brute phenomena, marks on paper, count as an institutional phenomenon, a test score. The meaning of a "fact" in the context of research is dependent on the meaning of a "fact" in the context of testing. At first this may seem a bit obtuse, and then it may appear obvious and apparently trivial; but it effectively deconstructs the distinction between theory and practice.

In a brute sense, what goes on in a testing situation? Students make marks on papers. Students hand these papers to a teacher who, at a later time, also marks on the same papers. The teacher hands the papers back to the students. Because of this some students are indulged and seem to be pleased. Others are deprived and seem discontent. I could continue in this fashion to "present a generalized description of the phenomena." It might also be possible to devise a theory or explanation to account for these physical movements.

Would it be an educational theory or explanation? No! Educational practice is not just physical movement. Educational practice is a set of activities constituted by rules, commitments, interests, and so forth. A theory or explanation of brute movements excludes socially constitutive factors. A theory or explanation is educational only if it accounts for what is educational about phenomena. Insofar as activities, rules, commitments, interests, ideologies, and power structures *constitute* educational practice; insofar as theories or explanations are attempts to represent practice; it *necessarily* follows that constitutive elements of practice are represented in some way in those theories and explanations. Educators surely are not interested in explanations of marks on paper; they are interested in the educational significance of test results. When it comes to empirically based theories of social practice, the theory/practice distinction erodes, because normative commitments and power structures that constitute practice must be found in theoretical representations of practice; otherwise they do not describe the phenomena. A final caveat on this point: interests, ideologies, and power arrangements are better camouflaged in some research findings than in others. For example, it is possible for ethnographic research to focus on and make explicit the normative structure of the environment (see Lane, 1962). Interests, ideologies, and power are more likely to remain implicit in quantitative studies, because constitutive elements of phenomena are several steps further removed from theoretical inferences (for more about this, see Chapter 6). Simply stated, the problem of hidden practical commitments in theoretical findings varies in terms of explicitness/implicitness, but, it should be noted, ethnographic studies do not always have the upper hand on this issue.

The theory/practice distinction can also be deconstructed in a more active way by drawing upon speech act theory and the later work of Wittgenstein (see Chapters 1 and 4). Together, they decisively reject a view of language as representational description. A theoretical formulation is a speech act and a description or explanation. Several things are done with theoretical formulations and explanations. First, a description is given, which may be true or false. Second, the description refers not only to brute movements or objects but to constitutive rules, commitments, interests, ideologies, and power structures. Third, insofar as utterances can reproduce practice, they do so. Theoretical statements and explanations, then, as speech *acts* reproduce the phenomena.

Research findings are speech acts. Here is an example: "Structuring the lesson and giving directions on task procedures were positively associated with high student scores" (Dunham & Lieberman, 1980, p. 20). This speech act has propositional value. To ascertain its propositional value, treatments, research design, and outcome measures can all be checked. The studies upon which it is based can be replicated. Threats to validity can be identified and eliminated. Educational researchers are skilled in each of these, and assessing the validity of knowledge claims is part of the research enterprise.

Several speech acts are performed. First, a generalized description is given of the relationship between lesson characteristics, such as structure, task descriptions, and student scores. Second, a normative description is given of the educational practice from which this finding comes: the lesson is structured, directions are given, evaluation is performed, students are scored, the lesson is broken into task procedures, the teacher controls the learning situation, and students receive and respond to stimuli. The generalization assumes these are nonproblematic and "given"; hence, the force of the description is to reproduce rules, interests, ideologies, and power arrangements that constitute the practice. Descriptions of practices without criticism endorse the practices described.

The theory/practice distinction has broken down in two related yet different ways. First, the distinction deconstructs in a relatively passive way. Educational researchers generate theories whose substantive content provides an empirically adequate generalized description of educational phenomena. Because such phenomena are socially constituted, empirically adequate descriptions explicitly or implicitly refer to those constitutive and normative elements. Second, theory and practice interpenetrate in an active way. Statements made and speech acts performed when empirically based theories are uttered reproduce normative components of a practice.

THE ANONYMITY OF PRACTICAL AND THEORETICAL DISCOURSE

Speech act theory attends to the analysis of utterances in a context of social institutions and conventions. Foucault attends to the governing social institutions and discursive-practices. The time-on-task finding cited above, for example, depends upon several background institutions and conventions for its meaning and force: the educational research enterprise, the institution of American schools, efficient management as an educational outcome, conventions of statistical analysis, conventions of learning objectives in the evaluation of educational outcomes, utilitarianism as a decision criterion in evaluation, and so forth. Foucault argues that power precedes speech and that discourse is governed by anonymous rules. When theoretical and practical discourses are viewed in this setting, the distinctions break down between theory and practice, between empirical theory and normative theory, between description of an action and prescription for a course of action, between explanation of social practice and justification of practice, and between fact and value. Knowledge does not exist apart from the constitutive interests that lead to its production. There is no clear, distinct line of demarcation between knowledge on one side and ideology, human interest, and power on the other.

Here are three illustrations. First, teachers and administrators work within preexisting discursive practices when students are tested. Activities such as the preparation of achievement tests, the administration of daily, weekly, or monthly instruments that measure student progress, the assignment of grades, the communication of results to students and parents, and the use of grades to place students in future classes *constitute*, and thereby necessarily constrain, what can legitimately be said about testing and evaluation. Likewise, research activities, whether concerned with item-response theory or social correlates of achievement, are constituted and constrained by existing discursive practices in fields as diverse as statistical theory and theories of social mobility.

Second, social practices identify who is authorized to make statements as well as which statements are appropriate and inappropriate. Susan Florio (1983) describes a collaboration between researchers and teachers studying writing instruction. After completing initial research into teaching elementary school writing (Clark & Florio et al., 1981) the researchers approached participating teachers with a proposal to collaborate democratically in reanalyzing the data. The purpose, Florio writes, was "to bring together members of different speech communities to deliberate on the problem of teaching writing and, perhaps, to create a new speech community marginal to the others" (1983, p. 5) The practical speech community of teachers and the speech communities of researchers/theorists were differently constituted, historically, culturally, and professionally. These differences played out in a variety of ways as the group worked together.

> What was striking and unanticipated in the Forum was not only how very differently members of our groups saw the research that we had

conducted and hoped to review and share, but how very differently they saw the Forum itself. Another surprise concerned how the institutional structures within which we worked supported those differences. (Florio, 1983, p. 6)

Finally, think of Foucault's account of discursive practices in the context of teacher education. Teacher education programs are constrained by state laws and university governance procedures. Such programs are limited by university requirements for disciplinary majors and minors. They are also shaped by past decisions about course requirements in professional education. Recall Shapiro's (1981) summary of Foucault, "statements make persons." Ongoing discursive practices constitute subjects (those who may speak) as well as objects (what may be spoken about).

The problem inhibiting critical practice is not centered in needing more and better research to represent more accurately what is going on and then applying the findings to practice. Attempts at representation actively contribute to the material reproduction of practice, because research findings are speech *acts* and their propositional content depends upon the practice described. Research findings that are simply reported materially reproduce normative, ideological, and power arrangements of practice.

Discursive-practices are at least partially anonymous and are enforced by power structures. They support a hierarchy in which theoretical knowledge is superior to practical knowledge. Discursive practices create subjects and places for speakers as well as objects that may be spoken about. Theoretical knowledge is separate neither from practice nor from its normative commitments and supporting power arrangements. Theoreticians and practitioners are each constituted by practices they seek to control. How is it possible to avoid the "viciousness" of the circle from practice that is observed to theory about such observations to future practice? How is it possible to avoid social-structural determination in representational theory and practice?

DIFFERENCES BETWEEN THEORY AND PRACTICE

To maintain that theory and practice are not opposed, separate, or distinct from each other is *not* to argue they are identical. A "generalized description of . . . phenomena" (Suppe, 1977, p. 223) is a description, not the thing itself. Likewise, educational testing in a classroom is a physical, material activity, not a linguistic account of it. Speech acts that constitute practice are obviously *different* from those that constitute theory. Teachers *command, request,* or *order* students to take tests. Researchers *describe* or *explain* different aspects of testing and evaluation phenomena. Descriptions and explanations implicitly contain commands, but descriptions are not commands. Teachers are concerned with idiosyncratic events in their totality when interacting with a student or class; the referent of an utterance is specific and unqualified. Researchers and theorists are concerned with theoretical constructs, variables, and classes of events that are general and highly qualified. Researchers must be self-conscious about what counts as what. What is an observation an instance of?

Alfred Schutz (1963b), although not writing in the tradition of speech act theory, writes about the difference between first-order constructs, such as speech acts of command, request, and order, and second-order constructs, such as speech acts of description and explanation. First-order constructs of everyday life are those we take for granted. Second-order constructs of social scientists explain, describe, and give accounts of first-order constructs and understandings. Wilfrid Sellars's (1963) distinction between manifest and scientific images of man-in-the-world roughly parallels that between first- and second-order constructs. The manifest image is of everyday life and its everyday meanings. The scientific image of man-in-the-world comes from descriptions, explanations, and accounts of the manifest image. Speech acts of practice and theory are different.

A second difference between practice and theory is the structure of each activity. Broadly speaking, they have a different syntax. What counts as sound argument, proper authority, appropriate norms, and reliable evidence are different for theory and practice. What is published in research journals is evaluated in terms of its scientific persuasiveness. How adequate is the research design, sample selection, treatment implementation, construct validity, measurement reliability, data analysis? Theoretical discourse attends to validity and meaning of theoretical terms, arguments, and research operations.

Practical discourse has different immediate interests from theoretical discourse. Because practical discourse often occurs face-to-face, there is less need to document and validate assertions. Tacit knowledge is not derogated; it is often elicited and elaborated. External validity of practical knowledge claims is not a major issue; it is often enough that they apply in the next classroom. Immediate and long-range purposes of practice and theory are often different, even though bound up with each other in common discourses-practices.

DISCOURSE AS OPPORTUNITY

Theory attempts to represent practice. It is ironic that as theory becomes more successful in representing practice, its substantive claims capture more of the constitutive and regulative elements of practice that break down the separation between theory and practice. Theory that successfully represents practice is the goal, but the goal becomes a problem if critical practice independent from the past is desired. Fortunately, practical and theoretical discourses are not identical with each other. They are not even identical with themselves over time or in different locations. *Differences among discursive practices provide insights important to criticism.*

If Foucault's account of discursive practices is correct, we are left with a deterministic view of social practice. But his analysis works much better for well-integrated and tightly coupled discourses, such as those of medicine, law, statistical analyses, and governmental bureaucracies, than for less well integrated and more loosely coupled discourses. It is to our advantage, therefore, that discursive practices are not always highly integrated or tightly coupled. Four points are worth making, each of which softens Foucault's argument. First, not all discursive practices are integrated to the same degree. For example, in the discourse of educational research journals terms tend to be well defined, rules of evidence widely agreed upon, criteria for appropriate statistical tests well known, and agreement on acceptable and unacceptable research designs and threats to validity prevalent. In other discourses, such as those found in classrooms, there is wider variation in what may be uttered, how arguments may proceed, and what is considered important. Second, when discursive practices and speech communities bump into each other, as it were, meanings and rules for proceeding must be negotiated and established. This happens when educational researchers present findings to classroom teachers and the methodological sophistication of the research community gives way for the sake of wider comprehension.

Third, anonymous, historical rules governing discourses can be challenged by those not fully socialized to them. For example, researchers with classroom experience can reject measures of educational achievement found in the research literature. Fourth, different background institutions will not police anomalous utterances with equal vigor. Those who edit research journals can entertain a fairly uniform discourse compared to teacher discussions of classroom experiences. Discursive practices, then, are often underdetermined. Their underdetermination requires negotiation of their rules of forma-

tion, transformation, structure, and meaning. This negotiation provides opportunity for critical discourse. Otherwise, we are left with a
withering and sterile determinism.

Habermas's theory of critical discourse can be used to capitalize
on discursive variations. Central to Habermas's thinking is the idea
that knowledge is informed by interests, ideology, and power. These
interests come from the constitution of the object of study (for example, classroom interaction, academic achievement, or racial integration) as well as from the constitution of the subject of study
(for example, the way educational researchers are trained and later
conduct their research). These impose material constraints on ideas
and what can be thought.

It is important to note that Foucault and Habermas mean somewhat different things by *discourse*. For Foucault, the term is used to
analyze systems of meaning and communication as they penetrate
from macrosocial practices to micropractices. Habermas identifies
social arrangements that constrain and distort communication. He
speculates about conditions that give individuals in face-to-face interaction, within small groups or collegial bodies, access to constraints
that makes discourse anonymous for Foucault. *Critical discourse* will
often be used in referring to Habermas's position.

Elaborating on Habermas (1979), imagine a conversation. It proceeds
smoothly as long as no one challenges what is said. Communicative
interaction depends upon four successful validity claims: the utterance must be understandable, the speaker sincere, the propositional
content true, and the normative content agreed upon. "Agreement is
based on recognition of the corresponding validity claims of comprehensibility, truth, truthfulness, and rightness" (p. 3). Conversation
proceeds apace as long as these validity claims are satisfied for speakers and hearers. If problems arise about understanding or sincerity,
these validity claims can be redeemed by further communication designed to clarify meanings or intentions.

But the remaining two validity claims, Habermas argues, can only be
redeemed discursively. The purpose of critical discourse is to resolve
the truth of a problematic belief or norm. McCarthy summarizes Habermas's position on discourse as "a willingness to suspend judge-
ment as to the existence of certain states of affairs that may or may not
be correct" (1973, p. 140). Critical discourse points toward institutionally unbound speech acts. Conditions for critical discourse are ideal
and counterfactual, that is, they posit a state of affairs that is counter
to social communication as we know it. They are unattainable for
Foucault and, as I will show, are also out of reach for Habermas.

Before this is seized upon as a weakness peculiar to critical discourse, it should be emphasized that research constructs such as those found in statistical analytic models, sampling procedures, measurement models, principles of research design, construct validity, and external validity posit one unattainable, ideal, counterfactual assumption after another without impeding the research enterprise.

As described by Habermas, discourse should be thought of metaphorically, with the pursuit of truth conceptualized in terms of ideal, face-to-face interaction. The purpose of discourse is to determine the truth of an utterance where

> the meaning of the truth or untruth of a statement does not consist in the conditions guaranteeing the objectivity of our experience but in the possibility of argumentative corroboration of a truth claim which is falsifiable in principle (Habermas, 1973, p. 166)

Truth is the goal of discourse, and it is a consensus about what is the case. The process by which consensus is brought about is designed to guard against distortions by the exercise of power. What any individual believes to be true may be in error, because we may be doing something other than what we think we are.

Critical discourse moves from an accepted consensus to a rational consensus. We find ourselves in the paradoxical situation in which constraints are required for radically free and critical discourse. The constraints are designed to minimize distorting influences of commitments, interests, ideologies, and power arrangements. Critical discourse—between, for example, practitioners and researchers-theorists—must be symmetrical and nondominated. All parties may initiate comments, challenge assertions, and question not only theoretical formulations but also metatheoretical and metaethical ones. It cannot be bound; it must be radically free, with only the best argument pursued. Strategic behavior, turning the search for truth into a conflict or competition, is not permitted; winning or losing is not the outcome of discourse. No votes are taken. The pursuit of the best argument is what is sought. These are necessary conditions for emancipation from past commitments, past practice, and social determinism.

Discourse is distorted by power and ideology if these conditions are not met. Some beliefs may be treated as nonproblematic because of institutional pressure, such as testing students regularly to estimate their achievement. Or some individuals may dominate not because of their arguments but because of their positional authority. Imagine, for example, a university-based teacher educator who presses behavioral objectives in art education on classroom teachers for the sake of accountability.

It is instructive to overlay conditions for critical discourse on the research enterprise. If perspectives of practitioners, students, and various minority groups are not accepted as valid, research may myopically turn in on itself. Likewise, if practitioners do not accept the validity of research insights, educational practice risks turning into an unreflective reproduction of ongoing practice. Teacher and administrator education programs that mediate theory and practice during an important stage of a practitioner's career should be structured so that the validity of theoretical and practical knowledge is mutually accepted.

Presumptions about hierarchical knowledge continually threaten open and critical discourse. Florio recounts a telling instance in her work with the Written Literacy Forum:

> In the Forum's early months we found, time and again, that we were hamstrung by the demands of our roles and by our taken-for-granted normative assumptions about teaching and research. What is more, we were not alone in all of this. After months of working together to achieve some consensus about our purpose, we took our messages about writing and its instruction to other groups—curriculum specialists, graduate students in research, teachers, and preservice teachers. Here we found that there were dramatic differences from group to group in both what were considered important findings to report from the Forum's work and in who had the authority to report them. (1983, p. 8)

> As our group addressed a large staff of curriculum specialists in an urban school district near Detroit, we watched the curriculum specialists whisper to one another, leave for early coffee, and show considerable restlessness while the teachers talked about writing instruction. Only during the question and answer period did these specialists appear satisfied when they would pointedly address the researchers to ask what the study "really found." (1983, p. 20)

Florio's experience illustrates institutional resistance to critical discourse. It also suggests certain limitations inherent in Habermas's theory of communicative competence. Curriculum specialists are hierarchically superior to classroom teachers; it is their job to be curriculum experts and bring their subordinates, who are classroom teachers, the latest news from the battlefront in the war against ignorance. University researchers, in turn, are higher in the hierarchy than curriculum specialists. They are front-line fighters against ignorance; research findings are the fruits of battle. This hierarchy is not supported simply out of respect for truth, however; there are an array of overlapping institutions behind it. For example, state certification requirements give university-based teacher educators and researchers power to accredit classroom teachers; the way school districts are organized makes curriculum specialists financially and professionally superior to classroom teachers; and curriculum specialists, often in combination with university-based experts, decide what textbooks and sequence of topics classroom teachers will follow. Florio and her colleagues were not just asking to alter conventional ways of thinking about teaching writing. They asked that the power arrangements upon which the accepted consensus was based be set aside.

Habermas shares with Foucault an important assumption: normative commitments, human interests, ideologies, and power arrangements infiltrate what we claim to know; in fact, knowledge would be impossible without them. Discourses are material practices, not simply interactions among people at the level of ideas. Habermas's analysis, as does Foucault's, rejects idealism and the separation of knowledge from power. But Habermas's solution is essentially idealistic. Crucial characteristics of critical discourse include symmetry, nondomination, nonexclusion of topics and comments, and so forth. These conditions refer to underlying power structures that legitimate certain topics and exclude others, that recognize some individuals as authorities and others as novices. The question is: Is conversation up to changing material conditions? As Florio writes about working with teachers in the Written Literacy Forum, "Put simply, I came to the realization that in a social world that is unequal, you don't get a democratic or open conversation simply by saying that everybody's free to talk" (1983, p. 8). Critical discourse turns out to be a material practice.

Habermas's conditions for critical discourse cannot be met. Our search for knowledge cannot proceed without normative commitments (the search for truth), human interests (someone must be interested, for whatever reason, in an object and its study), and power arrangements (if any asymmetries or inequalities exist, some modes and objects of study will be favored over others). What we know is shaped by these conditions. What would knowledge be if it were not informed and influenced by commitments, interests, and power? It would not be human knowledge. But just because the Habermasian conditions cannot be met does not mean they are not important or useful. If they do nothing else, they point out constraining effects of our institutions and discursive practices.

We are getting into curious territory with this line of argument. Our search for critical practice has led us to critical discourse that is itself material practice. Knowledge is distorted by the intrusion of interests, ideology, and power. But critical discourse cannot transcend these factors. Critical discourse as described by Habermas deconstructs as soon as it is advanced. It is self-contradictory because it attempts to avoid what cannot be avoided; it cannot eliminate structural conditions necessary for its own constitution. Whenever there is a temptation to think that distortions have been eliminated, one only needs to be reminded that the desire to eliminate distortions is also a normative commitment, or that the wish to make a true assertion about an object represents an interest in that object, or that what one can or cannot say about an object is constrained by how power is arranged in society. Habermas's notion of critical discourse deconstructs as surely as does Rivlin's view of PPBS expertise.

It is now time to return to the assumptions tested by Cohen and Garet, Rivlin's view of PPBS, and Weiss's assertion that program evaluation is rational, objective, and systematic. What is going on in these three cases? The idea that applied policy research leads to discrete policy decisions is at one with the idea that program evaluation is a rational activity. Cohen and Garet tested and Weiss criticizes idealistic arguments that ignore the materialism of discourse and posit that individuals and institutions respond to utterances as actions. Policy-makers accept the materiality of discourse, including the discourses-practices of program evaluation and applied educational research. Program evaluation may be rational, though not idealistically so, because power constrains what can be said and done. Rivlin's juxtaposition of technological expertise against common sense is a bit different. Technological expertise is theoretical knowledge because it does not have the "weaknesses" of commonsense knowledge. But, as we have seen, theoretical knowledge depends upon practice. Technological expertise depends upon commonsense knowledge. We can only decide whether expertise is useful in the context of practice by applying commonsense, practical, ethical, and political criteria. If we make the mistake of placing these forms of knowledge in opposition to each other by asserting the superiority of expert knowledge, we empower technicians to make practical and normative decisions and subvert efforts at critical discourse.

CONCLUSION

This argument is nearing its end, but before it does, it must be made more complex and more curious. From the outset one goal has been to explore the possibility of practice that is autonomous from the structures of the past, a practice freely chosen by individuals engaged in constituting their social world and institutions. This search led to the formulation of a critical discourse designed to reveal the distortive influences of interest, ideology, and power. The irony of critical discourse as an opportunity for autonomous practice, however, is that it requires a particular normative and material structure. The idea of autonomous practice is contradictory. Freedom requires structure; freedom without structure is chaos. The search for autonomy and freedom from oppressive social institutions and structures cannot proceed in the absence of a social structure. And we cannot be sure that any particular social structure intended to promote critical discourse is not itself oppressive. This does not mean, however, that all social processes and institutions are equally constraining and oppressive.

The idea of critical practice is at one with the idea of critical pragmatism. It is not something about which a technical handbook can be written. But some guidelines can be suggested for necessary but not sufficient conditions for critical discourse-practice or critical pragmatism. Some apparently necessary conditions can be suggested, but they will underdetermine what is required. The list will remain incomplete. What might be candidates for a list of necessary conditions? Here Habermas is particularly helpful. First, one might ask whose interests are being served by the practices of theoretical discourse as well as the practices of everyday life, although one should not expect definitive answers. If power, text, and speech are intertwined, then analysis and criticism necessary for critical practice must attend to how power influences, shapes, produces, and is produced by theoretical and practical discourses-practices. Second, everyone should be free to speak about their interests, beliefs, feelings, and so forth. Third, descriptions and explanations should be offered about the way subjectivities are conditioned and constrained by existing social structures. Fourth, alternative accounts of what is going on should be explored, regardless of their source. These, obviously, will constitute additional normative and material conditions for critical discourse.

Fifth, if authorities, such as educational administrators, are to be critical in a pragmatic way, they must consult beyond their legal and formal mandates (although authority will continue to be located in bureaucracies and social institutions). Sixth, one should watch for, indeed expect, contradictions and incompleteness in theory and practice. From time to time theoreticians and practitioners will make rhetorical claims that contradict the logic of their arguments and practices. Seventh, on the basis of critical discourse and analysis all "stakeholder" interests should be represented, a form of representation different from theories put forth as representational. Finally, "new" practices will, almost certainly, sooner or later exhibit contradictions and incompleteness, leading to a new round of analysis and criticism. An underlying theme is that "stakeholders" in a practice must learn to read discourses critically, including interests, ideologies, and supporting power arrangements. Often when people write about practice, the concern is with how deliberations are to be arranged (Schwab, 1983), or with information (the assumptions Cohen and Garet tested), or with data analysis and utility calculations (Rivlin's discussion of PPBS). If, however, a discourse or practice is to be critical, attention necessarily must be directed at what structures choices, actions, and utterances, not just at what is chosen.

Take another look at testing and grading. Those concerned with making testing more effective and efficient endorse actions, interests, ideologies, and power arrangements that constitute testing. Whose interests are being served by these practices? School administrators and teachers are well served, because they are held accountable by school boards, communities, state laws, and colleges and universities to provide an assessment of what students have learned. They, in turn, hold students accountable for learning certain material. Students who score high on subject-matter achievement tests are well served. Whose interests are not served by educational testing? Students who do poorly on exams. How well an individual student scores is influenced by the morally arbitrary natural allocation of social class, ethnicity, and so forth. Also, many scholarly interests are not well served by educational testing, because what filters into textbooks and tests is sometimes nothing more than a caricature of academic knowledge. The interests of teachers who teach subjects not well suited to objective testing, such as the humanities and fine arts, are not well served. Testing is a reifying process because it assigns words to things. But which words are assigned to which things serves the interests of some people better than others.

Critical discourse repeatedly interrogates texts and discourses-practices, keeping an eye out for contradictions and incompleteness between what is claimed and what is actually done thereby illuminating how they came to be what they are. I will offer two examples of curricular analysis that are excellent examples of deconstructive criticism. Michael Apple analyzes how certain prepackaged sets of curricular materials operate to deskill teachers. He describes deskilling in the context of workers as follows:

> Workers are continually deskilled (and, of course, some are "reskilled"). The skills they once had—skills of planning, of understanding and acting on an entire phase of production—are ultimately taken from them by management and housed elsewhere in a planning department controlled by management. (1982, p. 71)

As prepackaged sets of curricular materials are more widely used, teachers lose control of the practice of teaching to textbook authors and publishers. Everything a teacher needs to teach is provided. The teaching steps are built in as well as the testing apparatus.

> The goals, the process, the outcome, and the evaluative criteria for assessing them are defined as precisely as possible by people external to the situation. (Apple, 1982, p. 146)

> Skills that teachers used to need, that were deemed essential to the craft of working with children—such as curriculum deliberation and planning, designing teaching and curricular strategies for specific groups and individuals based on intimate knowledge of these people—are no longer as necessary. (Apple, 1982, p. 146)

Apple proceeds to point out some implications of deskilling: little interaction between teachers is required, teachers become divorced from the "actual stuff of their work," and schools become more like factories. By looking closely at the changing structure of teaching, a contemporary and technical view of teaching is deconstructed. Teachers do less teaching and more managing than before. The effect of prepackaged curricular materials is to remove control over teaching from the classroom in the name of efficiency. Teachers are not entrusted to teach.

A second example comes from Henry Giroux's analysis of literacy. Literacy, he argues, is currently discussed in technical terms separate from "the broader social, historical, and ideological forces that constitute the conditions for its existence" (1983a, p. 205). Contemporary approaches to literacy avoid its political dimensions. A technical approach to literacy assumes that schools are politically neutral sites, that there are no interests, ideology, and power arrangements in place. But we have repeatedly seen this is not the case. It is this "culture of positivism" that Giroux identifies. Insofar as literacy is viewed in the context of instrumental access to writing, reading, and language practices, students are denied access to the constitutive sources of the discourses in which they participate. If the structure of language practices remains hidden, students and teachers remain prisoners of dominant discourses-practices. Literacy presumably provides access to any kind of discourse, but instrumental and technical literacy actively prohibits access to interest, ideology, and power in what we say and do.

Descriptions and explanations of surface regularities endorse constitutive elements of those activities. But the educational profession is large and complex and is itself constituted by a number of discursive practices. They vary in interests, ideologies, and power arrangements. Constitutive and regulative rules of discourses-practices may be largely invisible to those fully socialized to them, but they are less so to those on the outside. As Florio demonstrates, powerful forces are opposed to exposing the nature of discursive rules or substituting different rules that might open the way to other topics or allow others to speak.

We may not be able to have autonomous practice, but critical practice and critical pragmatism are possibilities. If criticism is not to be short-circuited by anonymous constraints of dominant practices and structures, it must be radically open. Openness of discourse provides opportunities whereby knowledge and normative claims of individuals situated in different discursive practices can be utilized in a critical appraisal of practice. This is a tall order, but otherwise we are left with a social deterministic view of practice controlled by dominant interests and institutions. The field of curriculum, some would argue (see Chapter 7), is concerned with what students have an opportunity to learn. But if what students have an opportunity to learn is only considered on the surface of things, then the constituting discourses remain hidden and educational practice remains noncritical and naive. Such practice is produced by the relativism of historical, cultural, and geographical happenstance.

Critical practice and pragmatism are always in transit. More is involved than making existing discourses-practices work more efficiently. More is involved than talking to each other under ideal conditions. Whenever one thinks that distortive and coercive elements have been eliminated, the newest practices produced by reflective and critical discourse will deconstruct. This is no reason to despair, however, or to embrace social determinism. Critical practice involves at least two components. First, it involves the construction and deconstruction of educational texts and discourses-practices. It is continual movement between construction of a practice, which justifies why things are designed as they are, and deconstruction of that practice, which shows its incompleteness and contradictions. Second, construction and deconstruction of discursive practices reflect upon and analyze those activities. Critical discourse is continual movement between the constitution of a methodology designed to reveal distortive influences of interests, ideology, and power and subsequent criticism of that approach.

In the context of analyzing major developments in twentieth-century philosophy, Rorty (1980) argues a position strikingly similar to that outlined above. He gives a detailed and lively account of attempts by philosophers in the twentieth century to defend the notion that knowledge is representation of nature. After focusing on Wittgenstein, Heidegger, and Dewey, he concludes that edifying philosophy, where edification stands for "finding new, better, more interesting, more fruitful ways of speaking" (p. 360), is concerned that "the conversation should be kept going rather than to find objective truth" (p. 377). Normal conversation, empirically based research in the present discussion, is a search for truth, and its quest closes off conversation because certain hypotheses and assumptions are privileged. The privileged status of certain assumptions corresponds to Foucault's rules of a discursive practice and the limiting constraints of ideology and power. Edifying philosophy, critical discourse in my account, is abnormal conversation.

> To see keeping a conversation going as a sufficient aim of philosophy, to see wisdom as consisting in the ability to sustain a conversation, is to see human beings as generators of new descriptions rather than beings one hopes to describe accurately. . . . New directions may, perhaps, engender new normal discourses, new sciences, new philosophical research programs, and thus new objective truths. . . . The point is always the same—to perform the social function which Dewey called "breaking the crust of convention," *preventing man from deluding himself with the notion that he knows himself, or anything else, except under optional descriptions.* (Rorty, 1980, pp. 378–79; emphasis added)

One point of critical discourse and pragmatism is not only to illuminate conditions of normal discourse and conversation but also to acquire control over those conditions and structures and generate new ones by utilizing our best visions of what is beautiful, good, and true to build our communities.

The job of the professional educator, a challenging and exciting one, is to say where and on what terms deconstruction ceases. Will we

justify curricula that do not refer to minority or feminist history? Will
we support measures of academic achievement highly correlated to
social class and ethnicity? Will we proceed with a commitment to the
superiority of theoretical knowledge over practical knowledge? Will
in-service training sessions be a celebration of theoretical expertise
and control? Will theoretical/practical discourse be primarily one-way,
from educational researchers to classroom practitioners? Criticism is
subverted if research findings and the concerns they express are
ranked above tacit knowledge of teachers; or if maintenance needs of
schools as institutions are given superiority over interests of parents
and students; or if day-to-day needs of teachers and principals are
allowed to dominate agendas of researchers and theorists; and so
forth. The traditionally accepted superiority of theoretical knowledge
over practical knowledge supports conventional power arrangements
and inequalities in a way so powerful it is almost invisible. Power
structures will seemingly always be around, but they can be made
more explicit, criticized, justified, and rearranged.

Relating empirically based theory to practice assumes a prior understanding of research and theory. This brief discussion circumvent-
ed a number of important questions about empirical research. One
issue important in empirical investigations is construct validity, and it
will be analyzed in the next chapter. Construct validity is often treated
as marginal to educational discourses-practices, but I will argue for its
centrality. It is an instance of an idea and theme that has been
marginalized in contemporary education; yet whatever contribution
empirical research findings make to educational practice presumes
that issues of construct validity have been resolved.

CHAPTER 6

Construct Validity and the Discourses of Research

Knowledge is always inescapably complicit with the first-order myths and enabling fictions that underwrite its claims to truth. (Norris, 1985, p. 23)

The question is not about how to define words like "truth" or "rationality" or "knowledge" or "philosophy," but about what self-image our society should have of itself. (Rorty, 1985, p. 11)

It is arguable that social research methodology entered adolescence, if not maturity, in July 1955. This somewhat overlooked coming of age occurred with the publication of Lee Cronbach and Paul Meehl's "Construct Validity in Psychological Tests." Validity issues, such as criterion and content, had been part of the research literature for some time, but construct validity was new.

A construct is "some postulated attribute of people assumed to be reflected in test performance. In test validation the attribute about which we make statements in interpreting a test is a construct" (Cronbach & Meehl, 1955, p. 283). In 1971 Cronbach expanded, "A construct is an intellectual device by means of which one *construes* events. It is a means of organizing experience into categories" (p. 464). Constructs are the way experience is organized. Research findings are inferences from measurements to constructs and vice versa. Construct validation, then,

> is involved whenever a test [research measurement] is to be interpreted as a measure of some attribute or quality which is not "operationally defined." The problem faced by the investigator is, "What constructs account for variance in test performance?" (Cronbach & Meehl, 1955, p. 282)

Construct validity focuses attention on the juncture of words and things, concepts and objects, theory and practice, where social theory and research and theoretical constructs and research operations converge and diverge.

Arguments prefiguring construct validity had been made several decades earlier. Logical positivists of the Vienna Circle had argued that the goal of science was to speak correctly about the world, and Cronbach and Meehl explicitly followed in the tradition of logical positivism/empiricism.[1] Construct validity, in this reading, is concerned with speaking correctly and getting language use straight. What constitutes valid movement between constructs and research operations is foundational, if there is a foundation, to the entire enterprise of social theory and research and central to knowledge claims produced by empirical research. This chapter deals with three main questions: (1) How is construct validity portrayed in the mainstream methodological literature? (2) How is construct validity informed by alternative research traditions and schools of thought; namely, phenomenology, critical theory, Foucault's interpretive analytics, and Derrida's deconstruction? (3) What do these arguments imply for a maturing social research methodology?

MAINSTREAM RESEARCH METHODOLOGY

The story begins with Cronbach and Meehl. The immediate impetus for their essay came from ongoing activities of the Committee on Psychological Tests of the American Psychological Association. Because of previous dissatisfaction with treatments of validity, the committee set out, from 1950 to 54, "to specify what qualities should be investigated before a test is published" (Cronbach & Meehl, 1955, p. 281). In part, then, the mission was to regulate, police, and normalize discourse about testing.

Construct validity points toward *identity* between an attribute or quality being measured and a theoretical construct.[2] It is a question of meaning. What does a research operation mean? What does a construct mean? In light of the original positivist commitment, one speaks correctly about the world if one's constructs match phenomena being measured such that if research operations tap a theoretical construct and are appropriately labeled, the measurement has construct validity. Thus construct validity is identity.

This ideal is abandoned before fully being articulated.[3] Cronbach and Meehl write, "Persons who possess this attribute (associated meanings of a construct) will, in situation X, act in manner Y (with a stated probability)" (1955, p. 284). Construct validity may point toward identity but turns out to be far less. It is discursive at the moment of its introduction because any suggested identity between constructs and measurements is immediately qualified. One implication, an important one it turns out, is that the full power of logical argument, including the then-fashionable hypothetico-deductive model of explanation, cannot contribute fully to construct validity because the logical property of identity required for valid deductive argument is neither present nor available. The job of researcher-theorists, however, is to make arguments and explanations about one thing or another, and these arguments and explanations are now seen to be discursive and rhetorical as well as analytic and logical. The positivist interpretation of construct validity erodes at its inception.

Cronbach and Meehl anticipate this development: "Whether or not an interpretation of a test's properties or relations involves questions of construct validity is to be decided by examining the entire body of evidence offered, together with what is asserted about the test in the context of this evidence" (1955, p. 284). Identity gives way to probabilities, and "the entire body of evidence" as the seemingly straightforward simplicity of construct validity surreptitiously, or not so surreptitiously, becomes more complex.[4]

Construct validity, as readers steeped in the tradition realize, was always more than matching constructs to measurements. Locating constructs within sets of lawlike statements is also involved. Lawlike statements related to each other form theoretical schemata and theories. In order to validate research operations, one must state at least some lawlike statements in which a construct occurs and relate them, along with their key constructs, to other lawlike statements. Then it is determined whether measurements of the constructs are related to each other as hypothesized.

Construct validation occurs in the context of a nomological net, a set of related lawlike statements. This creates an interesting paradox, because nomological nets change. Identity, consistence, coherence, definition, and stability are valued and pursued in the context of change and instability. Cronbach and Meehl describe it as follows:

> A rigorous (though perhaps probabilistic) chain of inference is required to establish a test as a measure of a construct. To validate a claim that a test measures a construct, a nomological net surrounding the construct must exist. When a construct is fairly new, there may be few specifiable associations by which to pin down the concept. As research proceeds, the construct sends out roots in many directions, which attach it to more and more facts or other constructs. (1955, p. 291)

Consensus about the nomological net is required; otherwise ambiguity subverts efforts at clarity and there are several sources of ambiguity: (1) constructs may be inductive summaries in early stages of investigation; (2) psychological laws have a residue of vagueness; and (3)
there is the problem of interpreting failed predictions. "When a pre-
dicted relation fails to occur, the fault may lie in the proposed interpretation of the test or in the network. Altering the network so that it can
cope with the new observations is, in effect, redefining the construct"
(1955, p. 300). By this point, construct validation is explicitly discursive. This insight, I believe, is particularly important but has remained
relatively unexplored.

In 1959 Donald Campbell and Donald Fiske proposed convergent
and discriminant validation by a multitrait-multimethod matrix. Each
measurement instrument is a trait-method unit, that is, a particular
method is used to measure a specific trait (construct). More than one
method should be used to measure a trait; otherwise biases specific to
a method of measurement threaten inferences based on those measurements. More than one trait should be measured, because the
validity of a research operation is determined by traits clustering (cor-
relating) or remaining independent as hypothesized. Whereas Cronbach and Meehl locate constructs in a theoretical framework, Campbell and Fiske are more concerned with adequately measuring
constructs. These are not independent issues, even though one can
think of Campbell and Fiske as anchoring theoretical constructs with
measurement and observation—a vertical move, if you will, in terms
of abstractness/concreteness—and Cronbach and Meehl as stipulating
meanings by relationships among theoretical constructs—a horizontal
move (see Kaplan, 1964, p. 57ff). The meaning of a construct, as
developed by this line of argument, is determined by its location in a
structural matrix of vertical and horizontal connections.

In 1971 Cronbach expanded his characterization of validity in
Thorndike's *Educational Measurement*. "For some writers, *to validate*
means to demonstrate the worth of, but I intend to stress the openness of the process—i.e., *to validate* is *to investigate*" (p. 443). Constructs are used, he notes, whenever one classifies situations, persons, or responses (p. 462). And construct validity is the issue
whenever someone asks, "What does the instrument really measure?" The discussion is important, thoughtful, and in the tradition of
his earlier work with Meehl; validity is concerned with making sense
of a situation.

Cronbach also puts more distance between himself and logical
positivism by confronting ultra-operationalist criticism of construct

validity.[5] Operationalists claim that "a construct has scientific status only when it is equated with one particular measuring operation" (Cronbach, 1971, p. 480). Operationalists assert with a vengeance that validity is identity, which is, by the way, a perspective shared with educators who push for learning objectives defined in terms of behaviors. Behavioral objectives, Cronbach points out, deny the usefulness of constructs. He rejects this, rightly so in my opinion.

> The fact that construct validity can always accept negative evidence by reshaping the network is both its strength and its weakness. One can dispose of an anomaly by adding a conditional clause or an auxiliary construct. . . . To be sure, one can encumber the network to the point of unmanageability as the Ptolemaic astronomers did with epicycles and equants, but the cure is to invent a cleaner network not to banish constructs. (Cronbach, 1971, p. 483)

This intelligently moves construct validity away from logical positivism and ultra-operationalism. More broadly, rhetoric has ascended past logic in construct validation; that is, rhetoric in the sense of making persuasive arguments. There is also a pejorative use of rhetoric that attempts to be persuasive by using evidence selectively and appealing explicitly to biases and stereotypes. The shift toward rhetoric attempts to give convincing accounts of measurements and observations. But the discourse is limited to experts and implicitly promises solutions.

In 1974 Samuel Messick delivered a presidential address to Division 5 of the American Psychological Association on "The Standard Problem: Meaning and Values in Measurement and Evaluation." He showed that what measurements mean depends upon their validity and that construct validity is the *central* validity issue. Meaning, validity, and construct validity are interdependent. Puzzled by the low esteem in which construct validity is held by educational researchers, he speculates that it

> might be a product of the zeitgeist, for instance, a residual of the same ideological forces that nurtured behavioral modification in clinical psychology, behavioral objectives in pedagogy, performance-based criteria in teacher education, input-output assessment in program evaluation, and accountability in educational administration, namely a product- and outcome-oriented ideology, possibly a legacy of behaviorism and operationism, that views desired behaviors as ends in themselves with little concern for the processes that produce them or for the causes of undesired behaviors to be rectified. (1975, p. 959)

This might not be far off the mark (it seems plausible to me), but Messick offers a different explanation for the marginality of construct validity: educational tests are presumed valid on the basis of content validity. He quotes Cronbach on content validity:

> Content validity has to do with the test as a set of stimuli and as a set of observing conditions. The measuring procedure is specified in terms of a class of stimuli, an injunction to the subject that defines his task (i.e., what he is to try to do with the stimuli), and a set of rules for observing the performance and reducing it to a score. (Cronbach, 1971, p. 452)

Responses to stimuli are sampled, and application of a measurement rule, following classical measurement theory, transforms them into scores.[6] This raises several questions: (1) What purposes identify responses to be sampled? (2) What principles does the researcher use in defining the task? (3) Where do measurement rules that reduce observations to scores originate? (4) What interests are reflected in these measurement rules? (5) What alternative measurement rules are excluded? Answers to these questions reduce content validity to construct validity. Construct validity precedes content validity because one cannot be confident that the correct response universe has been sampled to suit one's purposes, whatever they may be, before one knows, at least in a general way, what construct(s) the stimuli represent. Furthermore, Messick continues, which measurements are used is a matter of purpose and value: "Even the very decision of whether or not to use a test for a particular purpose is aided by appeal to construct validity . . . because many of the possible ramifications of test use are inferable from the test's meaning" (1975, p. 962). In Messick's judgment construct validity is not just the "whole of validity from a scientific point of view" (with which I agree), but "even for purposes of applied decision making reliance upon criterion validity or content coverage is not enough, the meaning of the measure must also be pondered" (1975, p. 956).

The standard guide to quasi-experimental research design for many years was Donald Campbell and Julian Stanley's *Experimental and Quasi-Experimental Designs for Research* (1963), and their two major categories of validity were internal and external. Updated by Thomas Cook and Campbell (1979), internal validity expanded into internal and statistical conclusion validity, and external validity, into construct and external validity. If there is an anchor to this approach to validity in quasi-experimental design, in the manner of Messick's argument above, it is construct validity.

Statistical conclusion validity addresses the question: "Is the study sensitive enough to permit reasonable statements about co-variation?" (Cook & Campbell, 1979, p. 39). This concerns statistical power, sensitivity of measures, reliability of measures, reliability of treatments, homogeneity of respondents, and so forth. Prior to these issues, however, assumptions must be made about construct validity, such as: (1) the measurements tap the intended effect of the treatment; (2) the measurements record variation in the constructs of interest.

Internal validity is concerned with the following:

> Once it has been established that two variables covary, the problem is to decide whether there is any causal relationship between the two and, if there is, to decide whether the direction of causality is from the measured or manipulated A to the measured B or vice versa. (Cook & Campbell, 1979, p. 50)

Construct validity takes precedence over internal validity as it did over statistical conclusion validity for many of the same reasons. At its simplest, the problem is whether treatments representing a construct(s) produce observed effects or are effects caused by other factors or processes representing another construct(s). If these constructs become confused, research inferences will be in error.

External validity has to do with "(1) generalizing to particular target persons, settings, and times, and (2) generalizing across types of person, settings, and times" (Cook & Campbell, 1979, p. 71). Construct validity takes precedence over external validity because before one generalizes research findings to other persons, settings, or times, one must decide which constructs are involved in order to predict settings to which they are generalizable. Simply put, constructs must be explicated and elaborated in order to know which external generalizations are reasonable, warranted, or plausible.

Construct validity is central to what research findings mean, or, put a bit differently, the meaning of research findings depends upon settling, however provisionally, how theoretical constructs and measurements are linked. Construct-validity issues can be consciously settled by invoking principles of research methodology including reflection, interpretation, and criticism or be decided by default. Regardless of the manner by which construct validation is settled, it precedes, chronologically and epistemologically, other validity issues, inferences, and interpretations of research findings. If researcher-theorists default on construct validity, then inherited discourses of practice and theory assign meanings to constructs and measurements, and social reproduction will invisibly and effectively continue without conscious interruption.

It is useful to think of construct-validity discourse as a network of statements and activities paralleling Quine's (1953) view of scientific knowledge as a network of statements in which we are less likely to revise statements near the center than those near the edge (which are tested against experience). Meanings attributed to hypotheses and research findings are influenced and constrained by underlying assumptions about meanings assigned to constructs and measurements. Statements and practices of social research and what we take them to mean are subject to continual revision. The ongoing revision of what we think we know exposes the idea of positive knowledge, a goal of logical positivism, to be a seductive but elusive will-o'-the-wisp.

Construct-validity and research discourses are shaped, as are other discourses, by beliefs and commitments, explicit ideologies, tacit worldviews, linguistic and cultural systems, politics and economics, and power arrangements. Cronbach and Meehl anticipated such complexity but chose, for the most part, not to explore it. Construct validity as anchor to what social research undertakes and attempts to establish has generally been developed in the context of systematic quantitative research, for example, in terms of convergent and discriminant correlations (Campbell & Fiske, 1959) and principles of quasi-experimental design (Cook & Campbell, 1979).

Discourses about constructs and research are governed by explicit as well as tacit rules and are policed by those in a position to give and withhold indulgences. Rules of research discourses vary over time (educational "truths" of the nineteenth century are different from those of the twentieth), space (educational research in Western Europe is different in many ways from that in North America), profession (sociologists often arrive at inferences about schooling and education at odds with those of educators), and even within a profession (some teacher-effectiveness researchers produce "truths" that some ethnographers think specious and vice versa). What can and cannot be said is policed by relevant funding agencies, journal editors, senior faculty, and deans and department chairpersons. Different discourses produce different "truths."

There are other research traditions. There are other ways to analyze discourses. The flow and control of mainstream construct-validity discourse conceptualizes researchers as subjects, individuals as objects of research. Researcher-theorists regularly impose categories, constructs, statements, modes of argumentation, models, metaphors, literary allusions, descriptions, explanations, and theories on those they study. Research discourses-practices so constituted and reconstituted are designed to generate authoritative knowledge. Yet several questions can be asked of these discourses or any other, some of which have been raised in earlier chapters.

1. Who is authorized to speak?
2. Who listens?
3. What can be said?
4. What remains unspoken?
5. How does one become authorized to speak?
6. What utterances are rewarded?
7. What utterances are penalized?
8. Which categories, metaphors, modes of description, explanation, and argument are valued and praised; which are excluded and silenced?
9. What social and political arrangements reward and deprive statements?
10. Which metaphors, modes of argumentation, explanation, and description are valued?
11. Which ideas are advanced as foundational to the discourse?

If construct validity were reviewed to the present, some of these questions would surface. Cronbach (1986, 1987), for example, moves the argument toward contextualism (1986). Again, he rejects operationalism by emphasizing that measures are open to plural interpretations and that their interpretation is a project for a community instead of an individual (1987). The arguments in the following sections simultaneously pursue themes Cronbach has pressed, while breaking with them. They are a continuation and rejection of some of these ideas. Continuing and pursuing these arguments, in many cases, leads to their self-rejection.

From its inception, construct validity has been presented as discursive and rhetorical as well as empirical and logical. Construct-validity discourse and rhetoric, however, can take many forms other than those suggested by quantitative measurement, "principles" of experimental and quasi-experimental design, and statistical analysis and inference. Issues of construct validity are not confined within the province of quantitative researchers working in positivist-empiricist traditions. With this as foreground, phenomenological, critical-theoretical, interpretive-analytic, and deconstructive implications for construct validity will now be reviewed.

PHENOMENOLOGY AND INTERPRETATIVE RESEARCH

Mainstream conceptions of construct validity are set in the context of psychological and educational testing, wherein researchers are subjects and respondents are objects. An alternative conception of construct validity, even though this term is not used, is found in the qualitative traditions of phenomenology and interpretative research (Schutz, 1963a,b; Ihde, 1979; Lincoln & Guba, 1985).[7] Whereas logical-empiricist construct validity authorizes experts to nominate theoretical constructs and hypotheses, phenomenologists look to the "object" of the study for descriptive first-order constructs. What were formerly "objects"—for example, students, teachers, or educational administrators—are now subjects. Phenomenological concern attends to how subjects make sense of the world. How do students, teachers, and so forth interpret social practices in which they find themselves?

Phenomenologists adopting an attitude of *epoché*—wherein past beliefs, opinions, attitudes, experiences, ideologies, traumas, and frames of reference are bracketed, exorcised, and left behind—propose that the discourse of research emanate from subjects. Researchers are proscribed from imposing categories of observation on "objects" of study because "objects" are now subjects and are asked, watched, and recorded as they reveal their sense and understanding of the world. Subjects expose first-order constructs by which they organize and make sense of their daily lives. From first-order constructs researchers develop second-order scientific and explanatory constructs that account for first-order constructs.

A 1982 article by Jeffrey Shultz, Susan Florio, and Frederick Erickson demonstrates elements of construct validity from an ethnographic perspective as well as differences between ethnographic and mainstream research. They are concerned with discrepancy in communication exchanges between home and school and subsequent problems such differences create for students and teachers. Their construct of interest is "floor." Floor refers to "right of access by an individual to a turn at speaking that is attended to by other individuals, who occupy at that moment the role of listener" (p. 95). Students experiencing conflicting expectations between home and school about right of access in speaking could encounter, they point out, recurring interactional troubles at school. They begin with communicative competence, that is, "whatever the individual's practical knowledge . . . about how, when, and where to communicate, for what purposes" (p. 89). Because a communicative competence "package" can vary from one setting to another young children can experience conflicting "packages" at home and at school. the construct-validity issue concerns the meaning of the theoretical construct "floor" and appropriate ways to measure it.

They begin "looking for similarities and differences across the different kinds of contexts for interaction; or what Wittgenstein calls 'games'" (p. 93). Initially they consider and quickly discard comparing and contrasting situations—for example, resemblances between dinner at home and snack time at school—a strategy often followed in mainstream research to produce coding schemes and categories. There are superficial resemblances between dinner at home and snack time at school but little interactional resemblance between them. This identifies a crucial distinction between mainstream and phenomenological research that their quote from Wittgenstein highlights: "don't think, but look!" (p. 93). In order to look instead of think they shift to "contrasting patterns of behavior that could be loosely construed as aspects of *style or strategy*" (p. 94). The theoretical construct of *one* floor is abandoned when they *look* for interactional styles rather than *think* about interactions. Looking at videotapes of home dinner conversations reveals multiple conversational floors. This transforms the research question from what the conversational floor is to how many kinds of conversational floors there are and where they are. Working from videotapes and field notes, they observe four interactional patterns, with floor varying among them. Implications for teachers include the following:

> The differences in interactional etiquette obtaining between home and school create a situation in which quality schooling seems to be related directly to the school's recognition that it is not the sole educative force in a child's life. Acknowledgment of the existence and legitimacy of different learned systems of interactional etiquette entails acceptance of the existence and legitimacy of the nonschool cultures in which some of those systems are learned. Such recognition also amounts to a willingness for educators to think in terms of differing "kinds of competence," which change systematically from situation to situation, rather than thinking of "incompetence" or "deficiency." (p. 118)

A discourse about construct validity with emphasis on *looking* shifts locus of control and power from researchers to subjects.

Implications of this reallocation of power are sometimes subtle,

sometimes quite potent. Subjects do not tell researchers what to look
for or tell them what to research. They do not tell researchers what to
look at first or how to sequence their observations. They do not tell
them what words to use or constructs to deploy. Subjects gain power
because they are valued for themselves, when what they say and do is
accorded status, when their voice is acknowledged, and when they
are granted the "floor(s)."

Broadly put, ethnographic research grants power to introduce
constructs (first-order) to subjects who formerly were silent as objects.
It is not that they were not previously asked to respond, nor that their
responses were not recorded. Their responses, however, were to questions posed by others who had problems of their own to solve. Such
problems and questions may or may not capture the way subjects
make sense of and understand "their" world. Subjects' sense-making
provides the basis for theoretical constructs. Phenomenological and
interpretative research does not vacate the power of researchers; instead research authority *derives* from subjects and blurs distinctions
between subjects and objects. Construct validity remains concerned
with linkages among words and things, but the power to enunciate,
select categories, make arguments, choose metaphors, and propose
explanations shifts a bit from researchers to subjects, from the research literature to understandings of people in the world, from academic specialties (such as measurement and statistical analysis) to
tacit understandings. Phenomenologically based research produces
"truths" different from quantitative, statistically sophisticated research. The locus of power that makes "truth" possible shifts from
researchers as subjects to respondents as subjects.

One criticism sometimes directed against ethnographic research
has to do with external validity. If one samples only a few classrooms,
interactions, students, or teachers, how can one generalize with any
confidence to other settings, places, and times? The answer, of
course, is that one cannot generalize with confidence to nonsampled
settings, places, and times. This holds, by the way, for mainstream as
well as interpretative research. Coming back at mainstream researchers, ethnographers have an obvious retort. How can one generalize
with confidence to nonsampled settings, places, and times regardless
of sample size without satisfactorily solving problems of construct
validity? Mainstream researchers also face external validity problems,
although for different reasons.

Construct validity in phenomenological, and interpretative research remains discursive. The discourse is different from mainstream
conceptions and practices. Subjects of research as well as researchers

as subjects are central to the discourse, modes of argument looser, the range of metaphor wider, and the continuing social construction of our institutions and interactions explicitly acknowledged. The possibility of suggesting precise logical guidelines for what counts as understanding and explanation is rejected. Construct validation moves closer to life as experienced and lived, because secondary constructs of social researchers-theorists are explicitly derivative from and thereby validated by first-order constructs of everyday life.

CRITICAL THEORY AND RESEARCH

The mainstream approach to construct validity assumes that the positive body of knowledge (theory and research findings) brought to research is pivotal in revealing what is going on in a way undistorted by ideology and power. The phenomenological approach to construct validity assumes that subjects participating in social practices know and understand firsthand what is going on. There is a possibility that both assumptions are mistaken. This possibility underlies critical theory and research.

Human interests, histories, myths, ideologies, values, and commitments shape what researcher-theorists claim to know as well as everyday understandings. Social scientific constructs and those of everyday life are products of these and other influences. Effects of power on research activities and subjective understandings reduce some constructs to silence while enhancing others. Voices and silences of research discourse, whether originating with researchers or subjects/objects, can distort, bias, and oppress those who speak as well as those who listen.

Habermas's ideas about critical discourse, communicative competence, comprehensive rationality, and consensus theory of truth provide insights into construct validity.[8] Construct validation in critical discourse attempts to create conditions whereby biases and misperceptions of researchers and subjects/objects can be addressed and examined, if not overcome. Critical discourse sets out to determine the truth of an utterance when there is "the possibility of argumentative corroboration of a truth claim which is falsifiable in principle" (Habermas, 1973, p. 166). We can aspire to consensus, he contends, about what is the case in everyday life, such as schools and classrooms, or in social scientific explanations. The process by which consensus is realized can be designed to guard against distortions engendered by power, interest, ideology, commitments, and values.

Mainstream discussions of construct validity and interpretative research, to the contrary, are silent on many of these issues. Critical research assumes that beliefs of any (all?) individual(s) [researcher(s) or subject(s)] may be in error. We may always be doing something other than what we think we are.

Construct validity from a critical perspective moves from accepted to rational consensus about the meaning of research operations and the constructs they measure. All parties may initiate comments, challenge assertions, and question not only theoretical formulations but also metatheoretical and metaethical frameworks. Critical discourse pursues only the "best" argument and may not be limited. Strategic behavior, wherein search for truth turns into conflict, competition, or debate, is not permitted. Consensual agreement, not winning or losing, is desired. These are necessary conditions for emancipation from past constructs and understandings, past commitments, and past practices. Critical research avoids an adversarial approach to promoting and defending constructs and measurements. Interpretations and arguments of researchers *and* subjects may be questioned. Subjects may interrogate research interpretations, and researchers may interrogate subjective understandings. But the drama extends beyond the researchers and subjects immediately involved. Anyone may speak. For example, individuals only marginally interested in the research, constructs, and their application could prove most insightful. Critical construct validation is radically open and never settled.

Although critical theorists stress linkages between theory and practice, critical-theoretical writing, for the most part, remains abstract and philosophical (Geuss, 1981; Habermas, 1984), examples of critical research in education, such as Apple (1987), Anyon (1979), Bowles (1977), Popkewitz (1982), and Taxel (1980), notwithstanding. Frank Fischer (1985) advances the project of critical research by outlining and applying elements of critical theory to evaluations of Project Head Start. His argument and its implications illustrate many of Habermas's ideas. Building upon Habermas's conception of communicative competence, Stephen Toulmin's (1958) work on substantial arguments, and Paul Taylor's (1961) thinking on informal logic, Fischer outlines four phases of critical evaluation.

First, *research findings* that technically justify the program. These involve concerns of mainstream systematic, quantitative research or, in Habermasian terms, empirical-analytic questions. They question whether (1) the program fulfills its stated objectives; (2) there are secondary effects that work against program objectives; and (3) more efficient alternatives are available (Fischer, 1985, pp. 242–43). These questions, to use Cook and Campbell's terminology, deal with statistical conclusion and internal validity: "Was the control group adequate? Was sufficient attention paid to program variations? Was the sample random?" (Fischer, 1985, p. 243), as well as issues of benefit-cost and cost-effectiveness analysis. These are standard quasi-experimental design issues, and Head Start did not fare well when reviewed in these terms.

Second, *situational validation* of policy goals. Questions at this level deal with first-order normative issues. They include whether (1) the objective, standard, or rule is relevant; (2) such proposed rules are based in previous research; (3) other aspects of the context make this case an exception; and (4) goals that conflict are relevant (Fischer, 1985, p. 244). These questions touch upon phenomenological issues of subjective understanding and evaluation, and whether the understandings of researchers, subjects, and social groupings agree or even approach agreement. Criticisms of Head Start evaluations that reflected these issues probed the social relevance of focusing heavily upon reading scores as the most important outcome at the expense of "personal health, self-discipline, and socially responsible attitudes toward the community" (p. 245).

Third, *vindication of program values* at the societal level. This phase connects specific policy goals and outcomes to the larger society. This is what I call vulgar pragmatism, (sometimes called functionalism), which is discussed in Chapter 8. Questions involved include: (1) do program outcomes contribute to the efficiency of dominant social practices and institutions, and (2) are program outcomes politically acceptable (Fischer, 1985, p. 246)? Analysis at this level remains fundamentally instrumental, and dominant social values are accepted as valid. It could be argued here, for example, that Head Start programs should socialize children to dominant middle-class values. Of course, to the contrary, it can effectively be argued that middle-class values are not tightly organized into a coherent package. Also, there may be alternatives. Such counterarguments are addressed in the next phase.

Fourth, *rational social choice*. This phase of critical research questions the criteria and standards that previously had been accepted without question. They include: (1) are the outcomes equitable and just; (2) do they promote the advantage of all; and, if not, (3) is it possible to alter social practices and institutions to further the advantage of all (Fischer, 1985, p. 249)? By this point social criticism and political thought are legitimate contributors to construct validity and program evaluation. Alternative models of desirable social life are available, and we choose among them when constructs are validated and programs evaluated. Freedom, impartiality, and enlightenment precede rational social choice. John Rawls (1971) also argues this point. Critical research presupposes communicative competence among research-theorists and subjects and anticipates the ideal speech situation. Debate about constructs and programs will be rational in a comprehensive and critical, not simply instrumental, sense if these communication conditions are satisfied. Those who argue that Head Start outcomes are and should be ideologically justifiable contribute at this level.

Fischer's first phase is mainstream research as taught and practiced. The second phase reflects phenomenological and interpretative concerns. Phase three situates the first two in societywide context, and phase four introduces fundamental criticism of society *and* research. What reading scores mean and which theoretical constructs they tap, which were the most important of the initial dependent variables in Head Start evaluations, undergo radical change and reinterpretation as one moves from technical verification to rational social choice. A critical approach to construct validity quite different from phenomenological construct validity underscores the point that any observation or measurement taps numerous theoretical constructs (pick an approach, an interpretation, a criticism—"pick a card," but not just any card).

A critical approach to construct validity points out that in order to understand which theoretical constructs a reading score indicates, one must take one's eye off the score itself and look around it. Understandings of neither researchers (mainstream) nor subjects (phenomenology) locate measurements and meanings in terms of the larger society or possible alternative societies. Grounding and centering *the* meaning of constructs and measurements is illusory. This should come as no surprise, because boundaries limiting construct-validity discourse have yet to be justified. They are policed nonetheless. Mainstream and phenomenological discourse and constructs are normed and enforced, albeit differently. But when distinctions between research technique, methodological design, and social theory deconstruct, meanings of measurements and constructs are dispersed and deferred. The meaning of a reading score is not a straightforward technical matter to be settled at the level of technical verification. Reading scores can also be interpreted at levels, to use Fischer's categories, of situational validation, systems vindication, and rational social choice. Another way of putting this is to note that Cronbach's point that "to validate is to investigate" is far more open than it may have initially appeared.

Whereas critical theory locates research meanings and operations in contexts of social theory, society, and possible alternatives, the interpretive analytics of Foucault illuminates the force of history and power on what we say and do and how we are led to link words to things and theory to practice.

INTERPRETIVE ANALYTICS

Constructs and the discourses and practices within which they occur are objects of history. Researchers inherit discourses (only by becoming expert and certified does one become a researcher), and subjects inherit discourses (only by becoming socialized into preexisting discourses of everyday life does one become a member of a society, culture, or linguistic community). There is little choice about which discourses and practices we inherit; it is much like the choice we have in inheriting parents. One implication Foucault draws from this is that:

> we should try to discover how it is that subjects are gradually, progressively, really and materially constituted through a multiplicity of organisms, forces, energies, materials, desires, thoughts, etc. We should try to grasp subjection in its material instance as a constitution of subjects. (1980a, p. 97)

Two readings can be given to his use of *subject* and *subjection*. *Subject* refers to the way we think about ourselves and act, *and* it refers to discourses and practices that preexist us to which we are accountable. Put differently, we are subjects in *and* subject to discourses and practices. Our subjectivity, then, is a product of discourses and practices to which we are subject. This holds for researchers as well as for students, teachers, and administrators. Interpretive analytics emphasizes history and power in the production of the present and asks why researchers and those they study use the words, utterances, metaphors, analogies, and models they do when they make statements, arguments, and inferences.

Constructs and their validation are effects of power where *power* refers to asymmetries by which some people are indulged and rewarded and others are deprived and penalized. Effects of power produce subjectivities, constructs, discourses, and practices. Asymmetries of power and patterns of behavior with which they are associated reinforce ways of speaking among researcher-theorists. Foucault uses power in a productive sense as well as in a negative, coercive, and restrictive way. This is his general argument: power is often thought to operate as "censorship, exclusion, blockage and repression, in the manner of a great Superego, exercising itself only in a negative way," but, he continues, "if . . . power is strong this is because, as we are beginning to realise, it produces effects at the level of desire—and also at the level of knowledge. Far from preventing knowledge, power produces it" (1980a, p. 59). Researcher-theorists who *desire* to be productive, write proposals, secure grants, and contribute to the research literature attend to research norms, including those pertaining to constructs and measurements. When one desires to be a productive researcher-theorist, one produces knowledge that norms recognize as legitimate. Effects of power produce speech about construct validity as well as its silences. This is research as social reproduction.

Constructs, measurements, discourses, and practices are objects of history. From this perspective construct validity is situated in a power-knowledge nexus over which speakers have limited control. Taking the argument to its extreme, Foucault asserts that we know neither the origins nor the authors of our discourses (see Foucault, 1980b, pp. 113–38). Nor are the rules all known by which our constructs and metaphors can be deployed. Construct validity is thoroughly discursive, with the discourse a product of history and an effect of power and its consequences.

The argument can be stated more analytically. If statements and not things are true or false, then truth is necessarily linguistic; if truth is linguistic, then it is relative to language use (words, concepts, statements, discourses) at a given time and place; therefore ideology, interests, and power arrangements at a given time and place are implicated in the production of what counts as "true." "Truths" of a time and place are politically produced, and constructs and their measurement are tools of production.

Foucault pushes in the same direction as Habermas but offers little hope of expunging the effects of power on construct validation.

> My point is not that everything [constructs, categories, taxonomies, priorities, hierarchies, measurements, practices, discourses] is bad, but that everything is dangerous, which is not exactly the same as bad. If everything is dangerous, then we always have something to do. So my position leads not to apathy but to a hyper- and pessimistic activism. I

think that the ethico-political choice we have to make every day is to
determine which is the main danger. (Foucault, 1983, pp. 231–32)

Constructs, no matter whether they are first- or second-order, are
dangerous. Construct validity involves decisions about which constructs are dangerous and what dangers they pose.[9]

Foucault's argument leaves mainstream construct-validity operations, such as getting language use and methodological operations
straight and Fischer's technical verification phase, far behind. Our
constructs and their measurement are relative to time and place.
There is no final arbiter on correct language use or on matching constructs to measurements, because, as Foucault might put it, words do
violence to things. The failure to find a definitive arbiter or criterion is
known to philosophers as the failure to find a metanarrative, where a
metanarrative is a global, overarching, encompassing set of rules that
tell us, in the case of construct validity, the necessary and sufficient
conditions for the constructs and measurements we use and how to
use them. An antifoundational research methodology, suggested by
Foucault's analysis, points to political processes and institutions by
which truth is produced and instructs us to be prepared every day to
make ethico-political choices, about which constructs constitute the
main danger.

Mainstream approaches to construct validity, one might argue,
are technical choices based on expertise, rationality, and authoritative
knowledge—behind all of which lurk ethico-political choices. Implications of Foucault's interpretive analytics for construct validity locate
constructs historically and politically and attempt to validate ethico-
political choices by asking questions such as: Which ethico-political
choices are hidden? How are they hidden? How they can be illuminated? Decisions about construct validity cannot be disentangled from
ethico-political decisions. This does not argue against using devices
such as Campbell and Fiske's (1959) multitrait-multimethod matrix
but suggests that in many cases such techniques obfuscate, confuse,
and mislead more than they clarify and validate.

It is rare to find in the research literature theoretical constructs,
how they are measured, or the discourses within which we find them
treated as objects of history or as products of politics. Our legacy of
positivism continues to reinforce *a*contextual and *a*historical scientific
narratives of construct validation, hypothesis testing, and program
evaluation. Yet occasional histories of applied social research and
methodology illustrate some elements of Foucault's argument relative
to construct validity. One such history is Cohen and Garet's (1975)

revealing study, "Reforming Educational Policy with Applied Social Research." They succinctly state several hypotheses about applied social research and the rationalization of social policy and then review research on Head Start and compensatory education. Their hypotheses follow:

> One assumption is that policies consist of discrete decisions: Social research is expected to affect policy by influencing discrete choices among competing programs and methods. A second assumption is that applied research is more authoritative than ordinary common-sense ideas about social policy: Advances in the methodology of applied research are believed to bring corresponding advances in the authority and relevance of the knowledge available for decision making. Finally, on the basis of these assumptions, it often is argued that applied social research is justified because it provides the state with authoritative and objective evidence concerning costs and consequences of social policies: Research is expected to improve the effectiveness of social services. . . . *The main justification for applied research, however, rests on a belief that research will rationalize social policy.* (p. 20; emphasis added)

After surveying some ten years of research on compensatory educational programs, they conclude:

> 1. Most policy-oriented research, at least in education, tends to influence the broad assumptions and beliefs underlying policy, not particular decisions.
> 2. Better methodology and policy relevance in applied research in education have not produced more convergent findings. This is in part because most policy-oriented research concerns programs with broad and conflicting aims, but it is also attributable to methodological conflict among research approaches and to the fact that the advance of applied research tends to complicate and redefine issues. As a result, *improving applied research does not tend to produce more authoritative advice about social policy.*
> 3. The justification for applied social research carried out for the state cannot rest on the idea of instrumental rationality, because *applied research, at least in education, has not significantly increased the objective information base for decisions.* (pp. 39–40; emphasis added)

There was no support for rhetorical claims that discrete research findings enter into specific policy decisions.

Researchers and policymakers make rational choices and calculate strategies and actions while at every moment they are objects of history. Construct validity and evaluation discourses that constituted

Head Start evaluations were also historical objects shaped by the political environment (the Johnson administration's War on Poverty), contending ideologies, their histories, research traditions, and resources available to the participants. Together they produced desire and knowledge. Desire ranged from wanting to help disadvantaged children in a variety of ways to wanting to generate authoritative findings about teaching children to read. Conditions of poverty existed that some wished to ameliorate. This is inherited and is something to react against. Our constructs and discourses are inherited social constructions. Often, however, constructs and discourses of professional and everyday life are accepted with little analysis or criticism. For example, reading scores as an important outcome measure resulted from a conjunction of the War on Poverty (with its explicit need to demonstrate effectiveness of compensatory education programs) with discourses of social scientific research as a technology inherited from educational psychology and measurement. Cohen and Garet document Foucault's argument; in this case discourses of applied research had no single author, nor were they controlled by educational researchers.

The philosophical counterpart to the second part of their second conclusion (above) that social scientific research does not produce convergent findings is consistent with the Quine–Duhem thesis that Quine puts like this:

> It is misleading to speak of the empirical content of an individual statement . . . Any statement can be held true come what may, if we make drastic enough adjustments elsewhere in the system. . . . Conversely, by the same token, no statement is immune to revision. (Quine, 1953, p. 43)

Following up on Quine, construct validity is not found in an individual statement but in discourses and sets of statements. One implication of the Quine–Duhem thesis for construct validity is that construct and measurement meaning is equivocal. Cohen and Garet support this: "applied research in education . . . [has] not produced more convergent findings." Quine's apt metaphor is that "total science is like a field of force whose boundary conditions are experience. A conflict with experience at the periphery occasions readjustments in the interior of the field" (1953, p. 42). Individual evaluations of Head Start were definitive neither in estimating the worth of the program nor in influencing policy decisions, even though, taken together, they may have contributed to slowly changing attitudes toward compensatory education. Construct validity, as Cohen and Garet illustrate but fail to elaborate, cannot be separated from a history of the present.

Construct validity does not entail identity between constructs and measurements, and it extends beyond technical methodological considerations. Subjects as well as researchers have something to say. What subjects and researchers say (write) is located in an inherited context of time and place enforced by power relationships. What is said and written can be criticized. There are alternative interpretations and stories to tell. Construct validity, it turns out, cannot be disentangled from history, society, linguistic communities, and power any more than it can be separated from systematic research methodology.

There is yet another approach to discourse that produces different insights into construct-validity issues. If identity between constructs and measurements is not possible, is the meaning of constructs and measurements destined (condemned?) to dispersal and deferral? Deconstruction answers *yes*.

DECONSTRUCTION

Constructs draw boundaries between what is in and what is out, what is acceptable and what is not. In this way they operate ideologically. But claims about correctly inferring the meaning of measurements are substantially qualified by phenomenological, critical-theoretical, and interpretive-analytic criticism. Deconstructive criticism—deriving from the work of Derrida, among others—makes an analytic point about language and meaning that adds more qualifications. Whereas logically valid arguments begin with primitive (undefined) terms and premises that ground the remainder of the argument, Derrida argues that any such grounding and foundation are temporal at best and always fictional. For example, ideas such as educational excellence, structure of the disciplines, time on task, educational achievement, and equal educational opportunity are always based on prior ideas. Furthermore, meanings of constructs are *dispersed* in traces throughout language and texts in which they are found and *deferred* in time.

Somewhat surprisingly, a close reading of mainstream accounts of construct validity reveals these ideas not to be new, only ignored. For example: (1) More than "bridge principles" from logical positivism, Cronbach and Meehl emphasize discursive aspects of construct validity that link theory and observation. (2) Campbell and Fiske do not discuss meaning as identity because construct validity can be a correlational exercise. (3) Cook and Campbell explicitly acknowledge that meanings of constructs are theoretically dispersed. If construct validation as discourse had been directly confronted, deconstructive criticism would not presently be marginal to issues of construct validity.

Deconstructive analysis asserts that there is no firm, fixed, immutable grounding of constructs in observations. Mainstream accounts of construct validity acknowledge this as well. Deconstructive analysis argues that meanings are dispersed theoretically and observationally and deferred for later explication and clarification. Mainstream accounts agree. Deconstructive analysis assumes that there are always differences, such as in meanings, populations, treatments, and interaction effects. Again, mainstream accounts concur. Construct validity is a discursive process always in motion. Meaning is not based on identity between observation and construct or on immediate presence of observations. Deconstruction and mainstream views of construct validity agree: there is no immediate presence—unmediated perception of the world—that decides what measurements and observations mean once and for all.

Deconstruction has roots in the work of Nietzsche, and Allan Megill's discussion of Nietzsche on concepts (constructs) is illuminating.

> The world, in Nietzsche's view, is made up of absolutely individualized fragments: no thing, no occurrence, is exactly the same as any other thing or occurrence. Take, for example, a leaf. Every leaf differs, however slightly, from every other leaf. It follows that the concept *leaf* can only be formed through omission of these differences—an omission that Nietzsche holds to be entirely arbitrary. Thus, the concept *leaf* is a falsification of the reality of leaves. (1985, p. 49)

Constructs and concepts—this is where Cronbach and Nietzsche converge—are the way we view the world, and constructs cannot correspond to things because they are different from things. Constructs falsify things. The promise of validity as certainty, rigor, and positive knowledge is false and dangerous when paraded clothed in technical expertise.

Academic Learning Time (ALT) exemplifies the indeterminate nature of theoretical constructs. It was central to the Beginning Teacher Evaluation Study (BTES) (Denham & Lieberman, 1980):

> Time spent by a student engaged on a task that s/he can perform with high success and that is directly relevant to an academic outcome constitutes a measure of student classroom learning. We refer to time spent

under these conditions as Academic Learning Time (ALT). The basic components of ALT are allocated time, student engagement, and student high success (balanced with some medium success). (p. 10)

Student learning is measured by achievement test scores. A distinction crucial to the study is academic learning time/nonacademic learning time, with the former valued over the latter. Is this distinction, as they make it, stable and persuasive?

The dependent variable, after which the ALT model of instruction is named, is academic learning: "Achievement of the target students in each class was measured with a comprehensive achievement battery in reading and mathematics" (p. 13). They found:

> 1. "The amount of time that teachers allocate to instruction in a particular content area is positively associated with student learning in that content area" (p. 15),
> 2. "Reading or mathematics tasks . . . performed with high success is positively associated with student learning" (p. 16),
> 3. "Structuring the lesson and giving directions on task procedures were positively associated with high test scores" (p. 20).
> 4. "Teacher emphasis on academic goals is positively associated with student learning" (p. 21).

Related construct validity questions are: Which construct(s) are tapped by the standardized achievement tests? Do their achievement tests measure academic learning?

Achievement tests certainly measure information. They also measure skills. In Chapter 2 of *Time to Learn*, Borg's Tables 2.2 through 2.6 (1972, pp. 52–71) characterize academic learning in such terms as decoding blends and long vowels, decoding variant consonants, decoding complex patterns (spelling time), adding and subtracting (speeded test), linear measurement, and fractions. These categories represent important areas of achievement for elementary students. But if academic learning in this study bears any resemblance to academic knowledge and activities more generally, at least some of the following are involved: the ability to provide descriptions, generate explanations, make arguments, criticize arguments, tell stories (narratives) that combine different elements (observations, facts, events), reflect on the motives or values of oneself or others, analyze decisions, communicate clearly, state novel ideas (conjectures, hypotheses), and test conjectures against evidence. It is difficult to imagine academic learning without them. The Beginning Teacher Evaluation Study, by exclusion, classifies each of these as nonacademic learning. Their construct of academic learning contradicts itself, because their achievement tests *exclude* much that constitutes academic learning and skills.

This contradiction—that academic learning time deconstructs (the term *deconstruction* is not used, by the way)—is acknowledged in the following passage from Romberg:

> Academic Learning Time as defined is in large part dependent on the test items selected to measure achievement. Task relevance was not determined by curricular appropriateness, but by whether tasks were related to test items. Thus, work on study skills in reading or problem solving in math, for example, would not be coded as relevant, if corresponding items were not on the achievement battery. To the extent that many important curricular outcomes are difficult to measure, this too is a limitation of the model. (1980, p. 81)

BTES rhetoric claims to study academic learning; BTES logic excludes much that is academic learning. Thus, the construct *academic learning* deconstructs. The meaning of academic learning time as it drove the research operations of BTES is solved by appeal to achievement-test content. The meaning of academic learning, however, is deferred for another time.

Deconstruction makes the methodological point that there are foundational places neither to start nor to terminate a search for meanings. Furthermore, categorical distinctions desired by those who yearn for positive knowledge are, because of the nature of language, ambiguous and not so distinct. Categorical distinctions, such as academic learning time/nonacademic learning time, reflect dominant ideologies and power arrangements. This does not mean those critical of this distinction value nonacademic learning time. Instead, academic learning time narrowly circumscribed enhances control and centralization, it works to make the exercise of power more efficient, and it does not provide critical access to dominant ideologies and power arrangements. Deconstruction demonstrates an ever-present instability in meanings of constructs and measurements that structural interpretations obfuscate.

Empirically, multiple interpretations of constructs and measurements—for example, phenomenological, critical-theoretical, or interpretive-analytic—suggest that meanings of constructs are in flux, depending, perhaps, on methodology and one's point of view. Analytically, deconstruction shows that dispersed and deferred meanings of constructs and measurements are a property of language and texts. Lack of certainty, grounding, centering is one aspect of textuality and is not simply a product of politically motivated, extra-scientific criticism.

SUMMARY AND CONCLUSION

Construct validity is discursive. A construct and its measurement are validated when discourse is persuasive. Multiple discourses, ranging from rather standard and well-known approaches to measurement and research design to less widely known approaches of interpretation, criticism of various kinds, and deconstructive analysis, are implicated. A side note: the portrayal of construct validity and research in disputes between predominantly quantitative and qualitative approaches can be overly simple and misleading. Each has valuable contributions to make, but more is required than they separately or jointly offer. Furthermore, neither quantitative and qualitative approaches to construct validity and research nor critical research, interpretive analytics, and deconstruction are mutually exclusive, even though they can be so construed. Each produces a version(s) of things (Shultz, Florio, and Erickson, 1982, identified four explanations for the interactions they investigated). Sometimes these versions are reinforcing, at other times not. At times they build upon each other (phases three and four of Fischer's, 1985, schema for critical research build upon systematic, quantitative research *and* qualitative, interpretative research). Sometimes they are critical of each other (Fischer's rational social choice, Foucault's attention to the political production of truth, and deconstruction produce criticisms of each other as well as of mainstream and interpretative research). Someone might attempt to rank these approaches in terms of their importance for construct validity; there are many reasons not to expect such a ranking to be defensible (see Quine, 1969, for a general argument that subsumes this issue). There are better and worse ways to make arguments about constructs and measurements, but if there is *one* way to proceed that is superior to others the argument has yet to be made.

At the end of a chapter such as this, one occasionally encounters a diagram sketching how parts of the argument fit together. But consider what would be involved in such an illustration. In the center of the figure is the focus of construct(s) and measurement(s), say, a student reading. Because constructs and measurements are different from the reading student and attempt to capture the phenomenon, they are not in the center, they point to it. Off to the side, then, *observation* is circled or boxed. Also off to the side, *theoretical construct* is circled or boxed. The mainstream argument can be indicated by adding arrows that point from *theoretical construct* to *observation* to reading student. Adding interpretation or naturalistic investigation points the arrows from reading student to *observation* to *theoretical construct*. The quantitative and qualitative approaches are combined when the meaning of these bidirectional arrows is clarified and negotiated. A footnote to the diagram would indicate that these arrows connote some kind of "co-variation" or shared meaning, not identity, between constructs and measurements or measurements and phenomena.

Now critical research is added to the sketch. Activities of researchers and subjects occur in the context of ideology and interests. Ideology justifies each of these activities (reading, its measurement, and its interpretation). It is difficult to add ideology to the sketch, because it is everywhere and operates to justify different activities and interpretations that often conflict. If there is a single or simple dominant ideology, it could be added without much difficulty (a pyramid perhaps), but multiple ideologies and moments of dominance present problems. Power pervades what subjects do in addition to construct validity activities. Interpretations are normed and policed. How can this be added? More material than ideological, asymmetries of power relationships are found everywhere, often in shifting patterns. Power and ideology are both at the center and at the margins; they are ubiquitous. Constructs and measurements, it should be added, are *never* at the center. They are interpretative from the outset.

Still more must be added to complete the diagram. History must be represented. Our past creates desires and rewards that produce speech and action. Adding history to the sketch creates an additional problem. How should the contribution of history be diagramed? What captures movement from the past to the present? Does it move from the right to the left (neo-Marxists might prefer this)? Does it move from the left to the right (some conservatives might prefer this, and it is also the direction in which English sentences are read)? Or should it be depicted top to bottom, or vice versa? Effects of history, as with power and ideology, are everywhere.

More complications await us. Deconstruction challenges the linearity, clarity, certainty, and rhetoric of interpretations and criticisms that researcher-theorists, students, and others assign to "reading." Meanings of constructs and measurements are dispersed. Constructs and measurements are never at the center of the figure; they are always interpretations. Now they are interpretations in need of further interpretation. How could a diagram account for a decentered view of construct validation where meanings are not stable? For these and other reasons, a diagram is not included.

Some might object to the political bent and radical openness of these arguments. Issue might be taken with tracing histories of constructs or identifying their ideological connotations or uncovering the politics of research design. In general, these objections would bound discourses of construct validity and research. Boundaries cannot be drawn and enforced, however, without privileging beliefs and interests of one individual or group at the expense of others. Establishing boundaries and limiting discourses is a political act. Furthermore, boundaries exist only if they are enforced, and they are enforced by effects of power. It is imaginable that a mainstream researcher-theorist, to pick only one example, working in a systematic quantitative tradition would advocate limiting construct validity to applications of the multitrait-multimethod matrix and hypothesis testing. Methodological justifications can be offered, to be sure, but the move itself is overtly political because it silences other discourses, voices, and interests. Restricting discourses about constructs and their measurement on "methodological" and "theoretical" grounds betrays the political commitments of those in favor of the restrictions.

What counts as persuasive varies from time to time and place to place. Persuasiveness depends, in part, on the communities we live in and desire as well as on more traditional kinds of evidence and argument. Rorty describes, correctly I believe, what is involved:

> There are two principal ways in which reflective human beings try, by placing their lives in a larger context, to give sense to those lives. The first is by telling the story of their contribution to a community. This community may be the actual historical one in which they live, or another actual one, distant in time or place, or a quite imaginary one, consisting perhaps of a dozen heroes or heroines selected from history or fiction or both. The second way is to describe themselves as standing in immediate relation to a nonhuman reality. This relation is immediate in the sense that it does not derive from a relation between such a reality and their tribe, or their nation, or their imagined band of comrades. . . . Stories of the former kind exemplify the desire for solidarity, and . . . stories of the latter kind exemplify the desire for objectivity. (1985, p. 3)

Some mainstream approaches to construct validity promise stories of the latter kind, stories that desire objectivity. Cronbach and Meehl suspected, without stating it straight out, that objectivity would be elusive. Since 1955 the construct-validity literature has flirted with notions of objectivity but, again, never made the claim. If Rorty is correct that reflective human beings make sense of their lives by telling stories about either solidarity or objectivity and that our stories about objectivity are flawed, they nevertheless describe a community. The community is elitist, control-centralized, and criticism-limited to experts; the social context and historical setting of the community is not discussed; constructs (the way the community is conceptually organized) are chosen on neither ethico-political nor aesthetic grounds, but rather in terms of "scientific" criteria; and discourse is thought of as nonmaterial and descriptive-explanatory.

If Cronbach and Meehl led social research methodology into adolescence, it can be argued that the result has been arrested adolescence. Construct validity in terms of quantitative measurement and correlation was developed while a number of discourses that bear on hypothesized connections and assumptions between words and things went unexamined. One is entitled to ask what a more mature view of construct validity and research methodology might involve, even though maturity in construct-validation, as with other kinds of maturity, might prove evasive. What kind of community-solidarity would be described? In addition to the contributions of Cronbach, Meehl, Campbell, Fiske, Stanley, Messick, and Cook, the following hypotheses are involved (these are proposed as necessary but not sufficient conditions):

1. Construct validity and research are discursive (already part of the literature).
2. Discourses of research are linguistically, politically, economically, socially, culturally, and professionally relative.
3. Research discourses are material practices.
4. Meanings and truths situated in and promoted by quantitative, qualitative, critical, interpretive, and deconstructive studies are political products.
5. Tacit knowledge of subjects and social scientific knowledge of researchers are resources for discourse on construct validation.
6. Contributions of subjects and researchers should be subjected to radical criticism that traces meanings of what is said through language, texts, and social practices.
7. Construct validity decisions are ethico-political and aesthetic as well as social scientific.
8. Meanings of constructs, first- and second-order, are dispersed and deferred.

9. Validation includes studying why particular constructs, terms, metaphors, models, and explanations are privileged.
10. Validation includes studying social and material effects of constructs and their measurement.

Construct validity is identified neither by an object, because meanings of theoretical terms are dispersed throughout language, nor by a method, because correlational analysis, phenomenological investigation, critical discourse, interpretive analytics, and deconstruction give way from time to time to each other. Discourses of construct validity are, in part, discourses of power. Foucault is instructive here; one can almost imagine his following comment being directed precisely at construct validity in social research.

> A . . . methodological precaution . . . [urges] that the analysis should not concern itself with power at the level of conscious intention or decision; that it should not attempt to consider power from its internal point of view and that it should refrain from posing the labyrinthine and unanswerable question: "Who then has power and what has he in mind? What is the aim of someone who possesses power?" Instead, it is a case of studying power at the point where its intention, if it has one, is completely invested in its real and effective practices. (1980a, p. 97)

Real and effective practices include practices of construct validation and research as well as social practices targeted for investigation. Expanding upon Cronbach, construct validation is inquiry that interrogates words, statements, discourses, texts, and practices.

Construct validation is radical, critical, and pragmatic. It is pragmatic because it is concerned with giving *persuasive* (pragmatically convincing) accounts of what is going on. Whether an argument or story (about construct validity and research) is persuasive or not is determined against the context and background of communities of researchers, communities under investigation, and possible alternative communities. Constructs and conceptions mediate our experiences in descriptions, metaphors, models, and explanations. We do not have unmediated access to "brute" reality; our versions of things are, for better or worse, more or less adequate for our purposes. They invite criticism. Each approach to discourse and construct validity reviewed contributes information and perspective. But each is partial. From time to time one may desire or require only partial information, such as that provided by mainstream, naturalistic, or critical research, but partiality should not be mistaken for impartiality, incompleteness for completeness, bias for neutrality. Presently there are no guidelines (that I find persuasive) by which criticisms can be limited, even though guidelines abound in these (and other) genres about what constitutes better arguments.

Radical criticism is implicated. One sense of *radical* means to go to the root or origin. Certainly interpretive analytics and deconstruction push in this direction by asking basic questions, even though each denies foundational answers. Another sense of *radical* means considerable departure from the usual or traditional. Construct validity requires occasional departure from conventional practices of the past, or else the past will dominate the future. Construing construct validity as radical, critical pragmatism takes Cronbach and Meehl another step in the direction they headed in 1955.

Construct validity and validation is what those in authority choose to call it. If they choose to exclude phenomenological investigation, so be it. If they choose to exclude ideological criticism and discussions of power, so be it. If they choose to stipulate meanings for constructs and enforce them, so be it. But embracing what is in place does not free authorities from the strictures of inherited discourses. They simply are indulged for being in a privileged position. At bottom, construct validation is bound up with questions such as these: What justifies our theoretical constructs and their measurement? What kinds of communities are we building and how are we building them?

CHAPTER 7

Poststructuralism, Pragmatism, and Curriculum

> There is no power that is exercised without a series of aims and objectives. But this does not mean that it results from the choice or decision of an individual subject; let us not look for the head-quarters that presides over its rationality. . . . It is often the case that no one is there to have invented them [the rationality of power and its tactics], and few who can be said to have formulated them: an implicit characteristic of the great anonymous, almost unspoken strategies which coordinate the loquacious tactics whose "inventors" or decisionmakers are often without hypocrisy. (Foucault, 1980c, p. 95)

> With the linguistic resourcefulness and mobility accruing from an extreme language-scepticism, deconstruction had the capacity to come in under existing or emerging critical systems at their weakest point, the linguistic bad faith on which they were built. (Felperin, 1985, p. 110)

Curriculum is not derivative, as are many subfields of education, from other academic or applied disciplines. For example, educational psychology has roots in psychology; social foundations of education, in history and sociology; philosophy of education, in philosophy; the study of educational policy, in political science and the policy sciences; and educational administration, in the applied fields of business and public administration. Curriculum deals with problems that are uniquely educational in much the same way that instruction has its own special tasks. But instruction is confronted with the concrete situation of classrooms, students, content, and teachers. The tasks facing curriculum are less immediately demanding.

Such independence is rare. It is enviable, however, if one desires to chart one's course by picking and choosing among problems and orientations. But there are also costs. There is a sense of security, if not certainty, when it is possible to rely on an academic discipline to orient one's research, to help identify "important" problems, and to outline accepted research techniques and methodologies. Given the disciplinary independence of curriculum, it is not surprising that its history is marked by repeated turmoil and conflict, because it is always possible to question its purposes, beliefs, values, assumptions, metaphors, and orientations that fix its purpose and meaning.

An array of metaphors related to death and illness have been used to describe the field: in 1969 Schwab used the word *moribund*, in 1975 Dwayne Huebner wrote about a *wake*, and in 1980 Philip Jackson questioned the *existence* of a field of curriculum. But there was plenty of counterevidence that curriculum was alive and, if not well, at least kicking. There were heated exchanges among so-called reconceptualists, conceptual-empiricists, and traditionalists (Jackson, 1980; Pinar, 1980; Tanner & Tanner, 1979). Additionally, remnants of old positivist debates (Eisner, 1983; Phillips, 1983) and discussions of phenomenology (Macdonald, 1982; van Manen, 1982), critical theory (Anyon, 1981; Cherryholmes, 1980, 1982; Giroux, 1983a,b), and neo-Marxist criticism (Apple, 1982; Popkewitz, 1982) were explored in terms of curriculum. Curriculum, it is safe to conclude, is not dead. It is fair to ask, however, whether its conflicts and disagreements signify illness, moribundity, or death. These metaphors, I will argue, misconceptualize curriculum and its dynamics. Furthermore, its internal conflicts and turmoil are not anomalous but characterize all fields of study (for one argument along these lines, see Kuhn, 1974). It just happens that the disciplinary and task independence of curriculum exacerbates this condition.

This chapter proposes one argument to answer two questions: (1) Why has the study of curriculum been turbulent and full of conflict? (2) What is its central project? First, a definition of curriculum and then the 1960s movement to teach the structure of the disciplines will be described and given a poststructural reading. Then some implications of this for curriculum and education will be outlined.

One caveat before proceeding: any profession operates simultaneously at many levels. Some practitioners implement research findings and engage in the practices of the field on a day-to-day basis. Some researchers try to clarify and extend the knowledge of the field. Some trainers teach the literature, norms, and practices of the field to new entrants. Some developers work, in the case of curriculum, on new classroom materials and new approaches to school and classroom organization. Such different activities have distinct yet reinforcing discourses. They are concerned with different immediate tasks, while sharing larger goals and purposes. The substantive focus of this chapter is with curriculum knowledge, purposes, and goals; how a particular movement proposed to organize the field; why it was persuasive at the time; and why it failed to live up to its promise. This analysis, I submit, clarifies the dynamics of the study of curriculum.

WHAT IS CURRICULUM?

What is curriculum? Is it a program of studies? Course content? Planned learning experiences? Experiences "had" under the auspices of the school? A structured series of intended learning outcomes? A "written" plan for action? Or something more involved? This ground will not be covered in detail, since Mauritz Johnson (1967) and Robert Zais (1981), among others, have already analyzed and discarded many of these definitions.

Johnson defines curriculum as a structured series of intended learning outcomes. This is rejected for two reasons. First, Johnson's definition was selected in part because it distinguishes between curriculum and instruction, but this criterion is flawed because it presumes a categorical distinction between curriculum and instruction *before* curriculum is defined. Obviously, without a definition of curriculum it is not possible to know whether or not curriculum is distinct from instruction. Second, Johnson argues that curriculum cannot be defined *post hoc*; that is, it has to be defined before the act of instruction so that curriculum can guide instruction. Defining curriculum in this way has obvious instrumental and utilitarian appeal, but it places the study of curriculum, curriculum development, and so on at the service of immediate administrative and instructional demands. The functionalist nature of this definition is highlighted when one realizes that it would have administrative and instructional needs drive curriculum.

Zais, drawing on Hilda Taba's work, argues for a continuum between curriculum and instruction rather than a sharp distinction:

> The suggestion and central thrust of Taba's conception of curriculum, however, is that the broader (that is, more general) aspects of purposes, content, and method belong in the realm of curriculum, while the more proximate and specific aspects are properly allocated to teaching and instruction. (1981, p. 40)

Gail McCutcheon captures Zais's meaning with more fruitful results:

> By curriculum I mean *what students have an opportunity to learn* in school, through both the hidden and overt curriculum, and what they do not have an opportunity to learn because certain matters were not included in the curriculum, referred to by Eisner (1979, p. 83) as the "null curriculum." (1982, p. 19; emphasis added)

What students have an opportunity to learn refers to legitimate and approved communications and actions. What students do not have an opportunity to learn are those things off-limits. This definition refers to the substance of what students have an opportunity to learn and to the rules and procedures by which those opportunities are provided.

One might be tempted to criticize this definition because it includes everything: everything present and not present (p and *not p* in symbolic notation). This criticism both grasps and misses the point of the definition. It captures the point that when we have an opportunity to learn, our attention is directed toward an object and away from other objects. When students learn about the American Civil War, they are not learning about the French Revolution. Does this definition include everything and exclude nothing? No! The missed point is that what students have an opportunity to learn focuses attention on selecting an object of study and how it is presented to the exclusion of other objects. Students learn from excluded opportunities as well as from those overtly provided. But different things are learned, depending upon whether an object is present or absent. This distinction makes a difference. One task for the study of curriculum, in this view, is to discover how and why some opportunities are provided and others are bypassed. Curriculum, in part, is a study of what is valued and given priority and what is disvalued and excluded.

Curriculum defined as what students have an opportunity to learn has several advantages:

1. It acknowledges curriculum as a guideline for planning and evaluation, including intended learning outcomes.
2. It includes what students learn from school structure and organization; school administration is not *just* administration but is also part of the instructional system.
3. It includes what students learn from their peers, including what the Supreme Court discussed in *Brown* v. *Board of Education*.
4. It includes the fact that students learn from that which is excluded, from that which is not part of the discourse.

5. It avoids the error of distinguishing curriculum from instruction before defining curriculum.
6. It avoids making curriculum dependent on organizational needs of school administrators and teachers.

Structural analysis identifies categories and binary distinctions of an argument, myth, novel, poem, or, in the present case, curriculum theory, textbook content, curriculum guideline, or assessment test. Examples of binary distinctions that structure curriculum are achievement/failure, theory/practice, concept/fact, learner-centered/subject-centered, accountability/lack of accountability, terminal objective/intermediate objective, literate/illiterate, cognitive/affective, organization/disorganization, synthesis/knowledge of specifics, and sociocentric/egocentric. Several approaches to curriculum value the first over the second term in many of the preceding pairs, and which term is valued depends upon which transcendental signified is queen or king for a day. Some versions of humanistic education might be: learner-centered/subject-centered, practice/theory, lack of accountability/accountability, and affective/cognitive. Approaches to curriculum are topsy-turvy because these and other distinctions could be reversed and reversed again, depending upon the reigning transcendental signified. This is less likely to happen in other fields, such as educational administration or educational psychology, because their meaning is fixed, in part, by academic disciplines outside professional education, even if this dependence is unattributed. Privileged meanings that organize other fields also shift and change but often give the appearance of stability, or at least of slow evolution—not many Kuhnian revolutions having been reported recently. One point of Kuhn's (1974) analysis of scientific revolutions, although it is rarely read this way, is that a dominant paradigm functions as a transcendental signified until it is overthrown and replaced. A structural analysis of curriculum theory and practice offers insight into how the field is (or has been) conceptually organized, what the central tasks of the field are (or have been), and how curricularists are to go about their work (or have gone about their work). But, as pointed out in Chapter 3, structural assumptions contain elements that eventually undermine structural interpretations.

Poststructural analysis, in part, addresses questions about transcendental signifieds: Where do they come from? How were they produced? Why did they originate? What do they assert? Meaning is not centered or fixed because it is caught in a play of references between words and definitions. This can be seen in written texts, which give the appearance of stability but have no center, no transcendental signified, no transcendental semantic meaning. In curriculum we have seen a succession of candidates, and many educators hope, no doubt, that one will come along to organize now and for all time the study of what students have an opportunity to learn. This seems to be what educators have in mind when yearnings are expressed for "a" curriculum theory that will tell us what to do. But what would such a theory look like? How could it endure?

A POSTSTRUCTURAL ANALYSIS OF THE STRUCTURE OF THE DISCIPLINES

The succession of ideas put forward since World War II to serve as transcendental signifieds in curriculum attest to two things: (1) there has been a continuing search for a center to fix and ground thinking and arguments about curriculum, and (2) none has been found. In the early 1960s educators were urged to teach the structure of the academic disciplines. In many ways this was the highwater mark of structuralism and positivism in American curricular thought. The discursive practice of leading educators of the early 1960s is my concern here, not classroom discourse (which from this vantage point would certainly be hard to document). It is not clear to what degree national curriculum-development projects or teacher training institutes induced changes in classroom content or style. Textbooks published from the curriculum-development projects of that period eventually were used in classrooms across the nation, but classroom practices may have remained largely unchanged. The immense size, complexity, and decentralized nature of American education mitigates against quickly instituted, enduring changes. Foucault's approach to discursive practices provides a likely characterization of American education as an anonymous, powerful, slowly changing discourse that we inherit and over which we have little control.

It is always easy for politicians and laypeople to kick the educational system around, but at the end of the 1950s American education was particularly vulnerable due to national embarrassment over Sputnik I. On October 4, 1957, the Soviet Union launched the first artificial earth satellite. This was widely seen as a threat to the national security of the United States. It was important for the United States to compete technologically with and stay ahead of the Soviet Union. Therefore, for the sake of national security and in the name of patriotism, public education had to be upgraded.

How could schools be made better? One approach was "back to the educational basics." But making everyone proficient in reading, writing, and arithmetic was not going to save the nation. Another approach was to make schools more academic. What students henceforth had an opportunity to learn could be academically advanced, reflecting the structure of the disciplines. This was, perhaps, best expressed by Jerome Bruner.

In September 1959 a group of distinguished scientists, scholars, and educators met at Woods Hole on Cape Cod. The task was to consider how science education in primary and secondary schools might be improved. In 1960 Bruner reported their deliberations and recommendations in a small but very influential book, *The Process of Education*. A central theme was that students should be given "an understanding of the fundamental structure of whatever subjects we choose to teach" (p. 11). It was hypothesized that four outcomes would follow:

1. "Understanding fundamentals makes a subject more comprehensible" (p. 23).

2. "Learning general or fundamental principles ensure[s] that memory loss will not mean total loss, that what remains will permit us to reconstruct the details when needed" (p. 25).

3. "To understand something as a specific instance of a more general case—which is what understanding a more fundamental principle or structure means—is to have learned not only a specific thing but also a model for understanding other things like it that one may encounter" (p. 25).

4. "By constantly reexamining material taught in elementary and secondary schools for its fundamental character, one is able to narrow the gap between 'advanced' knowledge and 'elementary' knowledge" (p. 26).

This was a persuasive argument, advocated by distinguished scholars. The advantages were obvious to anyone seriously interested in educational achievement. Teaching the structure of a subject, tapping the center of disciplinary knowledge, was economic, in terms of the number of ideas to be learned, and long lasting in two ways, since there would be increased retention of what was learned and what was learned would become dated more slowly because of its fundamental character.

Two other discourses converged and contributed to the structure-of-the-disciplines movement. One was the explicit structural influence on education of Bloom et al.'s *Taxonomy of Educational Objectives* (1956). It was clearly stated by highly respected authorities that concepts were superior to facts; comprehension, to knowledge of specifics; application, to comprehension; analysis, to application; synthesis, to analysis; and evaluation, to synthesis. The valued and disvalued categories in discourse about educational objectives could not have been set forth more clearly. It was codified and certified. Not only was there a structure to the disciplines; there was also a structure to educational objectives. Conversely, the taxonomy assumed that subject matter had a structure conducive to such arrangement.

A third contributing discourse was Tyler's (1949) well-known rationale. Ten years before the Woods Hole Conference, Tyler applied principles of scientific management to education that showed educators how to think systematically: decide upon objectives, list learning experiences, organize learning experiences, and evaluate outcomes. Tyler's argument is a classic application of structuralism to education. Learning objectives by themselves mean little; but in a structure of organized learning experiences and evaluation, learning objectives contribute to systematic instruction. Likewise, by itself a measurement instrument used for evaluation has little significance; but in a structure of objectives and learning experiences, it can be given an interpretation straight off. By itself each stage of the Tyler rationale means little; the meaning of each stage depends upon differences from and relations to other parts of the process.

Structured interpretations were given to disciplinary knowledge, learning objectives, and curriculum. What had happened was remarkable: the disciplines had fundamental structures, which, if taught, had powerful and long-lasting benefits; learning objectives had been organized hierarchically; and systematic steps of scientific management had been applied to education. The interpretation of the Bloom et al. taxonomy and the Tyler rationale in support of teaching disciplinary structure was difficult to resist, to the degree resistance was considered. It all fit. Everything, from a curricular point of view, had seemingly fallen into place.

At this point a Foucauldian analyst might ask: How could it have turned out differently? Powerful discourses were operative. They reinforced each other: Bruner drew from positivist and logical-empiricist epistemology; Bloom et al., from educational psychology (also influenced by logical empiricism); and Tyler, from scientific (and efficient) management. Given the political imperatives of an internationally threatening situation, the discourse was set, limited, and legitimated. For a variety of reasons, each powerful and persuasive in its own way, teaching the structure of the disciplines had become for the time being the transcendental signified for the field of curriculum. It *centered* the system and it *fixed* meanings in education. Working from disciplinary structure, everything could be figured out, from objectives to evaluation. In retrospect, however, the idea of disciplinary structure was largely based on a positivist view of knowledge whose philosophical underpinnings had by then eroded.

The structure-of-the-disciplines argument seems to have presumed the following:

1. The structure of disciplinary knowledge was logically coherent and complete.
2. Disciplinary knowledge was logically valid and truth preserving, from first principles to testable hypotheses.
3. Disciplinary knowledge was factual and explanatory, not evaluative.
4. Scientific language was value neutral and passive in describing and explaining phenomena.

The first and second points assume a distinction between analytic and synthetic statements; the third, between facts and values; and the fourth, a view of language as passive and descriptive, not active or evaluative. An important consequence of the analytic/synthetic distinction is that a conclusion in a logically valid argument *necessarily* follows from the premises of the argument. Thus if a theory or explanation is stated in a valid deductive manner and its first principles are true, then its conclusion must also be true. It is easy to understand why this assumption is central to a structural approach to disciplinary knowledge. The latter two assumptions conceptualized knowledge and science somehow as separate from the world being described and explained.

Developments in modern logic by Quine (1953) and philosophy of language by Austin (1968) and Wittgenstein (1953) cut the ground from beneath these assumptions. Quine argued that it was not possible to account for truth-preserving natural-language arguments. (This depended on the notion of analyticity, which defied, then and now, clear characterization. See Quine, 1953, for the original argument.) Therefore it could not be shown that disciplinary knowledge was logically complete or truth-preserving. Austin and Wittgenstein, in different ways, showed that speech is action, not just description (which Austin called the descriptivist fallacy), and that value and institutional commitments infiltrate language and what is said. Disciplinary knowledge then, did not consist of passive, unambiguously truth-preserving factual arguments that excluded evaluation. A new account of disciplinary structure was in order. It was not forthcoming.

Not to be put off, many promoted curricula based on disciplinary structures that presumably were truth-preserving, objective, and cumulative, even though the precise nature of these structures, for good reason, was never spelled out. At Woods Hole there were six mathematicians, nine psychologists, four physicists, five biologists, and eight who represented history, classics, medicine, and cinematography. The issues discussed were philosophical to the core, but no philosophers participated. Elsewhere wars had been fought whose outcomes were important to a structural approach to the disciplines, but no one was there to report on battles, casualties, or outcomes.

These events illustrate Foucault's argument that power makes truth possible. The arguments of Quine, Wittgenstein, and Austin did not, nor would other contrary educational positions have been expected to, curb the structure-of-the-disciplines movement. The driving force was grounded in political exigencies internal as well as external to professional education, not in the substantive merits of the arguments.

Foucauldian analysis points to a continual movement from discourse (for example, Bruner's argument for a structural approach to curriculum) to history (for example, contemporary events within education and national and international political developments). That disciplinary structure became a transcendental signified for curriculum was an accident of history with no single author. Once it was in place, it determined who could speak and what could be said. Curricularists were not in control of their discourse; quite the reverse, dominant discursive practices dictated who was a curricularist. The discursive practice had shifted, and those who formerly had spoken with authority on curriculum were on the outside and those who had previously been on the outside of curriculum, for example, academic specialists, were now on the inside. And no one asked: Why not teach about racism, sexism, labor history, minority history, social inequality, or injustice. The configuration of power from several discourses, practices, and situations conferred upon the arguments of Bruner, Bloom et al., and Tyler the effects of truth. Power as well as truth had spoken, because power preceded and produced statements that were received as truth.

A deconstructive analysis in the manner of Derrida focuses less on the historical setting and more on the argument. One question is: What binary distinctions does a structure-of-the-disciplines approach advance and do they deconstruct? Disciplinary structure assumes the existence of a cumulative and hierarchical body of knowledge. It was assumed that academic scholars should set the educational agenda, and their assumptions about disciplinary structure led to a set of valued/disvalued categories. Some of these categorical distinctions were theory/practice, concept/fact, subject-centered learning/learner-centered learning, and cognitive/affective, with the first terms valued over the second. These distinctions separate what is central from what is marginal.

Are these distinctions stable? Of the theory/practice opposition, Michael Ryan (1984) writes, "All theory is either a theory of a past practice which it describes, or of a future practice toward which it aims, in addition to being itself a practice. Pure practice . . . is always itself a certain theory of practice" (p. 14; see Chapter 5 in this volume for an argument deconstructing the theory/practice distinction).

As for the hypothesized superiority of concepts to facts, it is well known that scientific concepts are not empirical unless they point to the possibility of factual observations. Conversely, factual observations are only possible given a conceptual background. Concepts and facts point to things in the world and depend upon each other. If concepts and facts are mutually constitutive, one is led to ask why educators would value scientific concepts over facts. When disciplinary concepts are valued over facts, the world as conceptualized by academicians is privileged over alternative conceptualizations, such as artistic, humanistic, aesthetic, and political ones, and facts highlighted by such alternative orientations are slighted.

As for subject-centered learning and learner-centered learning, learners do not exist without subjects and a subject to learn does not exist without previous learners. When subjects are valued over learners, the interests of learners who constituted the subjects (experts) are valued over the interests of other learners (students). It is simply the case that the subject-centered/learner-centered distinction privileges learners who are subject-matter experts.

Finally, let us address the cognitive/affective distinction. Presumably a cognitive emphasis values "objective" knowledge and an affective emphasis deals with values, feelings, attitudes, and opinions. But a cognitive orientation cannot exist without prior value judgments that single out some cognitions as more important or worthwhile than others. What is cognitive can be neither produced nor taught without reference to prior evaluations. The cognitive/affective distinction operates to hide prior value judgments. Those hidden commitments turn out to be the ones held by authorities and experts.

By 1970 a number of developments illuminated the shortcomings of a structure-of-the-disciplines approach to curriculum. It deconstructed, although this term was not used, when it became widely recognized that the rhetorical claims of Bruner exceeded the logic of his argument. First, as noted earlier, logical positivism and its successor, logical empiricism, each of which had contributed to the epistemological foundation for teaching disciplinary structure, could no longer sustain claims made on their behalf. No alternative interpretation of disciplinary structure had surfaced; given Kuhn's influential 1962 book on *The Structure of Scientific Revolutions* (cited throughout this book in its 1974 edition), coming as it did two years after Bruner's, one was sorely needed. Second, academics who sought in the early 1960s to map the structure of their respective disciplines were less than successful in doing so (Bruner, 1971). Third, the international political situation vis-à-vis the Soviet Union had changed. Fourth, domestic politics in the United States was now dominated by the civil-rights movement, the War on Poverty, and rising controversy over United States military involvement in Vietnam. Disciplinary structure no longer drove curriculum efforts. By the 1970s there were voices, including Bruner's (1973), asking why we were not teaching about racism, sexism, and social inequality and injustice. By the 1980s these demands, in turn, had almost been silenced as the cry shifted to educational "excellence." Forces external to professional education were making different demands from those voiced ten years earlier. Power was speaking again and this time telling a different story. What is considered true and authoritative often shifts as power moves, settles, and is relocated. That is what happened in curriculum.

CRITICAL PRAGMATISM AND CURRICULUM

Teaching the structure of the disciplines is one proposal among many that have been promoted to center, organize, fix the meaning of, and bring coherence to curriculum. The history of curriculum theory and practice can be read as a series of repeated invasions of organizing ideas that command attention for a while before they are turned out by the next invasion. Each new invader was beyond the control of any individual educator, reflected political events external as well as internal to education, represented prominent contemporary ideologies, and could be deconstructed. Proposed transcendental signifieds, such as teaching disciplinary structure, recede for at least two reasons: (1) the material, external events that push for their adoption disappear or become less demanding and/or new developments disrupt the discourse and its related practices, a Foucauldian hypothesis; and (2) the organizing persuasiveness of the idea is subsequently shown to be suspect, due either to direct criticism or indirect analysis, a Derridean hypothesis. The argument from Foucault tends toward a synthetic, empirical claim, whereas the Derridean is more analytic.

The study and practice of curriculum determines where and on what grounds opportunities to learn are provided and at what point the deconstruction of those opportunities will stop. Construction and deconstruction circle around a central question: Why do we provide an opportunity to learn about something in the first place? Curricula can help students gain insight into their discourses, into how knowledge and power create and recreate each other, or it can focus on accepting existing discourses along with their unique opportunities, constraints, and oppressiveness. Curricular constructions and deconstructive criticisms allow judgments to be made about objectives, learning experiences, the organization of learning experiences, and their evaluation—all of which are necessary in some fashion some of the time but should not be mistaken as transcendental. If poststructural criticism teaches nothing else, it teaches us to be suspicious of argumentative, knowledge, and policy claims based on appeals to precision, certainty, clarity, and rigor.

This argument may seem a bit curious, unsettling, and unfamiliar because academic and professional arguments are expected to begin with a question and end with an answer. Academic and theoretical arguments push toward certainty and promise identity, by identifying—if nothing else—what it is we are studying, if not truth. For example, it would seem that curriculum theory should tell us what curriculum is and authoritatively tell us what to do when it comes to developing, implementing, and evaluating curriculum. The poststructural lesson is to be suspicious of such authority. Much of the unfamiliarity and strangeness of poststructuralism recedes when applied to everyday life. Work, relationships, beliefs, skills, and we ourselves are not identical from one day, or even one moment, to the next or from one place to another. There are always differences. Theories and organizing principles put forward as transcendental signifieds are products of human activity; therefore they are necessarily marked by the uncertainties and transience of human efforts.

Think of social practice and theory allegorically. Social practice, in this case curriculum and education, may be compared to humanity after the Fall. What we do in everyday life is negotiated, compromised, contingent, subject to miscalculation, and flawed. Theories and first principles promise redemption. There is hope, an expectation, that theory will tell us what is good and what is true, how to make correct calculations and avoid errors. Because theory is produced by humanity in its fallen state, it should not be surprising, then, that it is also characterized by incompleteness, ambiguity, error, and contradiction.

How to proceed? Both constructors and deconstructors are needed. Some people are better at constructing, others at deconstructing. Constructors must realize that what is built is temporal, fallible, limited, compromised, negotiated, and incomplete or contradictory. Each construction will eventually be replaced. And deconstructive arguments must be shaped so that construction will be encouraged and follow. The field of curriculum has unwittingly experienced cycles of construction and deconstruction. These have been interpreted as illness, moribundity, and a foreshadowing of the death of the field. The hope of finding a purpose or cause that grounds work in curriculum and education and fixes its meaning once and for all, however, is misplaced. It appears to be fictional. But the continuing search for meaning and purpose and the subsequent deconstruction of the candidates that turn up need not cause despair. The realization that this is the nature of history, politics, and texts brings with it important changes in thinking about curriculum and education. If the structure, pardon my usage, of curriculum and how it moves continues to be unrecognized, however, elation is likely to be followed by despondency by elation by . . . with no basis for sustained insight or dialogue.

If discourse in the field is accepted as fragmented, pushed and pulled, contradictory and incomplete, responding to professional and political forces beyond our control, subject to deconstruction; and we consciously choose to constitute a dialectic of construction-deconstruction; then the nature of curricular discourse will change. Instead of talking about taxonomies of objectives, structures of disciplines, learning objectives, and what "a" curriculum theory would be like, the conversation will turn to what kind of society and schools we want, knowing full well that they constitute each other. Our concerns will be pragmatic and focus, as Rorty puts it, "about what self-image our society should have of itself" (1985, p. 11). For example, do we want to provide opportunities to learn a structure of the disciplines at the expense of teaching about the causes and consequences of racism, sexism, and social inequality and injustice? If the argument Bruner made in 1960 is compared to that he came back with in 1971 and 1973—that social issues should be moved closer to center stage in curriculum—we see the ebb and flow. Each argument was persuasive when it was made, but *the discursive practices and social structures that made each argument persuasive were never addressed*. How to get behind the discourse? How to get at what structures what we say? Why do we choose the words and make the statements we do?

Even though poststructural criticism is relatively new to discussions of social practice, even though it promises no final, transcendent meaning, it is still possible to outline what curriculum and education might look like when criticism feeds into pragmatic choices. Curriculum is what students have an opportunity to learn. What students have an opportunity to learn depends upon what they do not have an opportunity to learn. Power distributes opportunities and nonopportunities. And curriculum is intimately linked to educational administration and instruction, because each set of activities produces opportunities and constrains what can be learned. Curriculum is not more isolated than any other field of education. They are all part of a larger society and are moved to and fro by the same rhythms that shape our politics, music, business, technology, and so forth. Complaints about the illness, death, or moribundity of curriculum resulted from a failure to grasp these connections in combination with monumental expectations made of the field. It was as though curricularists were expected to tell educators what to do. But the acceptability of what was uttered would have reflected the contemporary interests of those in power, and there is little reason to think the rhetoric of the answer would have matched its logic. The study of curriculum is the process of rolling over one answer onto the next when asked what students should have an opportunity to learn. To expect curricularists to give a definitive answer to what students should have an opportunity to learn is to display an ignorance of the question and the field. Given this, what curricular strategies seem promising?

Curricular work takes place in a wide variety of settings with different scope and generality: there are the United States Department of Education, publishing companies that market textbooks nationwide, state departments of education, teaching-methods classes, school district curriculum committees, and individual classrooms. What is constructed at each level is shaped by what is inherited from previous social, organizational, or professional generations. Saussure states this general point very clearly, and here structural and poststructural thought converge and then separate:

> The word, though to all appearances freely chosen with respect to the idea that it represents, is fixed, not free, with respect to the linguistic community that uses it. . . . No individual, even if he willed it, could

modify in any way at all the choice that has been made; and what is more, the community itself cannot control so much as a single word; *it is bound to the existing language.* (1916/1966, p. 71; emphasis added)

Inherited discourses come into contact with each other, sometimes reinforcing, sometimes conflicting. A first step in a poststructural, critical, pragmatic strategy is to describe relationships between historical developments and political practices and curriculum theory and practice. For example, following up on the examples in Chapters 2 and 3, what were the historical and political conditions that made the Tyler rationale, the Bloom et al. *Taxonomy of Educational Objectives,* and Schwab's "Practical 4" persuasive? This should not be approached, however, in a simplistic and overdeterministic manner. Politics does not create curriculum out of whole cloth. Instead, power transforms discourses such that a category, like disciplinary structure, is given more salience and importance than others. International tensions did not create the notion of structure, but they did, however, assign an educational value it did not have before to disciplinary structure. Power creates opportunities for speech and discourse but does not create each category in the discourse. How does power shape curricular discourse and why are certain subjects privileged over others?

A second poststructural strategy follows from the point that power precedes curriculum discourse. Who, individually, or what group is rewarded and indulged and, conversely, who are those sanctioned and deprived? Who benefits under a curriculum organized in terms of disciplinary structure is easy to identify. Students from groups that did well in school would be expected to do well with an academic curriculum. Students from backgrounds that did not emphasize academic achievement would not be expected to do well. Academic specialists would be financially rewarded. Curricularists who argue humanistic or social-issue positions would be, for the time being, professionally marginalized.

A third poststructural move gives curricular discourse a close reading and analysis: Who listens? Who is excluded? What metaphors and arguments are deployed? Fourth, what are the dominant and valued categories? Since dominant categories cannot ground the logic of the system, it is only prudent to inquire into the values and ideologies that led to the choice of the organizing principles. Fifth, alternative interpretations of what students have an opportunity to learn should be generated, because it is a reasonable inference that subtexts tell stories different from those on the surface. Sixth, curriculum proposals, demands, and so forth should be examined in light of changes and developments in other disciplines, because their placement in a broader setting may provide insights into curricular discourses-practices, for example, that structural approaches to knowledge are not entirely defensible.

Structural approaches lend themselves to checklists; poststructural criticism defies the compilation of an enduring checklist. There are, to be sure, things to keep in mind in pursuing either Foucauldian or Derridean criticism, but it may be more productive to think of curriculum construction, the geneology of the construction, and its deconstruction more metaphorically. Poststructural criticism argues that linearity in text, organization, rationale, and argument is deceptive. Here are three metaphors offering contrasting yet dependent images useful in thinking about these things: normal and revolutionary science, normal and abnormal discourse, and canny and uncanny thinking. Although Kuhn in *The Structure of Scientific Revolutions* (1974) did not couch his account in poststructural terms, it roughly parallels the Derridean account. Scientific activity moves between normal science, which is governed by a paradigm that "stands for the entire constellation of beliefs, values, techniques, and so on shared by the members of a given community" or "denotes one sort of element in that constellation, the concrete puzzle-solutions . . . employed as models or examples" (1974, p. 175), and revolutionary science, which rejects and replaces paradigms. Normal science is, more or less, a hypothesis-testing activity wherein theories are elaborated and filled in. Occasionally the paradigm, the transcendental signified, breaks down. Scientific activity then takes on revolutionary overtones, and the search is on for a new set of governing principles and guiding puzzle-solutions, a new paradigm. Science, in this view, is movement between normal and rule-governed activity and a revolutionary search for new rules.

Normal and abnormal discourse is discussed by Rorty in *Philosophy and the Mirror of Nature* (1980). After recounting repeated failed attempts by twentieth-century philosophers to provide a foundation for knowledge, he notes that Wittgenstein, Dewey, and Heidegger came around to a common historicist message:

> Each of the three reminds us that investigations of the foundations of knowledge or morality or language or society may be simply apologetics, attempts to eternalize a certain contemporary language-game, social practice, or self image. (pp. 9–10)

This passes quite well as a general description of what was claimed for disciplinary structure in curriculum. In curriculum terms the search for "a" curriculum theory, "a" first principle, "an" organizing scheme, "an" evaluation procedure is an attempt to eternalize a particular social practice that is an accident of time and space. It represents an effort to deny our humanity by denying differences and movement.

Rorty devotes a fair amount of attention in his last chapter to education and edification, where *edification* stands for "finding new, better, more interesting, more fruitful ways of speaking" (p. 360). Edification begins with normal discourse dominated by "descriptions of the world offered by our culture (e.g., by learning the results of the natural sciences)" (p. 365). The move, then, is to abnormal discourse, which is always parasitic on normal discourse. On his final point he is worth quoting at length:

> The point of edifying philosophy is to keep the conversation going rather than to find objective truth. Such truth, in the view I am advocating, is the normal result of normal discourse. Edifying philosophy is not only abnormal but reactive. . . . The danger which edifying discourse tries to avert is that some given vocabulary, some way in which people might come to think of themselves, will deceive them into thinking that from now on all discourse could be, or should be, normal discourse. The resulting freezing-over of culture would be, in the eyes of edifying philosophers, the dehumanization of human beings. (p. 377)

Edifying discourse moves in and out from construction to deconstruction, from structure to its criticism, from normal to abnormal conversation and argumentation, always suspicious of certainty and precision.

Another way to think about structural and poststructural criticism is described by Culler in *On Deconstruction: Theory and Criticism After Structuralism* (1984). Building on work of J. Hillis Miller, he writes about canny and uncanny criticism about literature. The canny critic brings "literature out into the sunlight in a 'happy positivism'"(p. 23, quoting Miller). The uncanny critic pursues logical analysis into regions that are alogical and absurd, thus suggesting deeper meanings: "Uncanny post-structuralism arrives to waken canny structuralism from the dogmatic slumbers into which it was lulled by its 'unshakable faith' in thought and 'the promise of a rational ordering'" (p. 24). Being canny, shrewd, and clever about the world as it appears entraps, dehumanizes, and deludes us. Curriculum needs to be uncanny as well as canny.

It is time to bring the argument full circle and explain why historically the study of curriculum has appeared so turbulent. This has variously been interpreted as signifying illness, death, or moribundity, whereas other fields of education have seemingly displayed more stability. It is arguable that the disciplines from which educational psychology, social foundations of education, philosophy of education, educational policy analysis, and educational administration are, in part, derivative contribute to their apparent stability. Teacher education or instruction, as you will, attends to concrete situations. But curriculum is neither historically situated in the tradition of an academic discipline nor constrained by a concrete situation. The complexity of the demands thrust upon the study and practice of curriculum contribute to its looseness, its thrashing about, its contradictions, and its lack of a center, grounding, and foundation.

But the apparent stability of other fields in education and the lack of stability in curriculum are both illusory. Academic disciplines and the knowledge they produce are not stable, as Kuhn (1974) has persuasively demonstrated. But following a "scientific revolution," disciplines still have traditions and legacies. Questions shift and puzzle-solutions are discarded, but there is still some sense of what a field is about, whether it is philosophy or economics or political science. Transcendental signifieds for academic disciplines are in the long run fictional; but in the short run, say the length of an average professional career, they are stable. Life expectancy of foundational ideas may be longer in an academic discipline than in the field of curriculum for several reasons:

1. Academic disciplines are more loosely coupled to political events and exigencies, such as the surprise launching of an artificial earth satellite by the Soviet Union, than is the field of curriculum.

2. Research problems and tasks of disciplines are more closely framed and policed than the holistic tasks facing curriculum; for example, Kuhn argues that paradigms are often shared by communities of fewer than 100 members (1974, p. 178).

3. Disciplines do not have to respond to specific, immediate, and changing demands for excellence and performance as does professional education; for example, scholars can quietly admit within their community that they cannot solve a problem, as did political scientists who spent some 20 years trying to solve a problem known as Arrow's impossibility theorem. It turned out to be impossible to solve.

4. Whereas disciplines may reflect ideological orientations and problems of the larger society, such as a fixation on rational choice theories in microeconomics, psychology, and political

science, they are not continually confronted, as is curriculum, by the contradictions, frustrations, ambiguities, and, in some cases, helplessness of society.

The traditions, orientations, commitments, obligations, and, not least of all, focus of disciplinary and professional activity external to education give the appearance of stability to many fields in education. Curriculum does not have such a reserve.

Solid, immutable foundations do not exist for any of these endeavors. The absence of foundations is simply more noticeable in curriculum than in academic disciplines and other areas of professional education. The norm for curriculum, then, is not consensus, stability, and agreement but conflict, instability, and disagreement, because the process is one of construction followed by deconstruction by construction . . . of what students have an opportunity to learn. By explicitly adopting a poststructural attitude, educators will avoid the false hope of structural certainty and be in a stronger position to deal with, anticipate, and sometimes, perhaps, predict the fate of the latest proposal to guide curriculum. If the field of curriculum moves to a poststructural era along with its uncertainties, ambiguities, and criticisms, there is the promise of understanding more fully how we and others around us have become who we are. The possibility of such understanding brings with it the promise of increased freedom and power, increased freedom from existing social structures, and more power to create our societies and schools rather than the other way around.

CHAPTER 8

Education and Critical Pragmatism

It is true that we speak a public language, that we inherit versions, that talk of truth and falsity only make sense against the background of an "inherited tradition," as Wittgenstein says. But it is also true that we constantly remake our language, that we make new versions out of old ones, and that we have to use reason to do all this, and, for that matter, even to understand and apply the norms we do not alter or criticize. (Putnam, 1983, p. 240)

I believe, however, that I was quite explicit about the fact that nothing of what I said had a destructive meaning. Here and there I have used the word deconstruction, *which has nothing to do with destruction. That is to say, it is simply a question of (and this is a necessity of criticism in the classical sense of the word) being alert to the implications, to the historical sedimentation of the language we use—and that is not destruction. (Derrida, 1972, p. 271)*

Is there life after poststructuralism, and if so, what form might its institutionalization take? How may we carry on our critical and pedagogical practice under the pitiless gaze of deconstruction in particular, a doctrine that desanctifies our once sacred texts, destabilizes our secure hierarchies of authors and readers, classics and criticism, out of reliable relations, and demystifies our humanist vision of high cultural and moral purpose? With the cat so far out of the bag, what is our best strategy for survival? (Felperin, 1985, pp. 216–17)

Foucault was not the first to emphasize the importance of history and power in social theory, nor was Derrida the first to ask if the meaning of words is fixed. But their exploration of these and other arguments, along with the force of their scholarship, has produced insights that previously, perhaps, had only been glimpsed. It is possible, but by no means assured, that a critical pragmatism will result when poststructural insights are brought into our social and professional lives (see Rorty 1980, 1982, and 1985 for general discussions along these lines).

Links between poststructural analysis and a critical pragmatism involve the following. We are confronted with historical events, trends, and objects whose meaning is subject to continual reinterpretation. It is arguable that the apparent autonomy of our efforts to produce knowledge and control is oftentimes fictive and illusory. Our social and educational discourses-practices result, in substantial ways, from effects of power and its exercise. Furthermore, the meanings we ascribe to our lives, texts, and discourses-practices are continually dispersed and deferred. Our texts and discourses-practices continuously require interpretation and reconstruction. We choose and act, furthermore, without the benefit of positivist victories. Our choices and actions, in their totality, are pragmatic responses to the situations in which we and those around us find ourselves. They are based upon *visions* of what is beautiful, good, and true instead of fixed, structured, moral, or objective certainties. Poststructural analyses contribute criticism, which is sometimes radical, to our pragmatic choices.

In contrast to critical pragmatism, a second pragmatic orientation values functional efficiency. It is a vulgar pragmatism. This is pragmatism premised on unreflective acceptance of explicit and implicit standards, conventions, rules, and discourses-practices that we find around us. Eugene Rochberg-Halton (1986) captures its sense in stating that "it becomes too easy to lump pragmatism with the vulgar uses the word has assumed, so that one simply takes 'pragmatic' to mean pure utility or expediency" (p. 4). Vulgar pragmatism is socially reproductive, instrumentally and functionally reproducing accepted meanings and conventional organizations, institutions, and ways of doing things for good or ill. A distinction between being judgmental and being critical stakes out some differences between vulgar and critical pragmatism. When being judgmental, one forms an opinion or makes an estimation or decision by applying given criteria or standards. When being critical, one treats such criteria and standards themselves as problematic. Critical pragmatism results when a sense of crisis is brought to our choices, when it is accepted that our standards, beliefs, values, guiding texts, and discourses-practices themselves require evaluation and reappraisal. Subsequently, however, poststructural analysis and criticism turn into pragmatism that is as critical, unbounded, radical, visionary, and utopian *or* as vulgar, bounded, conservative, conventional, and traditional as we choose.

Vulgar pragmatism results when efficiency is pursued in the absence of criticism, when actions are privileged over thought, when practice is valued and theory disparaged, when practice is divorced from theory (as if that were possible) for the sake of making things work "better." Hostility to theory, as Eagleton puts it, "usually means an opposition to other people's theories and an oblivion to one's own" (1983, p. vii). Tyler's rationale and the Bloom et al. *Taxonomy of Educational Objectives*, however, have often been interpreted as the pursuit of efficiency absent a critical moment. Such interpretations and applications do not deal with the appropriateness of goals or content but with ways to become better organized, make everyone more accountable, and produce traditionally valued outcomes more efficiently. For example, this is the thrust of educational reform proposals that place increasing reliance upon testing in assessing educational outcomes. Standardized achievement tests thereby become the standard against which student, teacher, school, and system performance is evaluated. The task is to raise test scores. Efficiency is the underlying issue. The language is that of cost-effectiveness, how does one get more production out of fixed resources? Or, given increasing resources, how does one choose the most cost-effective educational strategy or strategies?

This is untamed functionalism and reinforces what is in place, including what counts as authoritative knowledge, methods of assessment, and educational excellence. By focusing on organizations and institutions (discourses-practices) that are to be maintained and made more efficient, production-oriented outcomes attempt to silence dislocations between home and school experienced by children from minority or disadvantaged families, existing social and economic inequalities, and conventional values that ignore or deprecate those who are socially and economically marginal. The vulgar pragmatism that pursues efficiency without criticism often promotes the advantage of those who are already advantaged while rhetorically claiming to aid those who are disadvantaged.

POSTSTRUCTURAL AND CRITICAL PRAGMATIC STRATEGIES

Strategies exist whereby at least some aspects of the exercise and effects of power can be read, interpreted, criticized, talked and written about, and evaluated. They can be employed critically and pragmatically from classrooms to work on research projects to teacher training programs. They do not suggest what researcher-theorists should tell teachers. They do not suggest what administrators should tell teachers. They do not suggest what politicians should tell educators. They do not suggest what teacher educators should tell practicing and prospective teachers. Instead, they suggest that *everyone* rethink what they say and do. Rethinking may rejuvenate commitment to conventional discourses-practices or it may lead to something quite different. To avail ourselves of possible choices, however, it is necessary to identify and criticize privileged themes in texts and discourses-practices as well as themes that are silenced. Textual themes and discourses-practices are privileged because, among other things, they are favored by power arrangements and supporting ideological orientations. The exercise of power that has no beginning produces texts and discourses and practices that have no authors. We deal with these by continually reading, interpreting, and criticizing them as we communicate about and evaluate them. Even though reading, interpretation, criticism, communication, and evaluation in the midst of power and history neither separately nor together constitute a sufficient or inclusive list of what critical pragmatism might involve, they are, nevertheless, worth (re)considering in terms of contemporary education.[1]

Reading

Textual consumption *and* textual production are important in contemporary education, though the latter, perhaps, is less acknowledged. Texts and discourses-practices impose values, categories, evaluations, and knowledge claims upon us. They exist to be consumed, to be accepted, to be acted upon, and we are who we are in important ways, individually and collectively, because of them. By closely reading the texts placed before us as well as our discourses-practices, the world, and ourselves, we acquire the ability to tell their stories and our own. Scholes makes the case in this way:

> We care about texts for many reasons, not the least of which is that they bring us news that alters our way of interpreting things. If this were not the case, the Gospels and the teachings of Karl Marx would have fallen upon deaf ears. Textual power is ultimately the power to change the world. (Scholes, 1985, p. 165)

Textual power as I will use the term is similar to other effects and exercises of power. Recall Eagleton (1983) on text, cited in Chapter 1: "Movement from "work" to "text" . . . is a shift from seeing the poem or novel [discourse-practice] as a closed entity, equipped with definite meanings which it is the critic's task to decipher, to seeing it as irreducibly plural, an endless play" (p. 138–39). Textual power is an asymmetrical relationship between readers and texts wherein readers, in experiencing texts, produce multiple readings, interpretations, and criticisms. Textual power is an asymmetrical relationship weighted on the side of the reader. If, to the contrary, readers (students, teachers, administrators, or researchers) conceptualize their job as discovering the *definitive* meaning of works placed before them, then the asymmetrical relationship between readers and works is weighted on the side of the latter (along with their dominant readings).

One is entitled to ask about the relationship between textual power and social change to which Scholes alludes. Is textual power a sufficient condition for social change? Not likely, because it is reasonable to expect that at least some existing material and textual practices will passively remain unscathed by the textual power of readers or will actively defeat and overwhelm efforts at change based on their readings. Is textual power a necessary condition for social change? Again, not likely, because social change can result from natural disasters, among other things, that are quite unrelated to textual power. Textual power, however, is a necessary condition for social change that reflects commitments, decisions, and actions of individuals, groups, and communities, because its multiple readings, interpretations, and criticisms provide leverage on the social world as we find it, a social world constituted by texts and discourses and practices. Without textual power we remain unwitting captives of texts and discourses-practices from the past. Without textual power we stand at a disadvantage in relation to our texts and discourses-practices.

A few, a very few, structures upon which contemporary education is premised have been analyzed and criticized in the previous chapters: Bloom et al.'s *Taxonomy of Educational Objectives*, Tyler's rationale for curriculum development, textbook meanings as identity between word and definition, utilitarian applications of research findings in guiding practice, correlational and hypothesis-testing approaches to construct validity, and curriculum content decisions made on the basis of disciplinary structure. Other structural claims are repeatedly advanced in published research, grant proposals, staff development workshops, teacher training programs, curriculum guidelines, and testing programs. Power arrangements may often be arbitrary, as Foucault argues; and structures, fictitious, as Derrida contends; but their stories are important in the organization and operation of our social world. It seems important, then, that we should read closely what we find around us as well as what is generally considered to be our canonical knowledge in the arts, humanities, social and natural sciences, and mathematics.

Reading is one step of textual practice and production: "Our job is *not* to intimidate students with our own superior textual production; it is to show them the codes upon which all textual production depends, and to encourage their own textual practice" (Scholes, 1985, pp. 24–25). Reading requires knowledge as well as skill: "The supposed skill of reading is actually based upon a knowledge of the codes that were operative in the composition of any given text and the historical situation in which it was composed" (Scholes, 1985, p. 21). Self-knowledge, along with knowledge of one's society, culture, traditions, politics, economics, and linguistic codes, is required.

Technical literacy, whereby one can process words on a page, is one, but only one, aspect of textual consumption and production. Reading produces texts *within* texts (Scholes, 1985). Stories in a text, discourse, and practice cohere because they connect to codes in language, culture, and society. Here is one story in Tyler's rationale for curriculum development. Curriculum planning and development should be orderly, organized, and accountable. By organizing the curriculum and putting it in order, teachers will become more efficient in what they do. Moreover, curriculum content covered in a systematic manner will help students learn more efficiently. If expected learning does not occur, changes and corrections can be made. This may not be an exciting story, but many find it plausible and persuasive.

One reads and consumes texts or discourses-practices when one can tell their stories: the stories within one's culture, society, government, economy, literature, art, gender, ethnicity, religion, or profession. Each of us continually consumes texts, albeit with different purposes, degrees of attention, levels of complexity, incompleteness, and command. The textual content traced in previous chapters included elementary textbooks, research findings, theoretical formulations, accounts of practice, theoretical constructs and their measurement, and curriculum decisions. Their stories submit to different tellings. For example, instead of the accounts I provided, they could have been told in terms of the history of domestic politics, technology, industry, and social elites; theoretical formulations, as explanations of discrete behaviors and outcomes; teaching, as instruction in the dominant and accepted views of knowledge and society; construct validity, as coherence among constructs and their measurement—a coherence with inherited research; and curriculum content, as something that is linear, cumulative, and structured. Stories such as these overlap, and the stories I have told in previous chapters overlap with each other. The fact that texts within texts are multiple yet overlap thematically bridges reading and interpretation. Reading, it turns out, is not categorically distinct from interpretation and criticism, nor are the latter two independent from each other.

Interpretation

Interpretation can build upon reading or upon previous interpretations or criticisms. Interpretation produces *text upon text*; it "is the thematizing of a text" (Scholes, 1985, p. 29).

> In thematizing a . . . text we move from the level of the specific events narrated . . . to a more general level of social types and ethical values. . . . The teaching of interpretation—*text upon text*—must include the basic principles recognized by our institutional practice. That is, we need to equip our students [ourselves] with the accepted strategies for moving from following a narrative ("within") to thematizing on ("upon"). (Scholes, 1985, pp. 29, 31)

Because one can tell a story without identifying its underlying thematic codes, interpretation is getting from "the said and read to the unsaid" (Scholes, 1985, p. 32). Interpretation locates stories and narratives in contexts larger than a sequence of events.

Social, cultural, and professional themes in the story told about the text within the text of Tyler's rationale, for example, include the following: progress is possible, progress is linear, linear planning is efficient, systematic evaluation improves efficiency, pursuit of efficiency is intrinsically as well as extrinsically valuable, and because bodies of authoritative knowledge implicitly contain valid first principles or ends of education, it is unnecessary to discuss them. These ideas link to yet larger themes that include Enlightenment ideals of progress, rationality, control, and cumulative knowledge; utilitarianism; logical positivism and empiricism; and individual accountability. The story within Tyler's rationale makes sense because its language, social codes, and themes are familiar, if not always explicit. It is not surprising, then, that reasonable and plausible themes within one culture, for example Anglo-American settings, often appear strange and implausible to those from different cultural backgrounds and vice versa.

Textual practice that only produces texts within texts and discourses-practices is not unlike a vulgar pragmatism, wherein readers are encouraged to become parasitic on existing and depersonalized structures. Reading as *experiencing* moves beyond textual assimilation to interpretation and criticism, with individuals exploring multiple voices of textual possibilities. Texts and discourses-practices often tell more than one story, each of which can have more than one interpretation, each of which can be subjected to more than one critical analysis. One cannot attribute just any story to a text or discourse-practice, however, because the opportunities and constraints for the stories that might be told and how they might be interpreted and criticized are shaped by which words are on the page, by background culture, historical events, professional activities, and research findings—by the everyday rules and activities of our discourses and practices.

Interpretation resonates sympathetically with John Dewey's thinking on experience and education. In "The Child and the Curriculum" he wrote:

> Development does not mean just getting something out of the mind. It is a development of experience and into experience that is really wanted. . . . There is, then, nothing final about a logical rendering of experience. Its value is not contained in itself; its significance is that of standpoint, outlook, method. . . . There is no such thing as sheer self-activity possible—because all activity takes place in a medium, in a situation, and with reference to its conditions. But, again, no such thing as imposition of truth from without, as insertion of truth from without is possible. (1902/1977, pp. 182, 184, 188)

Interpretative activities run counter to attempts at decontextualizing the knowledge that children confront in schools as well as to attempts at decontextualizing theoretical knowledge. Decontextual and ahistorical pressures remain strong. Simply put, they are a commanding component in contemporary education.

Surprisingly, but perhaps not too surprisingly, structural analysis in its canny and methodical way contributes to interpretation, because it identifies valued and disvalued categories upon which texts are organized and constructed and discourses-practices pursued. Accept, for a moment, two structuralist assumptions: (1) textual categories are relatively fixed for a time and (2) meanings are determined by relationships among these categories. Because structural analysis identifies binary distinctions, metaphors, models, modes of argumentation, inferences, and repetitions, it moves from the story and narrative to the background. Then, as a structural interpretation is extended, Scholes argues that "ultimate interpretation . . . must move from noting the cultural codes to understanding the attitude taken toward those codes by the maker of the text" (1985, p. 34). Put differently, does the author of record or practitioner support the proposed structure, offer a distanced commentary, or attempt to subvert it?

Interpretations can push in different directions. Linking the story or stories in Tyler's rationale to larger themes can lead one to draw upon neo-Marxist thought or rational-choice theory or approaches to scientific management or teacher-effectiveness research. Even though structural analyses are interest-relative and incomplete, dispersed and deferred, they are useful in identifying underlying values and commitments. Does criticism help resolve this multiplicity of voices? Yes and no.

Criticism

Criticism builds upon interpretations, readings, and other criticisms, not unlike the way interpretation builds upon readings, criticisms, and other interpretations. Criticism produces variant readings; for Scholes criticism produces *text against text*. But he warns that "the collectivity of academically sponsored scholars and teachers, is ill at ease with criticism" (1985, p. 35). He is not writing specifically about professional educators, but given the lack of criticism in education, educators would also seem to be "ill at ease with criticism" because it is practiced by its absence.

Teachers may or may not feel ill at ease with criticism but the practice of teaching often interprets what is to be learned in terms of positivist and structuralist readings where recall of fragmentary bits of knowledge is often the measure of performance and excellence. Critical moments are thereby subverted. Scholes puts it like this:

> It is a parable of all schoolrooms, is it not, and perhaps a parody of them as well. The student seems to be learning about the subject, but what he is truly learning is to give the teacher what he wants. He seems to be reporting about a real and solid world in a perfectly transparent language, but actually he is learning how to produce a specific kind of discourse, controlled by a particular scientific paradigm, which requires him to be constituted as the subject of that discourse in a particular way and to speak through that discourse of a world made visible by the same controlling paradigm. (1985, pp. 131–32)

The discourses of the controlling paradigm(s) appear as hard, brute characteristics of the world to which one becomes adapted and in which one becomes adept. Criticism provides important opportunities to break with dominant readings and interpretations; this likely is one source of discomfiture with criticism.

Criticism addresses texts and discourses-practices that present themselves as objectivistic, where "'objectivism' is a substantive orientation that believes that in the final analysis there is a realm of basic, uninterpreted, hard facts that serves as the foundation for all empirical knowledge" (Bernstein, 1976, p. 111). Objectivistic texts implicitly claim to *represent* things the way they are. If readers adopt a naturalistic attitude, they are encouraged by the objectivism claimed by a text or discourse-practice.

> As critics we need to confront both the naturalistic attitude—this is the way things are, people can't help themselves—and the objective detachment of the narration—this is the way things happen, I am just recording. (Scholes, 1985, p. 37)

Readers (students, teachers, scholars, parents, administrators) may feel ill at ease, threatened, defensive, or embattled when criticism challenges objectivistic and representative claims of a text. Such feelings notwithstanding, criticism points beyond objectivistic and naturalistic inclinations to read texts as representational.

Textual themes invoke cultural codes, valued categories, and ideological orientations. Criticism develops extratextual concerns by evaluating, discussing, examining, and questioning these codes, categories, and orientations. Textual themes adopt positions in social and educational debates. Criticism pursues those debates. Again, Scholes:

> I am suggesting that at some level, in some way, our students must be invited into these critical debates. . . . What this means in practical terms is that we must make available in the most efficacious form some of this critical controversy itself. The ability to criticize is a function of critical maturity. It must be learned by study and thought . . . we must start them on this path of development by showing them critics in action and encouraging them to produce their own critical texts—*not always and inevitably "against," but taking a stand outside the values and attitudes that have been identified . . . by reading and interpretation.* Criticism is "against" other texts insofar as it resists them in the name of the critic's recognition of her or his own values. (1985, p. 38; emphasis added)

Reading produces stories (among other things). Interpretation provides context. Criticism surfaces and evaluates that which narrative and interpretation has omitted, suppressed, devalued, silenced, and opposed as well as what has been claimed, asserted, and argued.

Eagleton describes criticism:

> Its task is to show the text as it cannot know itself, to manifest those conditions of its making . . . about which it is necessarily silent. It is not

just that the text knows some things and not others; it is rather that its very self-knowledge is the construction of a self-oblivion. (1983, p. 43)

Three approaches to criticism are suggested by arguments reviewed in earlier chapters:

1. Structural criticism illuminates counterstructures that texts and discourses-practices ignore or seek to silence.
2. In a Foucauldian genre, criticism produces histories and politics of the present, wherein texts and discourses-practices are effects of the exercise of power.
3. In a Derridean deconstruction, criticism exposes silences and gaps between that which is valued and disvalued, traces the sedimentation of meanings, and documents contradictions and ambiguities within texts and discourses-practices.

Consider these strategies one at a time. First, criticism can propose opposing counterstructures and counter–discourses-practices to those in place. Neo-Marxist criticism is often structural and oppositional in this manner. For example, Jean Anyon (1979) identifies important categories in the content of American history textbooks and argues for changes in what is valued and disvalued. Apple provides another illustration in discussing emerging school book clubs that market "junior Harlequin books [that] construct a model of femininity that is overtly 'classless' and 'raceless' and that harks back to definitions of women or girls as only finding fulfillment in the world of romance and commodities" (1986, p. 27). Authors and publishers of these books construct stories based on the oppositions classless/class and raceless/race, wherein women are portrayed in a classless and raceless society. Apple argues that class, race, and other important dimensions of contemporary society should be highlighted and brought to the foreground. Much remains unsaid about women, including the feminization of poverty, that can be written about and analyzed. His structurally oriented analysis provides the basis for critically advocating counterstructures in literature aimed at adolescents.

The arguments of Tyler, Bloom et al., and Schwab presented in Chapter 2 can likewise be criticized by advocating the reversal of the binary distinctions they promote. Instead of organization/lack of organization, evaluation/nonevaluation, accountability/nonaccountability, integration/nonintegration, legitimate knowledge/illegitimate knowledge (Foucault's *subjugated knowledge*), serious reflection/casual reflection, and subject-centered learning/student-centered learning, arguments can be made that value lack of organization (where learning is not defined exclusively by objectives), nonevaluation (where worthwhile learning is not measured entirely by achievement tests), nonaccountability (where attempts are not made to make teachers individually accountable for measurable student achievement), nonintegration (where attempts are not made to impose spurious structures on academic knowledge), illegitimate knowledge (where minority, labor, and feminist history, among other subjugated knowledge, is promoted), casual reflection (where learning and play are brought closer together and replace sober reflection), and student-centered learning (where the voices of students as readers, interpreters, and critics are valued, and reading as experiencing is promoted over reading as discovering).

Structuralist oppositional critics, neo-Marxist or otherwise, argue for replacing dominant structures with other structures. Humanistic educators might advocate distinctions and categories that minimize evaluation, deemphasize accountability, promote educational purposes not closely linked to measures of standardized achievement, and concentrate on student-centered learning. Critical educators might promote curriculum content previously thought either important enough to be silenced or unimportant enough to be ignored in areas such as racism, sexism, poverty, social injustice, and inequality. Structural criticisms, however, whether humanistic or critical, are themselves subject to poststructural criticisms.

Second, criticism can produce histories of the present in the style of Foucault. Foucault argues that writing history is *not* the writing of narratives. In "History, Discourse, and Discontinuity" he outlined the elements of such criticism:

1. Treat the past discourse not as a theme for a *commentary* which would revive it, but as a *monument* to be described in its characteristic disposition.
2. Seek in the discourse not its laws of construction, as do the structural methods, but its conditions of existence.
3. Refer the discourse not to the thought, to the mind or to the subject which might have given rise to it, but to the practical field in which it is deployed. (1973a, p. 235)

These methodological points about discourse—"its characteristic disposition," "its conditions of existence," and "the practical field in which it is deployed"—focus on relations between discourse and power and how effects of power produce texts and discourses-practices. Foucault investigates the "diversity *of the systems* and the play of *discontinuities* in the history of *discourses,*" (1973a, p. 235) in order to uncover how power operates in, through, and on discourses, institutions, and social practices.

Apple (1986) provides an example of criticism as a history of the present in his discussion of the political economy of textbooks. The economics of textbook publication pressures authors, editors, and publishers to produce books that will be profitable. The politics of state adoptions (primarily in Texas and California) place constraints on what to include and exclude. Teachers and school adoption committees have expectations about how textbooks should look and what they should include. Furthermore, expectations about textbook content are enforced by the content of statewide assessment tests and standardized achievement tests. Apple describes the "homogenization" of textbooks, which Foucault might attribute more generally to the anonymity of textbook discourses and practices. Additionally, from a Foucauldian perspective, none of the participants (authors, editors, publishers, state adoption committees, school adoption committees, teachers, students, parents) have many degrees of freedom in which to act (Cherryholmes, 1983). The political economy of textbooks is driven by several disparate yet reinforcing discourses-practices that produce "bland" textbooks that are strikingly similar. They are distinguished by design, writing style, pictures, graphs, maps, promotion, and marketing. They are relatively undistinguished by differences in content.

Popkewitz's (forthcoming) analysis of teaching and teacher education reform proposals provide a second example of Foucauldian criticism. It is tempting for educators to imagine that they are freely and rationally choosing programs to advance when they act as reformers. Some might call this the liberal illusion of social autonomy. Popkewitz argues that the reform proposals of the 1980s have resulted from the conjunction of several seemingly separate discourses-practices. At the federal level, there continues to be an expansion of statistical and research capability, which has increased in size since the end of World War II. It gained momentum during the late 1960s in the service of equal educational opportunity, although the emphasis on measurement and test performance now serves conservative political ends. At the state level, departments of education have expanded their surveillance of teacher education programs; for example, in Wisconsin the Office of Teacher Certification employed more than 20 persons in 1987, compared to just 2 in 1974, and its 1987 certification rules are contained in a program regulation booklet 209 pages long.

Among foundations, the Carnegie Forum for the Economy and Education is providing important support for the construction of a national teachers test. Among universities, the Holmes Group, a consortium of research universities, is promoting a fifth-year teacher education program and teacher testing. Furthermore, the dominant professional association, the American Educational Research Association, is, in turn, dominated by educational psychology, which currently emphasizes systematic quantitative measurement and research. Popkewitz cogently points out that the underlying power bases of these seemingly disjointed discourses-practices become more distant from those they police and control as they reinforce each other. Curiously, as individuals (teachers, students) become more visible through the measurement of their attributes (knowledge of teaching, knowledge of subject matter), the exercise of power that produces these measurements becomes more invisible. Those who are unreflectively caught up in the discourses-practices of reform engage in vulgar pragmatism, wherein standards and criteria are not problematic. Popkewitz's history of the present highlights the uncritical social determinism and reproduction that such reforms promote.

Interpretive-analytic criticism demonstrates how history and the exercise and effects of power work through, infiltrate, and shape what is said and done. It may attack liberal beliefs about our ability to make autonomous choices, but it also offers some chance of intervening in anonymous discourses-practices that move along seemingly beyond our control (no promises here). Additional examples of such criticism are found in earlier chapters: the ways in which past normative and ideological commitments and power arrangements produce textbooks (Chapter 4) and current educational practices and research (Chapter 5); the ways in which theoretical constructs and their measurement are shaped by prior research, power arrangements, and submerged political commitments (Chapter 6); and the historical and political contexts that push curriculum choices upon educators (Chapter 7).

Third, criticism can, in the style of Derrida, be pointedly deconstructive of rhetorical claims and favored textual, discursive, and practical categories. Again, several examples can be found in the preceding chapters: Schwab's rhetorical claims exceed the logic of his argument (Chapter 3); the categories of the Bloom et al. taxonomy, as well as Tyler's supposedly independent steps in curriculum design, are not mutually independent, nor do they produce linear planning (Chapter 3); the binary distinction between theory and practice proposed in utilitarian and incremental strategies cannot be sustained (Chapter 5); the meanings of theoretical constructs are continually dispersed and deferred (Chapter 6); and the presuppositions of a structure-of-the-disciplines approach to curriculum, including the distinctions between cognitive/affective, subject-centered/student-centered, and concept/fact, are fictitious (Chapter 7). The political projects of those who promote such strategies—projects of control, centralization, accountability, individualization, fragmentation of content, imposition of external arbitrary structures, and rational, linear planning—are thereby exposed, along with the contradictions and ambiguities of their proposals. Ideas proposed as transcendental, regardless of origin, are susceptible to deconstructive criticism. To provide another illustration of the insights deconstructive criticism can provide, consider the call by critical educators for emancipatory schooling. The importance critical educators attach to emancipation builds upon arguments from critical theory. Giroux summarizes it like this:

> The work of the Frankfurt School . . . is a sustained attempt to develop a theory and mode of critique that aims at both revealing and breaking with the existing structures of domination. Crucial to this perspective are an analysis and a call for the integration of the processes of emancipation and the struggle for self-emancipation. (1983a, p. 4)

Critical educators believe, as do I, that social oppression is an important characteristic and outcome of contemporary educational systems, even though it is often unintended as either characteristic or outcome. The emancipation/oppression distinction is a structural characteristic some of these critical analyses identify.

Social inequalities are present in our schools and social world. These inequalities and asymmetries privilege some social, ethnic, gender, linguistic, cultural, and economic groups over others. This privilege and dominance is reproduced in many ways: direct transfer of wealth; selective interpretation of history and culture; political socialization; differential effects of schooling, testing, and credentialing; and passing on career aspirations and tastes for high culture. Talk of social emancipation and self-emancipation proposes to break with current patterns of social dominance, reproduction, and oppression by rearranging existing asymmetries and inequalities.

Social differences, inequalities, classes, and stratification must be reduced, if not eliminated, if there is to be emancipation from social oppression. Social pluralism based upon class, language, culture, ethnicity, religion, politics, economics, and history, however, does not seem to be diminishing. There is reason to believe, to the contrary, that things could be going in the other direction, and there is little (no?) reason to believe these inequalities and differences will disappear of their own accord. Group identity involves shared commitments, interests, values, and ideology. These generate preferences. Group-based preferences are often different. Some of these differences produce social relationships and conditions that are oppressive.

If structural critics argue for emancipatory schooling, deconstructive critics ask if emancipation is categorically distinct from oppression. Rewards and indulgences, as well as punishments and deprivations, that constitute the effects and exercise of power as we find them must be changed if the oppressive conditions that educational discourses-practices privilege are to be ameliorated. Unless those who are privileged voluntarily and actively refuse the benefits of their position, oppressive conditions and situations are likely to continue. And, according to critical analyses, many of these conditions are not likely to be recognized either by the favored, oppressed, or various others. In order to emancipate individuals and groups from oppressive circumstances, conditions may, in some cases, have to be changed authoritatively and forcefully by using coercive strategies and actions.

Withdrawing advantages from those who are privileged is not likely to be a painless process, either for those doing the withdrawing or for those experiencing withdrawal symptoms. Desire for emancipation is a response to social injustice and oppression, yet movement toward emancipation is likely to require coercion that some (those not being emancipated) may find oppressive, because they will be deprived of opportunities and advantages to which they believe they are entitled. Coercion appears to be necessary for emancipation while simultaneously subverting emancipation. The emancipation/oppression distinction thereby deconstructs, and its deconstruction highlights an issue that critical educators tend to keep at the margins of their discourse: Which forms of domination (coercion, constraint) are justified in furthering which forms of emancipation? Vulgar pragmatists avoid the same question by excluding it altogether.

In certain ways interpretive-analytic and deconstructive criticisms reinforce each other. Derrida's concern with "the historical sedimentation of the language we use" (epigraph to this chapter) pushes in the same direction as the following comment by Foucault:

> Discourse is constituted by the difference between what one could say correctly at one period (according to the rules of grammar and those of

logic) and what is actually said. The discursive field is, at a specific
moment, the law of this difference. (1973a, p. 238)

Criticism can help map "the law of this difference." Looking for textual gaps attends to differences between what can be said and what is
said.

At these points Foucault's interpretive analytics and Derrida's deconstruction converge. Foucault highlights empirical, contingent circumstances by which transcendental signifieds are adopted and enforced. Derrida argues that transcendental signifieds that attempt to
norm and police texts are logically suspect and do not deliver on
rhetorical claims made for them. First principles, which are logically
suspect in Derrida's analysis, are, in Foucault's view, sometimes persuasive and adopted because of circumstances and situation and time
and place. Effects of power identify authoritative principles that guide
discourses-practices (Foucault), but there is often less and more to
these guiding principles than meets the eye (Derrida).

Deconstructive criticism and the subsequent construction of texts
and discourses-practices place people in the thick, if not center, of
things. In this connection, Leitch describes how Derrida links reading
and structurally oriented interpretation to criticism: "[Derrida] admits
and promotes the values of careful reading, particularly in the phenomenological and structuralist modes. At the same time he seeks
progress beyond such traditionalist practices" (1983, p. 175). Derrida
remarks on this:

> There are thus two interpretations of interpretation, of structure, of sign,
> of freeplay. The one seeks to decipher, dreams of deciphering, a truth or
> an origin which is free from freeplay. . . . The other, which is no longer
> turned toward the origin, affirms freeplay and tries to pass beyond . . .
> the reassuring foundation, the origin, and the end of the game. . . .
>   There are more than enough indications today to suggest we might
> perceive that these two interpretations of interpretation—which are abso-
> lutely irreconcilable even if we live them simultaneously and reconcile
> them in an obscure economy—together share the field which we call, in
> such a problematic fashion, the human sciences. (1972, pp. 264–65)

Structural themes, narrative history, linear planning, and models of
rational choice force order on things. Poststructural criticism shows
this orderliness to be tentative, provisional, contingent, incomplete,
and ambiguous. Themes and distinctions revealed by structural interpretations are thereby made problematic. And, as Derrida notes, we

live with these irreconcilable interpretations of interpretation simultaneously.

With some force Leitch puts the poststructural case, that affirms interpretative freeplay, this way: "To read closely in the deconstructive or *disfigurative* manner produces more reliable history than the history of historicists and archeologists, who champion carefully forged lies of order and continuity" (1983, p. 189). Multiple interpretations and criticisms are not likely to triangulate on a new "truth," "positivism," "theory," "program," "paradigm," or "structure" immune to dispersion, deferral, contradiction, or ambiguity. Instead, they are likely to identify complexity, disorder, and movement and bring to the foreground play, aesthetics, politics, criticism, and ethics that structures legislate against in the name of rationality and control.

Communication

We do not read, interpret, or criticize in isolation. We write and talk to each other. We continually interact, sometimes by way of reading, interpreting, and criticizing each other and ourselves, texts, discourses-practices, the state of the world. Assuming that we have something to say to each other—educators, at least, believe they do (it is part of their job)—a place to begin is with clarity and cooperation about accepted and traditional meanings, normative commitments, factual descriptions, empirical explanations, scientific theories, cultural beliefs, and ideologies, even though such clarity sooner or later is likely to become deceptive and misleading. One is tempted to think that efforts at clarity are useful only when communicating about valid and true conceptions, not about misconceptions. Let us, for the moment, assume the opposite. Even if our conceptions turn out to be misconceptions and our readings turn out to be misreadings and our theories cannot be shown to be probable or rationally justified (Popper, 1976), it is reasonable to premise interactions on conceptions, readings, and theories that, for the time being, are accepted as valid. Talking and writing with whatever clarity we can command will often be useful in exploring areas of ignorance that sometimes are found in the midst of mistaken certainties.

Communication is action as well as interaction; subject to multiple readings and interpretations; anticipatory of the ideal speech situation; bounded by time, place, and the exercise of power; and subject to deconstruction. From speech act theory come the points that saying something is doing something and that what is said, sometimes, can be true or false. From reception theory comes the point that multiple readings, interpretations, and criticisms are produced in the experience of reading. From Habermas's ideal speech situation comes the admonition to move toward understandings and beliefs in radically open and symmetrical interactions. From Foucault comes the insight that communications are governed by what discourses-practices permit. From Derrida comes the argument that meanings are dispersed and continually elude us, never to be pinned down once and for all.

These arguments, of course, are contradictory. Derrida denies Grice's clarity. The institutional context of speech act theory denies Habermas's ideal speech situation, even though the latter is premised on the former. Foucault denies Habermas's ideal speech situation because effects of power precede speech. Derrida denies Habermas's consensus except as a transitory moment of agreement. But Habermas does not let us forget the promise and power of Enlightenment ideals. Communication as a pragmatic enterprise is sometimes interpretative, critical, and pursued at cross-purposes; at other times it is valued for clarity and efficiency. At one moment clarity will be valued; at another, consensus; at another, conflict; at another, play; at yet another, an exploration of the historical sedimentation of meanings.

Grice's cooperative principle (1975) is useful (recall Chapter 4) when people wish to communicate clearly with each other about what they agree upon and think is important: (1) quantity (provide as much information as required and no more); (2) quality (avoid saying what you believe is false or for which you have no evidence); (3) relation (make it relevant); and (4) manner (be orderly, brief, clear, and avoid ambiguity and obscurity). Clarity, relevance, and brevity are valuable within contexts wherein "normal" readings, interpretations, and criticisms are desired and well defined. It seems reasonable to follow Grice from time to time by (1) premising communications on that which can be shared: language, terms, culture, beliefs, and information; and (2) pressing for clarity and cooperation, because multiple readings and interpretations, criticisms, contradictions, complexities, ambiguities, and deconstruction await us, if they wait at all.

Habermas (1979) argues that four validity claims are required for normal interaction (these are likely to be satisfied whenever Grice's principle is successfully implemented): sincerity, comprehensibility, truth, and normative agreement. If sincerity of either speaker or hearer is questioned, it is resolved by more interaction until one decides about the trustworthiness of the other. If comprehensibility is problematic (that is, if the words, arguments, and claims are not understandable), it is settled by more interaction until the need for clarification, elaboration, or explication is resolved. Problematic assertions about truth and normative acceptability are more involved and require more than normal interaction for their resolution. They are redeemed through critical discourse that is characterized by radical equality among participants: all interests should be represented, any question may be asked, any comment may be made, communication is symmetrical among participants, no strategic behavior (voting, debating) is allowed, and anyone may challenge metatheoretical and metaethical frameworks. Only the best argument is pursued, with an eye toward replacing an accepted consensus with a rational consensus.

This will be elaborated on briefly in terms of classroom interactions, but it can easily be generalized to staff development workshops, research proposals, teacher education programs, and other settings. Classroom interactions are fundamentally asymmetrical because of the teacher's authority. Teachers are authorities by virtue of their position because they are contractually obligated to provide instruction, to evaluate student progress, to assign grades, and to follow administrative directives. Teachers are also authorities because of their expertise resulting from greater education, training, and experience. Teacher authority militates against symmetrical interactions. A first necessary condition, then, is that the teacher be committed, or at least open, to critical discourse when normal interaction becomes problematic.

A second necessary condition requires teachers to share the norms of critical discourse with students. Students can be directly presented with norms of critical discourse that lead away from structural and positivist views of knowledge and meaning to critical reflection. Or these norms can be implicitly introduced into the classroom by employing them as fairly and consistently as possible. The latter is quite different, it should be noted, from inquiry activities that focus more narrowly on cognitive activities.

A third necessary condition for critical classroom discourse is authoritative instruction; that is, something authoritative must be asserted before it can be problematic. Foucault supports this idea in this comment on teaching: "The relation of teaching, that passage from the one who knows the most to the one who knows the least—it is not certain that self-management is what produces the best results; nothing proves, on the contrary that that approach isn't a hindrance" (1984, p. 379) Students should not be encouraged, however, to adopt a structural or positive or natural attitude toward authoritative teachings. Students should be discouraged from reifying or objectifying texts or discourses-practices, and, while being instructed authoritatively, it is important that students learn, for example, that values and norms are embedded in empirical generalizations, that "facts" are ideologically informed, and that power precedes speech.

A fourth necessary condition brings us to arguments. Even as there are generalized norms to determine the openness of a discourse, there are general criteria to evaluate the quality of analytic arguments. Habermas relies on Toulmin (1958), who divides arguments into (1) a conclusion to be justified, (2) data to support the justification, (3) a warrant that links data and conclusion, and (4) the backing for the warrant (see the discussion of Fischer in Chapter 6 for a variant of this). Learning to make and evaluate arguments is important for critical discourse, and everyone who wishes to participate needs the ability to make and distinguish better from worse arguments. Habermas instructs us to pursue only the best argument. This is well and good for awhile but eventually becomes problematic because, as Derrida points out, many arguments eventually contradict themselves. Even though Habermas writes of rational consensus about the "truth" of a matter based upon the "best" argument one should anticipate, if a "best" argument is ever agreed upon, its contradictions, ambiguities, and flaws will eventually surface, producing deconstruction and disagreement.

How far should consensus be pursued? In an interview shortly before his death Foucault commented directly on Habermas's idea of consensus:

> *Q.* If one can perhaps assume that the consensus model is a fictional possibility . . . it might in some sense be better, healthier, freer, whatever positive value one uses, if we assume that the consensus is a goal still to be sought rather than one that we simply throw away and say it's impossible to achieve.
>
> *A.* [Foucault] I would say, rather, that it is perhaps a critical idea to maintain at all times: to ask oneself what proportion of nonconsensuality is implied in such a power relation, and whether that degree of nonconsensuality is necessary or not. . . . The farthest I would go is to say that perhaps one must not be for consensuality, but one must be against nonconsensuality. (1984, p. 379)

This appears to be having one's cake and eating it too. Foucault anticipates the deconstruction of consensus yet rejects the idea of nonconsensuality. Even though consensus is idealistic and fictional, a continued lack of consensus is dangerous.

Movement from a situation characterized by Grice's clarity and cooperation to a situation where Habermas's validity conditions about truth and normative agreement are problematic opens the door to disruption, dissension, and disagreement without providing a means for closing it, even though Habermas discusses the possibility of rational consensus. This movement also captures much of the nature of education itself. Connections between ideas and knowledge cannot be bounded, constrained, and limited once introduced.

Evaluation and Judgment

Readings, interpretations, criticisms, and communications, for many different reasons, are evaluated and judged. Evaluations involve comparisons, sometimes of observations to each other or to agreed-upon standards or to both. These comparisons are often based upon utilitarian assumptions concerned with maximizing an outcome(s) for a group (House, 1976). Attention to the standards themselves is sometimes slighted, because evaluation research is beset with so many problems of validity (construct, internal, external, and statistical conclusion), reliability (treatment, measurement), and inference (statistical, metaanalysis, metaevaluation). In Chapter 6 it was shown that links between measurements and constructs are far from stable; this is also the case when outcomes are compared to standards. Evaluation problems have much in common with construct-validity problems, and parallels are easy to draw.

Even though Habermas and Rorty disagree on substantial issues, Habermas depicts what I have in mind regarding evaluation and judgment in describing one area of agreement with Rorty:

> Like Rorty, I have for a long time identified myself with that radical democratic mentality which is present in the best American traditions and articulated in American pragmatism. This mentality takes seriously what appears to so-called radical thinkers as so much reformist naivete. Dewey's "attempt to make concrete concerns with the daily problems of one's community" expresses both a practice and an attitude. (1985, p. 198)

The process and product of evaluations and judgments are part of our daily concerns. These concerns, repeating earlier arguments, are historically conditioned and reflect the exercise and effects of power. Keeping in mind that we cannot escape the time and place in which we find ourselves, Christopher Butler might well have made the following comment with respect to these standards:

> It nevertheless still make[s] sense to argue that we can make rational decisions on the margins between . . . discourses once we . . . [are]

aware of them. And that awareness may simply depend on our historic luck, the luck that preserves us from believing in Greek gods, or demons or witchcraft or whatever. We are lucky enough at present to realize that discourses such as those of overt ideology . . . are all relative to one another, and indeed that one of them may be dominant. (1984, pp. 128–29)

There seems to be little hope, however, that a definitive account or theory of evaluation, or even an adequate metatheory, is near at hand. Felperin's comment on 20 years of deconstruction in literary criticism is relevant to evaluation and judgment in education. Neither a common methodology, a common ideology, nor a meta- or master-discourse was produced. He speculates about

a "new historical dialect" . . . that draws on lexicons and grammars of several existing languages[2] holds diverse connotations for its speakers, and is sufficiently, though still imperfectly, shared to enable the haggle of exchange to go on more or less as usual, the dialect not of an interpretive community but of a mercantile tribe. (Felperin, 1985, p. 223)

But what substantive values are to be proposed for our standards? Is human dignity valued? Or liberty? Or equality? Or looking out for the least advantaged? Or tradition? Or security? Or possessions? Or democracy? Or higher standardized achievement scores? Values such as these provide a sense against which our evaluational and judgmental sensibilities are developed and tested. They do not constitute fixed standards against which evaluations and judgments are made. Attempting to negotiate a path through their conflicting claims and meanings quickly demonstrates that none of these values are candidates for transcendental status, even though some might argue otherwise. When texts that promote each of these are read closely, they often display an elusive complexity not unlike the complexity and covert texts in Tyler, Bloom et al., and Schwab (Chapter 3, this volume).

To illustrate such complexities, some issues involved in promoting human dignity will be reviewed. Conceptions of human dignity are important in shaping and planning what we say and do and in assessing what has been said and done; and, its complexity notwithstanding, I believe promoting human dignity is an important, if not the most important, educational goal. Having said that, what does it mean? Alternative conceptions of human dignity not only require interpretation and invite criticism; they are also ambiguous and contradictory. The resulting indeterminacy produces additional readings, interpretations, and criticisms. Harold Lasswell and Abraham Kaplan (1950) define human dignity as the satisfaction of eight human needs: power (participating in decision making), enlightenment (acquiring insight, knowledge, information), wealth (obtaining income and property), well-being (maintaining health, safety, security), skill (developing abilities to perform tasks), affection (giving and receiving love, friendship, solidarity), respect (attaining status, reputation), and rectitude (abiding by ethical or religious standards). These needs are interrelated, and pursuing human dignity involves continually making judgments about which of them are to be traded off and balanced against each other, since there is no prior reason to believe any two can be maximized at the same time, much less eight. If a decision criterion other than value maximization is used it likewise will require justification and application.

Another contemporary approach to human dignity focuses on justice and the design of social institutions. In updating thinking about the social contract, Rawls (1971) argues that individuals would rationally choose and agree on two principles of justice if everyone chose from an original position of self- and social ignorance. Rationality is thereby given a particularly interesting construction. One can be rational in a comprehensive and not self-interested sense only if factors that drive self-interest are excluded from calculation and choice. To achieve this, he asks us to imagine an original, foundational position from which people would choose principles of justice. A veil of ignorance characterizes this original position. The veil of ignorance excludes all forms of self- and social knowledge. This makes it "impossible to tailor principles [of justice] to the circumstances of one's own case" (1971, p. 18). It rules out knowledge of inclinations, aspirations, wealth, gender, skills, intelligence, and ethnicity, for example. Depriving everyone of this information produces an equality strikingly reminiscent of Habermas's ideal speech situation. Rawls writes:

> It seems reasonable that the parties in the original position are equal. That is, all have the same rights in the procedure for choosing principles; each can make proposals, submit reasons for their acceptance, and so on. Obviously the purpose of these conditions is to represent equality between human beings as moral persons, as creatures having a conception of their good and capable of a sense of justice. (1971, p. 19)

Given this version of an "ideal speech situation," Rawls argues that individuals would choose and thereby agree on the two following principles of justice: (1) "each person is to have an equal right to the most extensive basic liberty compatible with a similar liberty for others" (1971, p. 60) and (2) "social and economic inequalities are to be arranged so that they are . . . (a) reasonably expected to be to everyone's advantage, and (b) attached to positions and offices open to all" (1971, p. 60). Rawls's conception of human dignity is a variation on a familiar theme. Instead of imagining oneself in the place of another, one imagines oneself in some disembodied form with no information about one's person or place in society, while retaining the faculty of reason.

Raymond Geuss draws the following parallel between Rawls and Habermas (one can presume):

> The notion that social institutions should be based on the free consent of those affected is a rather recent Western invention, but one which is now widely held. The notions that an action is morally acceptable or a belief "true" if they would be the object of universal consensus under ideal conditions is an even more recent invention held perhaps by a couple of professional philosophers in Germany and the United States. (1981, pp. 66–67)

Rawls and Habermas articulate enlightenment and democratic ideals about human dignity. But if human dignity depends upon justice that requires consensus that can only be arrived at under ideal counterfactual conditions, in Rawls's case the original position and in Habermas's the ideal speech situation, disruptive disagreements should be expected. They could be about: What would people *really choose*? How would choices be *implemented*? How would choices be *interpreted*? Do the chosen social structures represent *correct interpretations*? Dispersal and deferral of the meaning of human dignity and justice result. The meaning of human dignity will be continually negotiated, renegotiated, applied, and changed. Its meaning will continually experience constructions and deconstructions that reflect historical and social conditions.

Daniel Bell builds upon the work of Rawls and others:

> We must insist on a basic social equality in that each person is to be given respect and not humiliated on the basis of color, or sexual proclivities, or other personal attributes. . . . We should reduce invidious distinctions in work, whereby some persons are paid by the piece or the hour and others receive a salary by the month or year. . . . We should assert that each person is entitled to a basic set of services and income which provides . . . adequate medical care, housing, and the like. . . . But one need not impose a rigid, ideological egalitarianism in all matters, if it

results in conflict with other social objectives and even becomes self-defeating. (1977, p. 627)

Bell anticipates criticism, deconstruction, and rejection of public policies embodying these ideas because any social arrangement judged fair and equitable at one time is a likely candidate for being judged unfair and inequitable at a later time.

Giroux's work, drawing from critical theory, sees emancipation from social oppression as central to human dignity and solidarity (the inner tensions in this view are discussed in the previous section on criticism). He advocates "struggle in the interest of self-emancipation and social emancipation" (1983a, p. 109) and "democratic practices, critical citizenship, and the role of the teacher as intellectual" (Giroux & McLaren, 1986, p. 215). Oppressive social relations deny human dignity and are not directly addressed in some of the positions mentioned above. His work highlights contradictory effects of schooling: schooling allied with oppressive discourses-practices contributes to loss of dignity; yet schooling can expose damaging beliefs and practices, thereby freeing individuals from frustrating social conditions and enhancing their dignity. Human dignity, in this reading, involves community and struggle.

These writers approach human dignity differently, yet in places they are complementary. There is little doubt, as well, that there are points of sharp disagreement. Disagreements are likely to flare up when statements of principle are interpreted and acted upon. Reading and interpreting theories of human dignity recall elements of reception theory (Chapter 4). When individuals read and provide accounts of human dignity, they are likely to highlight, suppress, and fill in textual gaps differently. One person's "rigid, ideological egalitarianism" is another's "fair and just society." Variation extends across time as well as across people. Interpretations, criticisms, or practices that I consider valid and beneficial today I might well decide are specious, flawed, and malevolent tomorrow. Educational discourses-practices result from "common," "agreed-upon," "dominant," "consensual," and "traditional" readings of human dignity, social equity, authoritative knowledge, social justice, literacy, democracy, cognitive skills, equal opportunity, and excellence that are subject to continual revision.

Human dignity can be promoted by attempts to be rational, orderly, organized, and emancipatory, but if we are to gain more control over our discourses-practices, human dignity should be treated as a regulative principle, guideline, and ideal. Any single interpretation of human dignity should not be treated as a definitive, transcendental, critical standard. We should guard against arguments that push in the direction of final solutions. Rorty is worth quoting at length on this issue:

> There is nothing wrong with liberal democracy, nor with the philoso-
> phers who have tried to enlarge its scope. There is only something
> wrong with the attempt to see their efforts as failures to achieve some-
> thing which they were not trying to achieve—a demonstration of the
> "objective" superiority of our way of life over all other alternatives. There
> is in short, nothing wrong with the hopes of the Enlightenment, the
> hopes [human dignity, community] which created the Western democra-
> cies. The value of the Enlightenment is, for us pragmatists, just the value
> of some of the institutions and practices which they have created. (1985,
> p. 16)

Efforts to enhance human dignity are bound up with Enlightenment hopes, liberal democratic values, and material and mental wel-
fare. They include providing for public health, aid to the indigent,
freedom of expression, legal due process, public education, universal
suffrage, mass and critical literacy, representative government, equal
educational opportunity, personal security, and protection of the rights
of minorities and the handicapped. These ideas and the practices
based upon them are not transcendental. They are inspired and materially produced by texts that have been projected onto the world in the
form of institutions, practices, and policies. Competing conceptions
of human dignity are continually judged against each other, and their
ambiguities and contradictions in turn enrich their further assessment
and development.

The comparisons of our evaluations and judgments are made
against standards *we* constitute. Rorty quotes, then comments upon, a
dramatic statement by Jean-Paul Sartre arguing this point:

> Tomorrow, after my death, certain people may decide to establish fas-
> cism, and the others may be cowardly or miserable enough to let them
> get away with it. At that moment fascism will be the truth of man, and so
> much the worse for us. In reality, things will be as much as man has
> decided they are. (Sartre, 1946, pp. 53–54)

> This hard saying brings out what ties Dewey and Foucault, James and
> Nietzsche, together—the sense that there is nothing deep down inside us
> except what we have put there ourselves, no criterion that we have not
> created in the course of creating a practice, no standard of rationality that

is not an appeal to such a criterion, no rigorous argumentation that is not
obedience to our own conventions. (Rorty, 1982, p. xlii)

Our decisions are made in terms of what *we* find persuasive. They are
made against standards and practices we have inherited and those we
have attempted to construct.

History and the effects and exercise of power cannot be excluded
from evaluations and judgments. Rawls and Habermas attempt to
deal with this issue when, respectively, they describe the original
position and ideal speech situation. Foucault seems not to be optimistic, to say the least, about dealing with power in our practices, because the anonymous exercise of power tends to reinforce its effects
(Chapter 5). But its exercise can sometimes be deployed in a struggle,
often more guerrilla warfare than open combat, to shape things differently in order to further the human dignity of everyone (whatever we
decide that means).

PRAGMATISM, FACTUAL COMPATIBILITY, AND RELATIVISM

Structural, instrumental, and utilitarian thought characterize the
educational texts and discourses-practices analyzed in preceding
chapters: the production and consumption of textbooks, relationships
among researcher-theorists and practitioners, relationships between
authoritative knowledge and practical knowledge, inferences about
theoretical constructs and research measurements, and the theory
and practice of curriculum. Social determinism is often unwittingly
embraced and social reproduction uncritically fostered when texts and
discourses-practices are approached with an eye to becoming expert
and facile in them. Poststructural analysis points beyond structure,
utility, and instrumentality. Our ability to shape and design the social
world can be enhanced, I hope, if we outline, examine, analyze, interpret, criticize, and evaluate the texts and discourses-practices that
surround us. This is a pragmatic undertaking and, for better or worse,
is as ambiguous and loosely conceived as pragmatism is as a school of
thought.

Pragmatism dominated philosophy in the United States from 1870
to 1920, yet it is not entirely clear what it is as a school of thought,
then or now (this ambiguity bears some resemblance to poststructural
thought) (Thayer, 1981). In a review of American pragmatism, Peter
Skagestad writes: "Little is gained, I think, by setting out . . . a definition of the word "pragmatism." Any formula which would be ac-

ceptable to all the major pragmatists would necessarily carry vagueness to an extreme" (1983, p. 364). Quine, a self-acknowledged pragmatist of sorts,[3] supports this: "It is not clear to me what it takes to be a pragmatist" (1981, p. 23). Regardless of the ambiguity that surrounds pragmatism, a number of points about it are worth making. Rochberg-Halton expresses a sense of pragmatism in the following:

> Pragmatism involves a conception of a critical public, free inquiry and communication, the growth of the imagination, and the embodiment of purposeful habits of conduct as essential not only to the realization of inquiry but to the ultimate goals of life as well. With its claim that all knowledge is inescapably fallible, it radically opposes the fundamentalist tendencies of this age of abstraction toward final solutions. (1986, p. 18)

It represents an orientation to thought and action, to discourse and practice that seeks to merge and synthesize different elements of our social world and ourselves rather than to fragment, dissect, and propose fundamental and lasting "solutions."

There are different ways of pragmatically going about things. One way is a vulgar pragmatism, introduced earlier in this chapter; roughly, it holds that a conception is to be tested by its practical effects. In this view, existing practices and institutions are accepted and become the standard. What is true and valued is what works in terms of what exists. This is another face of instrumentalism in pursuit of production and efficiency. Many reject this, as do I. This form of pragmatism is unreflective and dangerous, to reinvoke Foucault's warning about ideas and social practices. Ernest Gellner argues that pragmatism (that which I call *vulgar pragmatism*) is unjustifiably cheerful and opposed to a sense of crisis, where crisis calls "for a reevaluation of the very criteria of what is to count as a solution, for an overall reassessment of all the criteria of solutions themselves" (1981, p. 44). Gellner develops this theme in the following passage:

> It seems to me that [vulgar] pragmatism is indefensible, because radical cataclysms do occur. When they do, cheerfulness, in the sense defined— a happy reliance on the existing stock of tools and ideas, without any effort at a prior philosophy—simply is not a workable strategy. The pragmatist illusion that it *is* viable springs from an unacknowledged—and indeed unconscious—reliance on previous and successful efforts by "prior philosophers" to clear the ground in such crises, and *it is unwittingly parasitic on them.* (1981, p. 61; emphasis added)

Vulgar pragmatism is cheerfully parasitic on unexamined as well as examined texts and discourses-practices, even though nothing ever *seems* to remain unexamined. Vulgar pragmatism tests ideas and practices by comparing them to traditional and conventional norms with little or no sense of crisis or criticism. Vulgar pragmatists, to draw upon Eco one more time, promote local ideologies as global and past ideologies as those of the present and future. Such pragmatic attitudes are implicit in Tyler's rationale and explicit in Schwab's "The Practical 4" (see Chapters 2 and 3). However, reform proposals, educational and otherwise, often take structural and instrumental tacks, because reformers are uneasy with criticism that is not normalized, paradigmatic, or technical. Poststructural analysis and criticism break with vulgar pragmatism and the functionalist imperative described by Gellner.

Critical pragmatism draws, perhaps not too surprisingly, from a diverse intellectual heritage. A few ideas that contribute to critical pragmatism will be sketched. Rorty captures its spirit:

> The burden of my argument so far has been that if we get rid of traditional notions of "objectivity" and "scientific method" *we shall be able to see the social sciences as continuous with literature*—as interpreting other people to us, and thus enlarging and deepening our sense of community. (1983, p. 203; emphasis added)

Critical pragmatism continually involves making epistemological, ethical, and aesthetic choices (not necessarily in serial order or this order) and translating them into discourses-practices. Criticisms and judgments about good and bad, beautiful and ugly, and truth (small *t*) and falsity are made in the context of our communities and our attempts to build them anew. They are not decided by reference to universal norms that produce "definitive" and "objective" decisions.

Rorty identifies two broad paths along which we can proceed:

> One can emphasize, as Dewey did, the moral importance of the social sciences—their role in widening and deepening our sense of community and of the possibilities open to this community. Or one can emphasize, as Michel Foucault does, the way in which the social sciences have served as instrument of "the disciplinary society," the connection between knowledge and power rather than that between knowledge and human solidarity. (1983, pp. 203–4)

Think of these paths not as heading off in different directions but as criss-crossing in irregular and unexpected ways. They are not mutually exclusive. Furthermore, attending to Foucault's warning may be required for the success of Dewey's project.

Rorty groups William James with Dewey and Friedrich Nietzsche with Foucault. And he notes that Dewey and Foucault make similar criticisms of traditional notions of rationality, objectivity, method, and truth (1983, p. 204). Dewey is more optimistic than Foucault, no doubt about this; and Dewey focuses on democracy, freedom, and progress, whereas Foucault offers little in the way of a progressive politics. Rorty closes out his discussion of these two thinkers by telling us to follow Dewey's optimism, even though he is unsure about what Dewey offers beyond optimism. "Although Foucault and Dewey are trying to do the same thing, Dewey seems to me to have done it better, simply because his vocabulary allows room for *unjustifiable* hope, and an *ungroundable* but vital sense of human solidarity" (1983, p. 208; emphasis added). Critical pragmatism does not compare beliefs against traditional standards or something "objective" in order to produce rigorous decisions about positive knowledge or morally superior practice.

Pragmatism, critical or otherwise, must deal with two important questions: (1) Can factual research findings be incompatible? Put the other way around, if factual research findings are produced against different backgrounds, contexts, and interests, can their results be compatible? (2) Does pragmatism produce an unrelieved relativism? First, consider the question of factual compatibility in terms of Strawson on facts: "Facts are what statements (when true) state, they are not what statements are about" (1964, p. 38). Facts are linguistic; they are not objects. For our purposes, think of truth as unconstrained consensus about what is the case, as described by Habermas. Several important results follow. One set of results leads us to expect divergence among factual statements about the same phenomena. Suppe elaborates:

> To the extent that languages differ in what they are able to express, it follows . . . that languages differ in the facts they can assert. . . . To the extent that conceptual differences are reflected in language, it follows . . . that one's conceptual apparatus may limit the facts one can entertain . . . it follows . . . that differences in one's knowledge and beliefs affect the facts one can observe to be the case. (Suppe, 1977, p. 209)

In this view, facts are relative to language and language is relative to time and place. A second set of results from Strawson's approach to facts, however, leads us to expect compatibility, if not convergence, among factual statements:

> If it is assumed that all scientists are dealing with a common world and that an empirical proposition is empirically true if and only if it correctly describes that world, then it follows . . . that there cannot be incompatible facts; hence, no matter how different two persons are linguistically or conceptually, no matter how much their knowledge and beliefs differ, whatever facts they determine must be compatible. (Suppe, 1977, p. 209)

This answers or deflects much criticism that could be directed at critical pragmatism. Research findings, to the extent they are factual, are compatible. This means that factual systematic quantitative, interpretative, critical, or interpretive-analytic research findings (see Chapter 6), even though they might give the appearance of contradiction and (seemingly?) point in different directions, must be compatible. By focusing on the text of factual assertions, deconstructive analysis argues that often there is less and more to "facts" than structural or positivist readings would have us believe (this fuzzes up Suppe's characterization of truth a bit).

This places a strict qualification on what are called "crucial experiments" (Stinchcombe, 1968, Chapter 1). Research can provide information that operates as "decisive" in choosing among alternative theories or explanations *if* the theories or explanations make different predictions for a specific event, observation, or measurement. If, however, a quantitative researcher is interested in differential effects of instructional wait time and an interpretative researcher in how students gain the "floor" in classroom interactions, they may offer quite *different* yet *factual* accounts of the same classroom events. It remains to us, then, to choose which fact or combination of facts we will assume as a basis for our discourses and practices. These choices are made continually and, as with other choices, cannot be made without reference to *values and commitments* about which aspects of classroom interaction are important (facts, as discussed in earlier chapters, can be stated only after value judgments have been made about which phenomena are important to observe). The choices are pragmatic. They should be critical instead of vulgar. Values and preferences do not arise out of thin air, however; they are, among other things, effects of power and history. We choose and can make critical choices, but nevertheless we are bounced around and buffeted by the texts and discourses-practices of our time, which operate to tell us what is factual and what is not and then which facts are more important than other facts.

This may be unsettling in a society and profession that prizes empiricism. Suddenly it becomes clear that we never pull together "the" facts, because we are always pulling together "our" facts. Furthermore, gathering "our" facts is never *just* a technical and empirical matter, because practical (political, ethical, moral) and aesthetic dimensions are also involved, even though many professional discourses-practices go to great lengths either to run away from or hide the latter two. Because power, norms, commitments, and ideology operate through texts and discourses-practices, often almost invisibly, the practical and aesthetic dimensions of factual choices also approach invisibility. Given alternative factual descriptions, each of which is true (small *t*), *we choose*, unless we delegate these choices to textual and discursive-practical experts, which facts promote our best visions of ourselves, our communities, and the world. These are our choices, and if we let others make them for us, experts or not, that too is our decision.

One further point must be made, lest there be confusion on a related issue. Sets of methodological rules and guidelines are available for each type of research: systematic guidelines exist for quantitative, interpretative, critical, interpretive-analytic, and, yes, even deconstructive readings of research findings. These points of methodology identify and constrain what we, more or less communally, accept as factual and reject as nonfactual. Sometimes these rules come into direct conflict with each other, but more often they simply point in different directions. We choose the direction in which we wish to go (preferably it is somewhere between a rigid walk down a walled-off corridor and a random walk), and then, while we move along in a given direction for a time, the methodological rules and guidelines for that terrain tell us, in general and sometimes shifting ways, what to accept as factual or reject as nonfactual. And, as any accomplished researcher knows, these rules and guidelines change over time, although usually not very quickly. This is far from saying that we can choose whatever we wish to be a fact, because what qualifies as a fact is constrained both by the world and by a community of inquirers. Establishing boundaries around these methodological specialties legislates what counts as a fact. Policing some methodological rules to the exclusion of other sets of rules is a political as well as scientific activity and exposes the political as well as scientific commitments of the police. Critical pragmatism, on the other hand, would have us critically examine the commitments (normative, aesthetic, and political, in addition to scientific and technical) of these methodologies as well as the facts they produce.

Pragmatism must also answer to charges of relativism. A straight-

forward, simplistic relativism—"every belief is as good as any other,"
(Rorty, 1985, p. 5)—is, of course, self-refuting; if this statement is true,
then there is no reason to accept it as a guiding principle, since it is no
better than any other one. Unless some beliefs are better than others,
the arguments advanced in this book have no greater credibility than
those they attack (if I believed that, I would have saved myself a lot of
time and effort). Critical pragmatists reject this simplistic relativism
because it precludes judgments about how things could become better or worse, undercutting any sense of crisis itself. Along this line
and somewhat paradoxically, poststructural thought is not possible
without structural and analytic arguments that propose standards
that distinguish valid from invalid arguments, even though these
standards themselves are never unambiguously foundational.

A pragmatic view of knowledge and criticism that is sometimes
called relativistic is that "there is nothing to be said about either truth
or rationality apart from descriptions of the familiar procedures of
justification which a given society—*ours*—uses in one or another area
of inquiry" (Rorty, 1985, p. 6). This captures much of the Foucaldian
position. Bernstein puts it a bit differently:

> The basic conviction that when we turn to the examination of those
> concepts that philosophers have taken to be the most fundamental—
> whether it is the concept of rationality, truth, reality, right, the good, or
> norms—we are forced to recognize that in the final analysis all such
> concepts must be understood as relative to a specific conceptual scheme,
> theoretical framework, paradigm, form of life, society, or culture. (1983,
> p. 8)

Rorty (1985) calls this ethnocentric relativism and then asks why it
should be called relativistic at all. This is his argument:

> The pragmatist is not holding a positive theory which says that some-
> thing is relative to something else. He is, instead, making the purely
> *negative* point that we should drop the traditional distinction between
> . . . truth as correspondence to reality and truth as a commendatory
> term for well-justified beliefs. . . . As a partisan of solidarity, his account
> of the value of cooperative human inquiry has only an ethical base, not
> an epistemological or metaphysical one. (1985, p. 6)

On these terms a pragmatist like Rorty can be accused of ethnocentrism but not relativism.

Putnam (1983) charges, however, that Rorty's ethnocentrism is
culturally relativistic—no argument here—and that cultural relativism
turns into cultural imperialism. Putnam points out that if one's society

(Rorty prefers the liberalism of the North Atlantic community) determines "objective" standards of truth, then that society becomes the basis for evaluating other societies. Cultural relativism might, as Putnam argues, turn into cultural imperialism, but Putnam himself ends up not far away when he admits that we inherit versions and interpretations of the world (see epigraph to this chapter) and on that basis make decisions about what is good, true, and beautiful. He writes: "On this view (mine), then, "truth" (idealized justification) is as vague, interest relative, and context sensitive as *we* are" (Putnam, 1983, p. xvii). His idealized justification or idealized warranted assertibility

> *is* a kind of realism, and I mean it to be a *human* kind of realism, a belief that there is a fact of the matter as to what is rightly assertible for us, as opposed to what is rightly assertible from the God's eye view so dear to the classical metaphysical realist. (Putnam, 1983, p. xviii)

This idealized justification turns out to be realism *and* relativism.

> There are two points that must be *balanced*, both points that have been made by philosophers of many different kinds: (1) talk of what is "right" and "wrong" in any area only makes sense against the background of an *inherited tradition*; but (2) traditions themselves can be *criticized*. (Putnam, 1983, p. 234)

I agree. This is what I call critical pragmatism.

There are other responses to charges of relativism. Consider what is required for a text or discourse-practice to be nonrelative. Nonrelativistic discourses-practices require a nondeconstructible grounding idea or concept. Unless some system of thought or program transcends time and place, the charge that critical pragmatism or poststructural analysis and criticism are relativistic is empty, because every other system of thought will likewise be relative to changing situation and circumstance. It may be comforting to think of centers, grounds, and foundations for what we say and do, but that is not the same as establishing those centers, grounds, and foundations; this is a case in which it is easier said than done.

Pursuing this line of argument in the context of education, let us *assume* the existence of foundational principles denied above, let us *grant* principles that neither derive from localized power arrangements nor deconstruct. In order for these principles to be applied and become operative, however, they must be read and interpreted. For example, in order to follow the Bloom et al. taxonomy, one must read or at least be aware of it and interpret its story or stories. To simplify further, imagine the authors of the taxonomy telling us, to the best of their ability, their intentions and *exactly* how they believe the taxonomy should be read, interpreted, and applied. *But these statements of intention and application, yet another text, still require interpretation themselves.* Interpretations and thematic links change as individuals and situations change. Intentions and applications are relative to situations, unless, of course, one hypothesizes an absolutist position that admits *no* exceptions and embraces legalistic, technical enforcement. But new situations continue to arise. A legalistic rulebook to cover all past situations and new situations as they occur would be a large book indeed. Furthermore, it would be impossible to write unless one knew the future, and whether one knows the future is an empirical question whose answer must be deferred. In any case, new rules for new situations remain *relative* to them and must be interpreted.

Relativism is an issue for structuralists because they propose structures that set standards. Relativism is an issue if a foundational structure *exists* that is ignored in favor of expediency, leisure, profit, career advancement, recreation, or exploitation. A Derridean might argue, however, that the issue is one of *differance*, where meanings are dispersed and deferred. If dispersion and deferral are the order of the day, what is relative under structuralism is differance under deconstruction. If there is a foundation, there is something to be relative to; but if there is no foundation, there is no structure against which other positions can be "objectively" judged. If, to the contrary, it is shown that meanings can be judged against unchanging, nondeconstructible structures or foundations or first principles or presence or identity, then poststructural arguments will be undermined. Another way to think of this is that logical positivists set out to write a metanarrative of positive knowledge in order, at least, to recognize what it means to "speak correctly about the world." They failed. Critical pragmatism and poststructural thought will be shown to be relativistic if and when this failed project or another one with a similar goal is successfully completed.

Poststructural analysis and criticism contribute interpretation, criticism, and evaluation to a pragmatism that possesses a sense of crisis. We are as much a product of time and place as are the texts and discourses-practices around us. We make decisions about beliefs and actions against this background. A vulgar and naive pragmatism, functionally reproducing things for good or ill, plays itself out if we remain uncritical and unreflective and attend only to what is "practical." Critical pragmatism is realistic because it begins with what is in place. Critical pragmatism is relativistic because it is relative to what is in place.

CONCLUSION

Professions are constituted by what is said and done in their name and through which the effects and exercise of power operate. Criticism offers opportunities to expose the benevolent and constructive operations of power as well as those that are malevolent and destructive. In many ways, some of which have been discussed earlier, contemporary education is constructed on outmoded and dangerous structural, utilitarian, and instrumental assumptions. They are outmoded because they make rhetorical claims for textbooks, teaching, research, and practice that their logic subverts. They are dangerous because they rhetorically promise foundational, final, and efficient answers about which their logic is silent. They dehumanize by demanding that we adjust to structures imposed upon us while remaining silent about the exercise of power within those structures. Basing educational discourses-practices on unacknowledged and unqualified structural principles that bring with them functional and instrumental imperatives invites disillusion and defeat. These privileged structures, however, can be identified, read, interpreted, criticized, talked and written about, accepted, rejected, modified. If we can be critically pragmatic in the construction, deconstruction, construction . . . of how we live and together build communities using our best visions of what is beautiful, good, and true, then the unreflective reproduction of what we find around us, including some of its injustices, might be tamed and changed a bit.

> *First thesis:* We know a great deal. And we know not only many details of doubtful intellectual interest but also things which are of considerable practical significance and, what is even more important, which provide us with deep theoretical insight, and with a surprising understanding of the world.
> *Second thesis:* Our ignorance is sobering and boundless. Indeed, it is precisely the staggering progress of the natural sciences (to which my first thesis alludes) which constantly opens our eyes anew to our ignorance, even in the field of the natural sciences themselves. This gives a new twist to the Socratic idea of ignorance. . . . We also discover that where we believed that we were standing on firm and safe ground, all things, are in truth, insecure and in a state of flux. . . .
> *Third thesis:* It is a fundamentally important task for every theory of

knowledge, and perhaps even a crucial requirement, to do justice to our first two theses by clarifying the relations between our remarkable and constantly increasing knowledge and our constantly increasing insight that we really know nothing. (Popper, 1976, pp. 87–88)

Any discipline worthy of the name must offer its reasons for saying and doing what it does, reasons which will be deemed valid or invalid, embraced or rejected, only according to the norms of the historical community within which they are offered, and not according to those of some utopian order of ultimate rationality or imminent socialism. This counsel of liberal scepticism—some would call it pragmatism—may not enable us to avoid the gross, obvious errors of interpretive subjectivity and cultural ideology that have beset criticism, as its historical condition, from the beginning. But what counsel for criticism could do that? (Felperin, 1985, p. 222)

NOTES

REFERENCES

INDEX

ABOUT THE AUTHOR

Notes

CHAPTER 1

1. Power is a concept that has had little currency in North American social science since the mid-1960s. A few comments on why this is so and why power has a central place in this argument are in order. Political science is the discipline that was most concerned with the concept of power, and power has had a central place in modern political thought from Machiavelli through Hobbes and Locke and into the middle of the twentieth century. In *An Essay Concerning Human Understanding*, Locke refers to power primarily as a relational concept, "powers are relations, not agents" (Book II, chapter 21), and power as a relational concept is retained to the present. Friedrich (1963, p. 159ff) expands on this in pointing out that power is to some extent a possession and to some extent a relation because power is often applied to institutionalized power relationships. Lasswell and Kaplan support Friedrich in stating, "Power is here defined relationally, not as a simple property" (1950, p. 75), and their formal definition captures a sense of power often found in the literature: "*Power* is participation in the making of decisions: G has power over H with respect to the values K if G participates in the making of decisions affecting the K-policies of H" (p. 75). Dahl builds upon this idea with his intuitive sense of power: "A has power over B to the extent that he can get B to do something that B would not otherwise do" (1961, p. 344). Pursuing this analytic exercise, the power that Dahl expresses in terms of base, means, amount, and scope (1961, p. 345) is described by Lasswell and Kaplan in terms of domain, scope, weight, and coerciveness (1950, p. 74).

Simon (1961) builds upon Lasswell and Kaplan in looking at the exercise of power as an "influence process," and "this definition involves an asymmetrical relation between influencer and influencee" (1961, pp. 365–66). He adds that a social structure is a system of asymmetrical and dynamic relationships. In concluding his discussion Simon anticipates that power is likely to be a troublesome concept for social researchers:

> The phenomenon (power and influence) we wish to measure is an asymmetrical relation between the behavior of two persons. We wish to ob-

serve how a change in the behavior of one (the influencer) alters the behavior of the other (the influencee).

We have seen that in most situations, all sorts of reciprocal power relations are present, and that their observation is complicated by the anticipation of reactions. The more accurate the predictions of participants in the system of the reactions of others, the more difficult it becomes to observe influence. *Our main hope must be that human beings will remain fallible in their predictions.* (1961, p. 375; emphasis added)

Put differently, power becomes less visible and tractable in research as social systems become more integrated. *Social integration* here is used in the sense that individuals have a great deal of knowledge about their social practices, accept them, and seek to fit into and abide by them. This is precisely the situation with well-developed professions and social practices such as those that constitute contemporary education. Simon does not argue that power and influence are not present in such professions and practices, it is just that they cannot easily be observed.

Dahl, Simon, and March (1966) were interested in defining power so that it could be used empirically in behavioral research. Some attempts were successful. Shapley and Shubik (1961) devised a method for measuring power in a committee system and Dahl (1961), for estimating power in the U. S. Senate. These were qualified successes at best. March, in a provocatively titled essay, "The Power of Power," argues persuasively that, based on an evaluation of six decision-making models, power was of little theoretical or empirical significance. He summarizes as follows:

> The class of social-choice situations in which power is a significantly useful concept is much smaller than I previously believed. . . . Although *power* and *influence* are useful concepts for many kinds of situations, they have not greatly helped us to understand many of the natural social-choice mechanisms to which they have traditionally been applied. (1966, p. 68)

After the mid-1960s, the study of politics proceeded with the concepts of power and influence relegated to the margins of research and theory, a curious and surprising result.

Putting this in some perspective, Dahl, March, and Simon approached social research and theory in a tradition dominated by logical positivism and empiricism. They were concerned with reducing the measurement of power to one-on-one situations, developing predictive models, and elaborating deductive explanations. It turns out that the methodological individualism of the first goal is overly restrictive and leaves out factors such as the group-related properties of culture, morale, and ideology; traditional uses of metaphor; linguistic meanings; and consideration of alternative forms of explanation and modes of discourse—in short, exclusive focus on the individual ignores the contextual opportunities and constraints that structure individual choices and actions. Furthermore, methodological individualism lacks a metatheory that justifies accepting subjective preferences and existing conditions as the *beginning* or *origin* of meaningful social behavior. May Brodbeck cogently argues:

> Sometimes the phrase "methodological individualism" is applied . . . to the view that the laws of the group sciences are in principle reducible to those about individuals . . . [but this] is a matter of fact. And matters of fact cannot be legislated into existence. In other words, the empiricist commitment to *definitional* methodological individualism does not logically imply a commitment to *explanatory* methodological individualism, that is, to reduction. (1968, pp. 301–2)

Valid natural-language, deductive explanations and the role of prediction in social theory, the second and third goals, have subsequently been shown to be problematic at best. (See Quine, 1953, for a critique of the first and Scheffler, 1960, for an analysis of the second.) It turns out that the criteria by which the concept of power was found wanting are flawed themselves. In any case, these political theorists never argued that power and influence were not important. They simply could not develop theoretical and operational ideas about power satisfactory to a view of science consistent with logical positivism and empiricism. Logical positivism and empiricism have since been discarded, and there are many reasons, I submit, to take another look at power and its effects, especially in the context of contemporary education. I agree with Simon that the more integrated the social system, the less visible the effects of power. This is also central to the work of the French scholar Michel Foucault, which is discussed in Chapter 3 and several times thereafter. Simon and Foucault agree about the ubiquity of power in social systems. After agreeing on this, however, they go in different directions: (1) Simon rejects the concept of power, and (2) Foucault makes it central to his work. The arguments in this book are set in the latter tradition.

One way to think about this is in the context of microeconomic thought, where it is assumed that individuals have subjective preferences or likes and dislikes that they can, at least, rank order. Given an existing utility function, Simon, along with March and others, argues that power as a concept is of limited use in explaining and predicting individual choices. No disagreement here, and this is largely a result of structuring a view of social science around methodological individualism and individual choice. There is an alternative. Instead of only looking for effects of power on individual choices, one can look for effects of power on the formation of individual preferences. Social, political, and material asymmetries reward and punish and are institutionalized in relationships in social structures. Individuals in those settings adapt to those asymmetries and patterns of reward and punishment, or they are not likely to succeed. I will argue that many options in terms of instruction, the processing of research findings, the validation of theoretical constructs, and approaches to curriculum are excluded from contemporary educational practice and, furthermore, that the asymmetries and inequalities of our institutions and the relationships they foster have a lot to do with this.

2. The term *hegemony* is related to the way I will mention, from time to time, the constitution of subjectivities. Apple summarizes hegemony as "the common-sense meanings and practices that are so deep-seated in people as to appear as the 'only way the world can be,' even though that world may be unequal or repressive" (1981, p. 496). I do not use hegemony in this analysis for two reasons. (1) It would inject neo-Marxist criticism explicitly into the discussion, and that would push the argument in directions I choose not to take at the moment, even though I find much of value in various neo-Marxist analyses. (2) Neo-Marxist criticism can be quite structural and programmatic and is as susceptible to poststructural and deconstructive readings as are mainstream educational texts. Sorting all of this out at this point would unnecessarily burden and complicate what follows.

3. This idea of the recursiveness between individual choices and behavior and social outcomes and stability roughly parallels Giddens's theory of structuration. (See Giddens, 1979, Chapter 2.)

4. Paulo Freire expresses comparable ideas in the following passage:

> Reading is not exhausted merely by decoding written word or written language, but rather anticipated by and extending into knowledge of the world. Reading the world precedes reading the word, and the subsequent reading of the word cannot dispense with continually reading the world. Language and reality are dynamically intertwined. The understanding attained by critical reading of a text implies perceiving the relationship between text and context. (1983, p. 5)

The time ordering of reading the world prior to the word may be difficult to argue, certainly given Wittgenstein's arguments against the possibility of private language. That language is separate from reality, as Freire suggests, is, I think, more literary allusion than intended literally. That reading the world and the word are inseparable, however, is something we both firmly believe.

5. Metanarratives are narratives about narratives. Similarly, "A metalanguage is a language used to talk about another language (called an object language) and to specify the syntax and semantic interpretations of sentences in the object language" (Suppe, 1977, p. 35n). Likewise, "the aim of a metalogic is to develop methods for the appraisal of logical methods" (van Fraassen, 1971, p. 2).

6. For a distinguished treatment of the absence of a final grounding metanarrative, see Quine's "Ontological Relativity" (1969).

CHAPTER 2

1. An exception is Gibson's *Structuralism and Education* (1984), which argues for educators to employ structural approaches in their work.

2. Some of these points are discussed in Piaget, 1971, pp. 1–16.

3. See Seung, 1982, pp. 10–13, for a discussion of binary opposition versus binary distinction.

CHAPTER 3

1. The bodies of thought that are called *structural* and *poststructural* will sometimes be referred to as *structuralism* and *poststructuralism*. *Ism* in this context is a literary device and does *not* refer to a political ideology, although important political as well as educational consequences follow from each position.

2. Interpretive analytics to describe Foucault's work comes from Dreyfus and Rabinow (1983, p. 122). Foucault variously refers to his project as an *archaeology* or *genealogy*, but interpretive analytics moves beyond the static, descriptive implications of either term. Of Foucault's interpretive understanding they write:

> Interpretive understanding can only be obtained by someone who shares the actor's involvement, but distances himself from it. This person must undertake the hard historical work of diagnosing and analyzing the history and organization of current cultural practices. The resulting interpretation is a pragmatically guided reading of the coherence of the practices of society. It does not claim to correspond either to the everyday meanings shared by the actors or, in any simple sense, to reveal the intrinsic meaning of the practices. (1983, p. 124)

History and social practices are read in terms of each other.

CHAPTER 4

1. From time to time I will analyze examples taken from an elementary social studies series of which I was a senior co-author. The criticism should not be read as second guessing or as belated reservation about the quality of the series, because that is not the case. While working on the project, however, I came to appreciate Foucault's characterization of discursive practice in an immediate way. This is not an argument against textbooks. It is not even an argument about textbooks. They are convenient and important to deal with, however, because of their strategic location in American education. I will analyze and comment on the way textbooks treat meaning and meanings and I will do so by referring to work with which I am very familiar.

2. Putnam refers to this idea as follows:

> We teach a child a word, say "table," by showing him the object and by using the word in various ways in the presence of that object (or, rather,

kind of object) until the child comes to "associate the word with the object. . . . (As an ordinary language remark about, say, pedagogy, it is unproblematical; for, in such a context, the notions of an "object" and of "showing someone an object" and of "associating a sound with a kind of object" are all taken for granted, as part of the linguistic background we assume.) (1983, p. viii)

3. These questions are not singled out as particularly exemplary but as illustrative of the different discursive directions to which a text, in this case its questions, can point. Teaching can emphasize structural or poststructural elements at will.

4. Several differences distinguish the approaches to meaning discussed above. Granting that, it remains possible to divide them *roughly* into two groups. By structuralism I will refer to traditional word meaning, linguistic structuralism, truth-conditional semantics, early speech act theory, and institutionally bound speech acts. Poststructuralism will include later speech act theory, Wittgenstein's later work, noninstitutionally bound meanings of Habermas, Foucault's account of discursive practices, Derrida's deconstruction, reception theory, and Eco's semiotics. Grice's pragmatics leans toward the latter while valuing the former. This is not a neat grouping and it breaks down in places, but it makes the argument of the next section more concise and coherent than would otherwise be possible. Understanding some nuances of linguistics and philosophy is useful, but too many nuances sometimes create unnecessary confusion.

CHAPTER 6

1. See Shapiro, 1981, Chapter 1, for an overview of logical positivism as speaking correctly about the world. See Cronbach and Meehl, 1955, p. 290, for references to Braithwaite, Carnap, Feigl, Hempel, and other prominent logical positivists/empiricists.

2. Construct validity might point toward identity between theoretical terms and measurements, but by 1955 explicit definition of theoretical terms had been rejected by philosophers of science. A bit of logical-positivist history makes clear how Cronbach and Meehl took up where original positivist tenets had broken down. Positivism attempted to eliminate metaphysics from science. Suppe puts the positivist position like this:

> Since metaphysical entities are not . . . observational entities, the terms used to describe them cannot be observation terms, and so must be theoretical terms. But, theoretical terms are allowed [into scientific theories] only if they can be provided with correspondence rules which give them explicit phenomenal definition, and so the objectionable metaphysical entities cannot be introduced into scientific theories. (1977, p. 13)

These explicit definitions "are called *correspondence rules* since they coordinate theoretical terms with corresponding combinations of observation terms"

(Suppe, 1977, p. 12). There are two problems with explicit definitions. The first was identified in the 1930s by Carnap (1936, 1937), who, as Suppe notes, pointed out that dispositional terms such as *fragile* or *soluble* or *engaged time* are clearly cognitively significant but cannot be described by explicit definition in observational terms. They can be described, however, under certain test conditions. Explicit definitions and correspondence rules were then replaced by operational definitions in which *"the concept is synonymous with the corresponding set of operations"* (Suppe, 1977, p. 19). Operational definitions create a second problem because more than one experimental procedure can produce measurements of *fragility* or *solubility* or *academic learning time*. Surely a different theoretical term will not be assigned to each measurement: academic learning time *a*, academic learning time *b*, . . . , academic learning time *n*. The result is that identity between theoretical terms and measurements either as explicit definition or correspondence rule or operational definition reduces to *partial definition*. Suppe puts it a bit more formally, "The terms in V_T [theoretical vocabulary] each are given a partial interpretation in terms of V_O [observational vocabulary] by reduction sentences" (p. 23). Cronbach and Meehl reflect these developments by rejecting operationalism when they begin to puzzle out what is involved in construct validity and the role of partial definition in social research.

3. Two years earlier Quine (1953) wrote a devastating critique of empiricism as reductionism. Cronbach and Meehl intelligently avoided such a claim.

4. Rorty (1980) documents the failed attempts to portray knowledge as representation of nature. Cronbach and Meehl were prescient in avoiding this claim, but thoughtful, experienced researchers would not be expected to fall into this trap, at least in its extreme form.

5. The influence of logical positivism extends beyond ultra-operationalism. For example, formal theories in microeconomics or positive theory (a fortuitous name for this field of study) in political science make positivist claims that are quite different from those asserted by ultra-operationalists. In the case of microeconomics or positive political theory, the construct validity problem takes the form of assigning meanings and interpretations to theoretical terms that are defined by each other in uninterpreted formal systems.

6. This general characterization of measurement is repeatedly found in the literature. Nagel wrote the following about measurement more than 50 years ago:

> Measurement has been defined as the correlation with numbers of entities that are not numbers. . . . From . . . [a] larger point of view, measurement can be regarded as the delimitation and fixation of our ideas of things, so that the determination of what it is to be a man or to be a circle is a case of measurement. (1932/1960, p. 121)

Coombs discusses a similar idea in his theory of data:

> An interpretive step on the part of the scientist . . . is required to convert the recorded observations into data . . . a classification of observations

in the sense that individuals and stimuli are identified and labeled. (1967, pp. 4–5)

He continues by noting that conclusions "even at the level of measurement" (p. 5) are a consequence of theory.

Finally, Kerlinger (1973) cites Stevens (1951) and Campbell (1952) in dealing with the foundations of measurement. Stevens writes, "In its broadest sense, measurement is the assignment of numerals to objects or events according to rules" (1951, p. 1), and Campbell notes that measurement is "the assignment of numbers to represent properties" (1952, p. 110). There is a fair amount of agreement on defining measurement. There is a fair amount of disagreement on what measurements mean. Construct validity is concerned with the latter.

7. Ihde (1979) is a very readable introduction to phenomenology, and Schutz (1963) provides more details. Lincoln and Guba (1985) is a distinguished contribution to this literature. Phenomenology is used in a generic sense here. Ethnography, field research, and interpretative research are also included in this category.

8. Thomas McCarthy (1978) has written a thorough and critical introduction to the work of Habermas. He is also Habermas's major translator into English. For Habermas's development of some of the ideas that follow, see Habermas (1984).

9. Concluding a discussion of controversy surrounding mental testing, Cronbach makes this observation along the same lines:

The spokesmen for tests, then [1920s] and recently, were convinced that they were improving social efficiency, not making choices about social philosophy. Their soberly interpreted research did place test interpretation on a more substantial basis. But they did not study the consequences of testing for the social structure—a sociological problem that psychologists do not readily perceive.

The social scientist is trained to think that he does not know all the answers. The social scientist is not trained to realize that he does not know all the questions. And that is why his social influence is not unfailingly constructive. (1975, p. 13)

Bringing Foucault's analysis to bear on this issue: Where do social science questions come from? What historical conjunctions and disjunctions produced our theoretical constructs? What dangers do they pose?

CHAPTER 8

1. Ideas in the following three sections have been developed from Scholes, *Textual Power* (1985, Chapter 2).

2. For approaches to research, see Chapter 6; languages of research and

practice, see Chapter 5; ways of using textbooks, see Chapter 4; and curriculum proposals, see Chapter 7.

3. For example, Quine argues that deciding whether a scientific problem resides in the conceptual scheme of the scientist or is a matter of empirical fact is a constrained yet ultimately pragmatic choice.

> The issue over there being classes [scientific] seems more a question of convenient conceptual scheme; the issue over there being centaurs, or brick houses on Elm Street, seems more a question of fact. But I have been urging that this difference is only one of degree, and that it turns upon our vaguely pragmatic inclination to adjust one strand of the fabric of science rather than another in accommodating some particular recalcitrant experience. Conservatism figures in such choices, and so does the quest for simplicity. (1953, p. 80)

References

Althusser, Louis. *For Marx*. London: Allen Lane, 1969.

Anyon, Jean. "Ideology and United States History Textbooks." *Harvard Educational Review*, 49 (August 1979), 361–86.

———. "Social Class and School Knowledge." *Curriculum Inquiry*, 11 (Spring 1981), 3–42.

Apple, Michael. "On Analyzing Hegemony." In Henry Giroux, Anthony Penna, and William Pinar, eds., *Curriculum and Instruction*, 109–23. Berkeley, CA: McCutchan, 1981.

———. *Education and Power*. London: Routledge and Kegan Paul, 1982.

———. *Teachers and Texts: A Political Economy of Class & Gender Relations in Education*. New York: Routledge and Kegan Paul, 1986.

Austin, J. L. *How To Do Things with Words*. New York: Oxford University Press, 1968.

Ayer, Alfred. *Language, Truth, and Logic*. New York: Dover, 1946.

Barbut, Marc. "On the Meaning of the Word 'Structure' in Mathematics." In Michael Lane, ed., *Structuralism: A Reader*, 367–88. London: Jonathan Cape, 1970.

Barthes, Roland. *Mythologies*. London: Jonathan Cape, 1972.

Bell, Daniel. "On Meritocracy and Equality." In Jerome Karabel and A. H. Halsey, eds., *Power and Ideology in Education*, 607–34. New York: Oxford University Press, 1977.

Benne, Kenneth. "Authority in Education." *Harvard Educational Review*, 40 (August 1970), 385–410.

Benveniste, Emile. *Problems in General Linguistics*. Miami, FL: The University of Miami Press, 1971.

Bernstein, Basil. "Social Class, Language, and Socialization." In Jerome Karabel and A. H. Halsey, eds., *Power and Ideology in Education*, 473–86. New York: Oxford University Press, 1977.

Bernstein, Richard. *The Restructuring of Social and Political Theory*. New York: Harcourt Brace Jovanovich, 1976.

———. *Beyond Objectivism and Relativism: Science, Hermeneutics, and Praxis*. Philadelphia: University of Pennsylvania Press, 1983.

———, ed. *Habermas and Modernity*. Cambridge, MA: MIT Press, 1985.

Bloom, Benjamin S., et. al. *Taxonomy of Educational Objectives: Cognitive Domain*. New York: David McKay, 1956.

Borg, Walter. "Time and School Learning." In Carolyn Denham and Ann Lieberman, eds., *Time to Learn*, 33–72. Washington, DC: U.S. Department of Education, 1980.

Borges, George Luis. *A Universal History of Infamy*. Translated by Norman Thomas di Giovanni. New York: Dutton, 1972.

Bourdieu, Pierre. "Cultural Reproduction and Social Reproduction." In Jerome Karabel and A. H. Halsey, eds., *Power and Ideology in Education*, 487–510. Oxford, England: Oxford University Press, 1977.

Bowers, C. A. "Culture Against Itself: Nihilism as an Element in Recent Educational Thought." *American Journal of Education*, 93 (August 1985), 465–90.

Bowles, Samuel. "Unequal Education and the Reproduction of the Social Division of Labor." In Jerome Karabel and A. H. Halsey, eds., *Power and Ideology in Education*, 137–52, New York: Oxford University Press, 1977.

Brewer, Gary, and deLeon, Peter. *The Foundations of Policy Analysis*. Homewood, IL: The Dorsey Press, 1983.

Brodbeck, May. "Methodological Individualisms: Definitions and Reduction." In May Brodbeck, ed., *Readings in the Philosophy of the Social Sciences*, 363–97. New York: Macmillan, 1968.

Bruner, Jerome. *The Process of Education*. Cambridge, MA: Harvard University Press, 1960.

———. "The Process of Education Revisited." *Phi Delta Kappan*, 52 (1971), 18–21.

———. *The Relevance of Education*. New York: Norton, 1973.

Burgess, Anthony. "Let's Talk Nonsense." *The New York Times Book Review* (August 9, 1987), 1, 24–25.

Butler, Christopher. *Interpretation, Deconstruction, and Ideology*. Oxford, England: Clarendon Press, 1984.

Campbell, Donald, and Fiske, Donald. "Convergent and Discriminant Validation by the Multitrait-Multimethod Matrix." *Psychological Bulletin*, 56 (March 1959), 81–105.

Campbell, Donald, and Stanley, Julian. *Experimental and Quasi-Experimental Designs for Research*. Chicago: Rand McNally College Publishing, 1963.

Campbell, Norman. *What is Science?* New York: Dover, 1952.

Carnap, Rudolf. "Testability and Meaning." *Philosophy of Science*, 3 (1936), 420–68.

———. "Testability and Meaning." *Philosophy of Science*, 4 (1937), 1–40.

Cherryholmes, Cleo H. "Social Knowledge and Citizenship Education: Two Views of Truth and Criticism." *Curriculum Inquiry*, 10 (June 1980), 115–41.

———. "Construct Validity and the Discourses of Research." *American Journal of Education* 96 (May 1988).

———. "Discourse and Criticism in the Social Studies Classroom." *Theory and Research in Social Education*, 9 (Winter 1982), 57–73.

———. "An Exploration of Meaning and the Dialogue Between Textbooks and Teaching." *Journal of Curriculum Studies* 20 (January–March 1988), 1–21.

_____. "Knowledge, Power, and Discourse in Social Studies Education." *Journal of Education*, 165 (Fall 1983), 341–58.

_____. "A Social Project for Curriculum: Post-Structural Perspectives." *Journal of Curriculum Studies* 19 (July–August 1987) 295–316.

_____. "Theory and Practice: On the Role of Empirically Based Theory for Critical Practice." *American Journal of Education*, 94 (November 1985), 39–70.

Cherryholmes, Cleo H., Manson, Gary, et. al. *McGraw-Hill Social Studies: Kindergarten Through Grade Six*. New York: McGraw-Hill, 1979.

Clark, C. M., and Florio, S., with Elmore, J. L., Martin, J., Maxwell, R. J., and Metheny, W. *Understanding Writing in School: A Descriptive Study of Writing and Its Instruction in Two Classrooms*. Final Report of the Written Literacy Study (Grant No. 90840) funded by the National Institute of Education, U.S. Department of Education. East Lansing, MI: Institute for Research on Teaching, Michigan State University, 1981.

Cohen, David, K., and Garet, Michael. "Reforming Educational Policy with Applied Social Research." *Harvard Educational Review*, 45 (February 1975), 17–42.

Cook, Thomas, and Campbell, Donald. *Quasi-Experimentation: Design and Analysis Issues for Field Settings*. Boston: Houghton Mifflin, 1979.

Coombs, Clyde. *A Theory of Data*. New York: Wiley, 1967.

Cronbach, Lee. "Test Validation." In Robert Thorndike, ed., *Educational Measurement*, 2d ed., 443–507. Washington, DC: American Council on Education, 1971.

_____. "Five Decades of Public Controversy Over Mental Testing." *American Psychologist*, 30 (January 1975), 1–14.

_____. "Five Perspectives on Validity Argument." In H. Wainer and H. Braun, eds., *Test Validity for the 1990s and Beyond*. Hillsdale, NJ: Erlbaum, 1986.

_____. "Construct Validity after Thirty Years." In R. L. Linn, ed., *Intelligence: Measurement, Theory, and Public Policy*. Urbana: University of Illinois Press, 1987.

_____, and Meehl, Paul. "Construct Validity in Psychological Tests." *Psychological Bulletin*, 52 (July 1955), 281–302.

Crosman, Robert. "Do Readers Make Meaning?" In Susan Suleiman and Inge Crossman, eds., *The Reader in the Text: Essays on Audience and Interpretation*, 149–64. Princeton, NJ: Princeton University Press, 1980.

Culler, Jonathan. "The Linguistic Basis of Structuralism." In David Robey, ed., *Structuralism: An Introduction*, 20–36. Oxford, England: Clarendon Press, 1973.

_____. *On Deconstruction: Theory and Criticism After Structuralism*. Ithaca, NY: Cornell University Press, 1984.

Dahl, Robert. "The Concept of Power." In Sidney Ulmer, ed., *Introductory Readings in Political Behavior*, 342–62. Chicago: Rand McNally, 1961.

Davidson, Donald. "Truth and Meaning." In Jay Rosenberg and Charles Travis, eds., *Readings in the Philosophy of Language*, 450–66. Englewood Cliffs, NJ: Prentice-Hall, 1971.

Denham, Carolyn, and Lieberman, Ann, eds. *Time to Learn*. Washington, DC: National Institute of Education, 1980.

Derrida, Jacques. "Discussion: Structure, Sign and Play in the Discourse of the Human Sciences." In Richard Macksey and Eugenio Donato, eds., *The Structuralist Controversy*, 247–72. Baltimore: The Johns Hopkins University Press, 1972.

———. *Positions*. Chicago: The University of Chicago Press, 1981.

———. *Of Grammatology*. Baltimore: The Johns Hopkins Unversity Press, 1982.

Dewey, John. "The Child and the Curriculum." In Arno Bellack and Herbert Kliebard, eds., *Curriculum and Evaluation*, 175–88. Berkeley, CA: McCutchan, 1977. Originally published 1902.

Dreyfus, Hubert L. "Knowledge and Human Values: A Genealogy of Nihilism." *Teachers College Record*, 82 (Spring 1981), 507–20.

Dreyfus, Hubert L., and Rabinow, Paul. *Michel Foucault: Beyond Structuralism and Hermeneutics*. Chicago: The University of Chicago Press, 1983.

Eagleton, Terry. *Criticism and Ideology*. London: Redwood Burn Ltd., 1982.

———. *Literary Theory: An Introduction*. Minneapolis: University of Minnesota Press, 1983.

Eco, Umberto. *Semiotics and the Philosophy of Language*. Bloomington: Indiana University Press, 1984.

Eisner, Eliot. *The Educational Imagination*. New York: Macmillan, 1979.

———. "Anastasia Might Still be Alive, but the Monarchy is Dead." *Educational Researcher*, 12 (1983), 13–24.

Fay, Brian. *Social Theory and Political Practice*. London: George Allen and Unwin, 1977.

Felperin, Howard. *Beyond Deconstruction: The Uses and Abuses of Literary Theory*. Oxford, England: Clarendon Press, 1985.

Finch, Henry Le Roy. *Wittgenstein—the Later Philosophy: An Exposition of the Philosophical Investigations*. Atlantic Highlands, NJ: Humanities Press, 1977.

Fischer, Frank. "Critical Evaluation of Public Policy: A Methodological Case Study." In John Forester, ed., *Critical Theory and Public Life*, 231–57. Cambridge, MA: MIT Press, 1985.

Florio, Susan. "The Written Literacy Forum: An Analysis of Teacher/Researcher Collaboration." Paper read at the 1983 AERA Meetings, Montreal. Mimeographed. East Lansing, MI: College of Education.

Foucault, Michel. *The Archaeology of Knowledge*. New York: Harper Colophon Books, 1972.

———. "History, Discourse, and Discontinuity." *Salmagundi*, No. 20 (Summer–Fall 1973a), 225–48.

———. *The Order of Things*. New York: Vintage Books, 1973b.

———. *Madness and Civilization: A History of Insanity in the Age of Reason*. New York: Vintage Books, 1973c.

———. *The Birth of the Clinic: An Archaeology of Medical Perception*. New York: Vintage Books, 1975.

_____. *Discipline and Punish*. New York: Vintage Books, 1979.

_____. *Power/Knowledge*. New York: Pantheon Books, 1980a.

_____. *Language, Counter-Memory, Practice*. Ithaca, NY: Cornell University Press, 1980b.

_____. *The History of Sexuality*. Vol. 1. New York: Pantheon, 1980c.

_____. "On the Genealogy of Ethics: An Overview of Work in Progress." In Hubert Dreyfus and Paul Rabinow, eds., *Michel Foucault: Beyond Structuralism and Hermeneutics*, 2d ed., 229–52. Chicago: University of Chicago Press, 1983.

_____. "Politics and Ethics: An Interview." In Paul Rabinow, ed., *The Foucault Reader*, 373–79. New York: Pantheon Books, 1984.

Freire, Paulo. "The Importance of the Act of Reading." *Journal of Education*, 156 (Winter 1983), 5–11.

Friedrich, Carl. *Man and His Government*. New York: McGraw-Hill, 1963.

Fukumoto, Elton. "Pragmatism and Critical Theory." Ph.D. dissertation, University of California at Los Angeles, 1984.

Gandy, Robin. "'Structure' in Mathematics." In David Robey, ed., *Structuralism: An Introduction*, Oxford, England: Clarendon Press, 1973.

Gellner, Ernest. "Pragmatism and the Importance of Being Ernest." In Robert Mulvaney and Philip Zeltner, eds., *Pragmatism: Its Sources and Prospects*, 41–66. Columbia: University of South Carolina Press, 1981.

Geuss, Raymond. *The Idea of a Critical Theory: Habermas and the Frankfurt School*. Cambridge, England: Cambridge University Press, 1981.

Gibson, Rex. *Structuralism and Education*. London: Hodder and Stoughton, 1984.

Giddens, Anthony. *Central Problems in Social Theory*. Berkeley: University of California Press, 1979.

_____. "Reason Without Revolution? Habermas's *Theorie des kommunicativen Handelns*." In Richard Bernstein, ed., *Habermas and Modernity*, 95–121. Cambridge, MA: MIT Press, 1985.

Giroux, Henry A. "Toward a New Sociology of Curriculum." *Educational Leadership*, 37 (December 1979), 248–53.

_____. *Theory and Resistance in Education*. Boston: Bergin and Garvey Publishers, 1983a.

_____. "Theories of Reproduction and Resistance in the New Sociology of Education." *Harvard Educational Review*, 53 (1983b), 257–93.

Giroux, Henry, and McLaren, Peter. "Teacher Education and the Politics for Engagement: The Case for Democratic Schooling." *Harvard Educational Review*, 56 (August 1986), 213–38.

Grice, H. P. "Logic and Conversation." In Peter Cole and Jerry Morgan, eds., *Syntax and Semantics*. Vol. 3, *Speech Acts*, 41–58. New York: Academic Press, 1975.

Habermas, Jürqen. "A Postscript to Knowledge and Human Interests." *Philosophy of Social Science*, 3 (1973), 157–89.

_____. *Communication and the Evolution of Society*. Boston: Beacon Press, 1979.

_____. *The Theory of Communicative Action*. Boston: Beacon Press, 1984.

_____. "Questions and Counterquestions." in Richard Bernstein, ed., *Habermas and Modernity*, 192–216. Cambridge, MA: MIT Press, 1985.

Hawkes, Terence. *Structuralism and Semiotics*. Berkeley: University of California Press, 1977.

Hirsch, E. D. *Validity in Interpretation*. New Haven, CT: Yale University Press, 1967.

Holub, Robert C. *Reception Theory: A Critical Introduction*. London: Methuen, 1984.

House, Ernest. "Justice in Evaluation." In Gene V. Glass, ed., *Evaluation Studies Review Annual*, Vol. 1, 75–100. Beverly Hills: Sage Publications, 1976.

Huebner, Dwayne. "The Moribund Curriculum Field: Its Wake and Our Work." *Curriculum Inquiry*, 6 (1976), 153–66.

Hunter, Madeline. *Rx Improved Instruction*. El Segundo, CA: Tip Publications, 1985.

Ihde, Don. *Experimental Phenomenology: An Introduction*. New York: Paragon Books, 1979.

Inglis, Fred. *The Management of Ignorance: A Political Theory of the Curriculum*. New York: Basil Blackwell, 1985.

Iser, Wolfgang. *The Implied Reader*. Baltimore: The Johns Hopkins University Press, 1974.

Jackson, Philip W. "Curriculum and its Discontents." *Curriculum Inquiry*, 10 (1980), 28–43.

Jay, Martin. *The Dialectical Imagination: A History of the Frankfurt School and the Institute of Social Research, 1923–1950*. Boston: Little, Brown and Company, 1973.

Johnson, Mauritz. "Definitions and Models in Curriculum Theory." *Educational Theory*, 17 (Spring 1967), 127–40.

Kaplan, Abraham. *The Conduct of Inquiry*. San Francisco: Chandler, 1964.

Kempson, Ruth M. *Semantic Theory*. New York: Cambridge University Press, 1977.

Kerlinger, Fred N. *Foundations of Behavioral Research*. New York: Holt, Rinehart & Winston, 1973.

Kliebard, Herbert. "The Tyler Rationale." *School Review*, 78 (February 1970), 259–72.

Kuhn, Thomas S. *The Structure of Scientific Revolutions*. 2d ed. Chicago: The University of Chicago Press, 1974.

Lambert, Karl, and Brittan, Gordon. *An Introduction to the Philosophy of Science*. Englewood Cliffs, NJ: Prentice-Hall, 1970.

Lane, Michael. "The Structuralist Method: Structure and Structuralism." In Michael Lane, ed., *Structuralism: A Reader*, 11–42. London: Jonathan Cape, 1970.

Lane, Robert. *Political Ideology: Why the American Common Man Believes What He Does*. New York: Free Press of Glencoe, 1962.

Lasswell, Harold, and Kaplan, Abraham. *Power and Society*. New Haven, CT: Yale University Press, 1950.

Leitch, Vincent B. *Deconstructive Criticism: An Advanced Introduction*. New York: Columbia University Press, 1983.

Levi-Strauss, Claude. *Elementary Structures of Kinship*. Boston: Beacon Press, 1969a.

_____. *Mythology. Vol. 1, The Raw and the Cooked*. London: Jonathan Cape, 1969b.

Lincoln, Yvonna, and Guba, Egon. *Naturalistic Inquiry*. Beverly Hills, CA: Sage Publications, 1985.

Locke, John. *An Essay Concerning Human Understanding*. Oxford, England: Clarendon Press, 1924. Originally published 1687.

Lyotard, Jean-François. *The Postmodern Condition: A Report on Knowledge*. Minneapolis: University of Minnesota Press, 1984.

Macdonald, James B. "How Literal is Curriculum Theory?" *Theory Into Practice*, XXI (Winter 1982), 55–61.

McCarthy, Thomas. "A Theory of Communicative Competence." *Philosophy of the Social Sciences*, 3 (1973), 135–56.

_____. *The Critical Theory of Jürgen Habermas*. Cambridge, MA: MIT Press, 1978.

_____. "Translator's Introduction." In Jürgen Habermas, *Communication and the Evolution of Society*, i–xxiv. Boston: Beacon Press, 1979.

McCutcheon, Gail. "What in the World is Curriculum Theory." *Theory Into Practice*, XXI (Winter 1982), 18–22.

Mager, Robert. *Preparing Instructional Objectives*. Belmont, CA: Fearon Publishers, 1975.

Man, Paul de. "Professing Literature: A Symposium on the Study of English." *Times Literary Supplement* (December 10, 1982), 1355–56.

March, James. "The Power of Power." In David Easton, ed., *Varieties of Political Theory*, 39–70. Englewood Cliffs, NJ: Prentice-Hall, 1966.

Megill, Allan. *Prophets of Extremity: Nietzsche, Heidegger, Foucault, Derrida*. Berkeley: University of California Press, 1985.

Messick, Samuel. "The Standard Problem: Meaning and Values in Measurement and Evaluation." *American Psychologist*, 30 (October 1975), 955–66.

Nagel, Ernest. "Measurement." In Arthur Danto and Sidney Morgenbesser, eds., *Philosophy of Science*, 121–40. New York: World Publishing, 1960. "Measurement" originally published 1932.

Norris, Christopher. *Deconstruction: Theory and Practice*. New York: Methuen, 1982.

_____. *The Deconstructive Turn*. New York: Methuen, 1983.

_____. *Contest of Faculties: Philosophy and Theory After Deconstruction*. New York: Methuen, 1985.

Ochoa, Anna; Cherryholmes, Cleo; and Manson, Gary. *McGraw-Hill Social Studies: Studying Cultures*. New York: McGraw-Hill, 1979.

Parsons, Talcott. *Structure and Process in Modern Societies*. Glencoe, IL: The Free Press, 1960.

Peirce, Charles S. *Collected Papers*. Cambridge, MA: Harvard University Press, 1931–58.

Phenix, Philip. *Realms of Meaning*. New York: McGraw-Hill, 1964.

Phillips, D. C. "After the Wake: Post-Positivistic Educational Thought." *Educational Researcher*, 12 (May 1983), 4–12.

Piaget, Jean. *Structuralism*. London: Routledge and Kegan Paul, 1971.

_____. *The Child's Conception of the World*. London: Collins Fontana, 1976.

Pinar, William. "A Reply to My Critics." *Curriculum Inquiry*, 10 (Summer 1980), 199–205.

_____. "The Reconceptualization of Curriculum Studies." In Henry Giroux, Anthony Penna, and William Pinar, eds., *Curriculum and Instruction*, 87–97. Berkeley, CA: McCutchan, 1981.

Popper, Karl. "The Logic of the Social Sciences." In T. W. Adorno, ed. *The Positivist Dispute in German Sociology*, 87–104. New York: Harper Torchbooks, 1976.

Popkewitz, Thomas. "Craft and Community as Metaphors for Social Inquiry Curriculum," *Educational Theory*, 27 (Fall 1977), 310–21.

_____. *Paradigm and Ideology in Education*. New York: The Falmer Press, 1984.

_____. "Teaching and Teacher Education Reforms: Reconstituting a State Bureaucratic Apparatus and Forming a Political Discourse." Madison, WI: College of Education of the University of Wisconsin at Madison, 1988.

Putnam, Hilary. "The Analytic and the Synthetic." In H. Feigl and G. Maxwell, *Minnesota Studies in the Philosophy of Science*, Vol. III, 350–97. Minneapolis: University of Minnesota Press, 1962.

_____. "The Meaning of 'Meaning'." In H. Putnam, ed., *Mind, Language, and Reality*, 215–72. New York: Cambridge University Press, 1975.

_____. *Meaning and the Moral Sciences*. London: Routledge and Kegan Paul, 1978.

_____. *Realism and Reason*. Cambridge, England: Cambridge University Press, 1983.

Quine, W. V. O. *From a Logical Point of View*. Cambridge, MA: Harvard University Press, 1953.

_____. "Ontological Relativity." In W. V. O. Quine, ed., *Ontological Relativity and Other Essays*, 26–68. New York: Columbia University Press, 1969.

_____. "The Pragmatists' Place in Empiricism." In Robert Mulvaney and Philip Zeltner, eds., *Pragmatism: Its Sources and Prospects*, 21–40. Columbia: University of South Carolina Press, 1981.

Rabinow, Paul, ed. *The Foucault Reader*. New York: Pantheon Books, 1984.

Rajchman, John. "Philosophy in America." In John Rajchman and Cornel West, eds., *Post-Analytic Philosophy*, ix–xxvii. New York: Columbia University Press, 1985.

Rajchman, John, and West, Cornel, eds. *Post-Analytic Philosophy*. New York: Columbia University Press, 1985.

Rawls, John. *A Theory of Justice*. Cambridge, MA: Harvard University Press, 1971.

Rivlin, Alice M. *Systematic Thinking for Social Action*. (Washington, DC: The Brookings Institution, 1971.

Rochberg-Halton, Eugene. *Meaning and Modernity: Social Theory in the Pragmatic Attitude*. Chicago: The University of Chicago Press, 1986.

Romberg, Thomas. "Salient Features of the BTES Framework of Teacher Behaviors." In Carolyn Denham and Ann Lieberman, *Time to Learn*, 73–94. Washington, DC: U.S. Department of Education, 1980.

Rorty, Richard. *Philosophy and the Mirror of Nature*. Princeton, NJ: Princeton University Press, 1980.

———. *The Consequences of Pragmatism*. Minneapolis: University of Minnesota Press, 1983.

———. "Solidarity or Objectivity?" In John Rajchman and Cornel West, eds., *Post-Analytic Philosophy*, 3–19. New York: Columbia University Press, 1985.

Ryan, Michael. *Marxism and Deconstruction*. Baltimore: The Johns Hopkins University Press, 1984.

Sabine, George H. "The Two Democratic Traditions." *The Philosophical Review*, 61 (October 1952), 451–74.

Said, Edward. *Beginnings: Intention and Method*. New York: Basic Books, 1985.

———. *The World the Text and the Critic*. Cambridge, MA: Harvard University Press, 1983.

Sartre, Jean-Paul. *L'Existentialisme est un Humanisme*. Paris: Nagel, 1946.

Sarup, Madan. *Marxism/Structuralism/Education*. New York: The Falmer Press, 1983.

Saussure, Ferdinand de. *Course in General Linguistics*. New York: McGraw-Hill, 1966. Originally published 1916.

Scheffler, Israel. "Explanation, Prediction, and Abstraction." In Arthur Danto and Sidney Morgenbesser, eds., *Philosophy of Science*, 274–87. New York: World Publishing, 1960.

Scholes, Robert. *Textual Power*. New Haven, CT: Yale University Press, 1985.

Schutz, Alfred. "Concept and Theory Formation in the Social Sciences." In Maurice Natanson, ed., *Philosophy of the Social Sciences*, 231–49. New York: Random House, 1963a.

———. "Common-sense and Scientific Interpretation of Human Action." In Maurice Natanson, ed., *Philosophy of the Social Sciences*, 302–46. New York: Random House, 1963b.

Schwab, Joseph, "The Concept of the Structure of a Discipline." *The Educational Record*, 43 (July 1962), 197–205.

———. "The Practical: A Language for Curriculum." *School Review*, 79 (November 1969), 1–24.

———. "The Practical 4: Something for Curriculum Professors To Do." *Curriculum Inquiry*, 13 (Fall 1983), 239–66.

Searle, John. *Speech Acts*. Cambridge, Cambridge University Press, 1969.

———. "Austin on Locutionary and Illocutionary Acts." In Jay Rosenberg and Charles Travis, eds., *Readings in the Philosophy of Language*, 262–75. Englewood Cliffs, NJ: Prentice-Hall, 1971.

Sellars, Wilfrid. *Science, Perception, and Reality*. New York: Humanities Press, 1963.

Seung, T. K. *Structuralism and Hermeneutics*. New York: Columbia University Press, 1982.

Shapiro, Michael J. *Language and Political Understanding*. New Haven, CT: Yale University Press, 1981.

Shapley, L. S., and Shubik, Martin. "A Method for Evaluating the Distribution of Power in a Committee System." In Sidney Ulmer, ed., *Introductory Readings in Political Behavior*, 384–86. Chicago: Rand McNally, 1961.

Shultz, Jeffrey J.; Florio, Susan; and Erickson, Frederick. "Where's the Floor? Aspects of the Cultural Organization of Social Relationships in Communication at Home and in School." In Perry Gilmore and Allan A. Glatthorn, eds., *Children In and Out of School*, 88–123. Washington, DC: Center for Applied Linguistics, 1982.

Simon, Herbert. "Notes on the Observation and Measurement of Political Power." In Sidney Ulmer, ed., *Introductory Readings in Political Behavior*, 363–75. Chicago: Rand McNally, 1961.

————. *Administrative Behavior*. 3d ed. New York: The Free Press, 1976.

Simon, Roger. "Curriculum Study and Cultural Politics." Paper read at the American Educational Research Association Meetings, April 1985, Chicago. Mimeographed. Toronto, Canada: The Ontario Institute for Studies in Education.

Skagestad, Peter. "American Pragmatism." In Guttorm Floistad, ed., *Contemporary Philosophy: A New Survey*. Vol. 4. *Philosophy of Mind*, 363–86. The Hague, The Netherlands: Martinus Nijhoff Publishers, 1983.

Stevens, S. S. "Mathematics, Measurement, and Psychophysics," In S. S. Stevens, ed., *Handbook of Experimental Psychology*, 1–49. New York: Wiley, 1951.

Stinchcombe, Arthur. *Constructing Social Theories*. New York: Harcourt, Brace & World, 1968.

Strawson, P. F. "On Truth." In George Pitcher, ed., *Truth*, 32–53. Englewood Cliffs, NJ: Prentice-Hall, 1964.

Suppe, Frederick. *The Structure of Scientific Theories*. Chicago: The University of Illinois Press, 1977.

Taba, Hilda. *Curriculum Development*. New York: Harcourt Brace Jovanovich, 1962.

Tanner, Daniel, and Tanner, Laurel N. "Emancipation from Research: The Reconceptualist Prescription." *Educational Researcher*, 8 (June 1979), 8–12.

Tarski, Alfred. "The Semantic Conception of Truth." In Leonard Linsky, ed., *Semantics and the Philosophy of Language*, 13–49. Chicago: University of Illinois Press, 1952.

Taxel, Joel. "The Direction of the American Revolution in Children's Fiction: A Study in Sociology of Social Knowledge." Ph.D. dissertation, University of Wisconsin at Madison, 1980.

Taylor, Paul W. *Normative Discourse*. Englewood Cliffs, NJ: Prentice-Hall, 1961.

Thayer, H. S. "Pragmatism: A Reinterpretation of the Origins and Consequences." In Robert Mulvaney and Philip Zeltner, eds., *Pragmatism: Its*

Sources and Prospects, 1–20. Columbia: University of South Carolina Press, 1981.

Toulmin, Stephen. *The Uses of Argument*. Cambridge, England: Cambridge University Press, 1958.

Tyler, Ralph W. *Basic Principles of Curriculum and Instruction*. Chicago: The University of Chicago Press, 1949.

_____. "Personal Reflections on The Practical 4." *Curriculum Inquiry*, 14, (Spring 1984), 97–102.

Ulmer, Gregory. *Applied Grammatology: Post(e)-Pedagogy From Jacques Derrida to Joseph Beuys*. Baltimore: The Johns Hopkins University Press, 1985.

van Fraassen, Bas C. *Formal Semantics and Logic*. New York: Macmillan, 1971.

_____. *The Scientific Image*. Oxford, England: Clarendon Press, 1980.

van Manen, Max. "Edifying Theory: Serving the Good." *Theory Into Practice*, XXI (Winter 1982), 44–49.

Visser, N. W. "Structuralism." In Rory Ryan and Susan van Zyl, eds., *An Introduction to Contemporary Literary Theory*, 53–65. Johannesburg, South Africa: A. D. Donker, Ltd., 1982.

Vuicich, George; Stollman, Joseph; Cherryholmes, Cleo; and Manson, Gary. *McGraw-Hill Social Studies: Understanding the United States*. New York: McGraw-Hill, 1979.

Weber, Max. "Bureaucracy." In H. H. Gerth and C. Wright Mills, eds. *From Max Weber: Essays in Sociology*, 196–244. New York: Oxford University Press, 1958.

Weiss, Carol. "Evaluation Research in the Political Context." In Elmer L. Struening and Marcia Guttentag, eds., *Handbook of Evaluation Research*, Vol. 1, 13–26. Beverly Hills, CA: Sage Publications, 1975.

West, Cornel. "The Politics of American Neo-Pragmatism." In John Rajchman and Cornel West, eds., *Post-Analytic Philosophy*, 259–75. New York: Columbia University Press, 1985.

Williams, Raymond, "Base and Superstructure in Marxist Cultural Theory." In R. Dale, *Schooling and Capitalism: A Sociological Reader*, 13–49. Urbana, IL: University of Illinois Press, 1952.

Wittgenstein, Ludwig. *Philosophical Investigations*. Oxford, England: Basil Blackwell, 1953.

Zais, Robert S. "Conceptions of Curriculum and the Curriculum Field." In Giroux, Penna, and Pinar, eds., *Curriculum and Instruction*, 31–49. Berkeley, CA: McCutchan, 1981.

Index

About the Author

Cleo H. Cherryholmes is Professor of Political Science at Michigan State University. He received his bachelor's degree from Yale University, master's degree from Kansas State Teachers College, and doctorate from Northwestern University. He has published in the *American Journal of Education, Journal of Curriculum Studies, Curriculum Inquiry, Journal of Education, Theory and Research in Social Education, Theory Into Practice*, and *Social Education*. He currently teaches courses in social research methodology, public policy analysis, curriculum theory, politics of schooling, and philosophy of social science.